The AMETHYST MINING INSCRIPTIONS of WADI EL-HUDI

PART I: TEXT

Ashraf I. Sadek

British Library Cataloguing in Publication Data

Sadek, Ashraf I
The amethyst mining inscriptions of
Wadi el-Hudi. - (Modern Egyptology series).
Part 1: Text
1. Egyptian language - Inscriptions
2. Hudi Valley - Antiquities
I. Title II. Series
493'.1 PJ1526.W3

ISBN 0-85668-162-8

Published by ARIS & PHILLIPS LTD, Warminster, Wilts, England.

Printed in England by BIDDLES LTD, Guildford, Surrey.

CONTENTS

FOREWORD

In the great periods of their history, the ancient Egyptians proved to be eager and enterprising explorers of the awesome, tawny deserts that hem in the green ribbon of populated land bordering the Nile. For over a century now, students of ancient Egypt have had easy access to the records of major expeditions mining turquoise in Sinai and quarrying hard stone in Wadi Hammamat. Most recently, an Egyptian expedition has unearthed proof of ancient Egyptian installations on and near the shore of the Red Sea, sites that served as bases for their voyages south to the land of Punt or Pwenet.

Among the valuable records from these and other such sites both East and West of the Nile valley, the inscriptions of Wadi el-Hudi deserve a prominent place. The amethysts that their authors anciently secured went into royal jewellery, which for taste, refinement and technique, must rank among the finest produced anywhere. But since the pioneer publication in 1952 by the late lamented Professor Fakhry, this group of texts has been all but totally ignored by Egyptologists. Lacking the easy convenience of translations, notes and critical apparatus in that work, most students have been unwilling to grapple with the acute epigraphic problems of these irregular cursive texts.

However, as Dr. Sadek's work shows, the effort to restore these texts to the canon of written sources of direct value to Egyptology has proved to be thoroughly worthwhile, amply rewarding the efforts expended, as I have had opportunity to discover personally while intermittently studying these texts with the author in the last few years. Henceforth, no-one need have reason or excuse to ignore these texts. Throughout this new edition, the solutions proposed in readings and translations are furnished with essential background support, and are offered on the sensible basis of adopting the least remarkable, most mundane readings and interpretations feasible: thus, unsound novelties without a future are substantially avoided.

We may consider the version of the texts here published by Dr. Sadek as being, if not definitive, as near to that ideal as is likely to be attained for a long time to come. It has been fascinating to share in some measure in the fuller epigraphic 'recovery' of these inscriptions, and is now a real pleasure to commend this edition of them to all who are interested in any aspect of ancient Egyptian history, exploration, administration, social structure, statistics, prosopography, philology and technical enterprise in the vigorous, bustling epoch of the Middle Kingdom in the opening centuries of the second millenium BC.

K.A. Ḳitchen
(Reader in Egyptian & Coptic, University of Liverpool)

PREFACE

The present work represents the fully revised version of a doctoral thesis (III cycle) presented at the Sorbonne in June 1977 on the mining inscriptions of Wadi el-Hudi. These texts were first published as a whole by the late Professor Ahmed Fakhry in 1952. His was a pioneering work, executed and published under great difficulties, and he himself hoped that this important body of texts would some day receive further treatment. This work is intended to fulfil his wish in some measure at least, by offering an improved edition of these inscriptions so that they may take their rightful place as part of the total historical resources for the Egyptian Middle Kingdom. The work is in two volumes, Text and Plates. This division is a practical one, with the double advantage of making the normalised texts (with translations and commentary) available as promptly as possible, and of facilitating easy comparison between texts and plates which is impossible for such cursive texts when all is bound together in one volume.

Having been already interested in Middle Kingdom inscriptions, I welcomed Dr. Labib Habachi's original suggestion to study the Wadi el-Hudi inscriptions. I now take this opportunity of expressing my thanks to all those who made possible the realisation of this work.

Thus, my thanks go to Professor Jean Leclant as supervisor of my thesis at the Sorbonne.

My especial thanks go to Mme. Professor C. Desroches-Noblecourt, whose contributions both material and intellectual greatly helped me to attain my aim, and also to her assistants at the Louvre.

It is appropriate also to pay a warm tribute to the late Professor Jacques Vandier, whose encouragement I enjoyed from the beginning of my studies in France until his death.

Facilities for my research in the Salle Champollion I owe to the liberality of its director, Professor G. Posener.

The kindness of Dr. K. A. Kitchen in contributing a Foreword on the importance of these texts gives me much encouragement. I desire to express here my deep gratitude to him not only for introducing my work to a wider audience and for help and advice at all stages, but also for so willingly undertaking to autograph the hieroglyphic texts specially for this publication.

My work has also benefited materially from the help kindly afforded by the following: M. J.-Cl. Degardin and Mme. Abeles, Collège de France; Prof. S. Allam, University of Tübingen; Prof. J.-L. de Cenival, Keeper at the Louvre; M. Chappus, Chief Keeper, Musée des Monuments Français, and M. Charcosset of that museum; Mme. Blanc, geologist at the Centre de Recherches sur les Monuments historiques; the late Mr. Boutros Nosseih, Director of the Aswan Museum; M. Georges Soukiassian; and by no means least Mlle Sylvie Mouillot, who typed the original French version and gave other much appreciated practical help.

Finally, my thanks go to the publishers for making this work so readily available to students of ancient Egypt.

Ashraf Iskander Sadek
Liverpool, 1979

ABBREVIATIONS

ASAE	*Annales du Service des Antiquités de l'Egypte,* Cairo.
Belegstellen	see under *Wb.*
BIFAO	*Bulletin de l'Institut Français d'Archéologie Orientale du Caire,* Cairo.
Blu, *Unt.*	Elke Blumenthal, *Untersuchungen zum Ägyptischen Königtum des Mittleren Reiches, I, Der Phraseologie*, Berlin, 1970 (= *Abhandlungen der Sächischen Akademie der Wissenschaften zu Leipzig, Phil.-Hist. Klasse*, Band 61, Heft 1).
BM	British Museum.
BSFE	*Bulletin de la Société Française d'Egyptologie*, Paris.
CdE	*Chronique d'Egypte*, Brussels.
CMH, *or* Couyat & Montet	J. Couyat, P. Montet, *Les inscriptions hiéroglyphiques et hiératiques du Ouâdi Hammâmât*, 2 vols., Cairo, 1912-13 (= *Mémoires de l'Institut Français . . . du Caire*, 34).
CRIPEL	*Cahiers de Recherches de l'Institut de Papyrologie et d'Egyptologie de Lille*, Lille (Etudes sur l'Egypte et le Soudan anciens).
F., Fakhry	Ahmed Fakhry, *The Inscriptions of the Amethyst Quarries at Wadi el Hudi*, Cairo 1952. (Service des Antiquités de l'Egypte: The Egyptian Deserts.)
Faulkner, *Dict.*	R.O. Faulkner, *A Concise Dictionary of Middle Egyptian*, Oxford, 1962.
Gardiner, §	A.H. Gardiner, *Egyptian Grammar*, 3rd ed., Oxford, 1957, usually cited by paragraph.
Hellström *(Rock Drawings)*	P. Hellström et al., *The Rock Drawings*, one vol. in two parts, 1970 (Scandinavian Joint Expedition to Sudanese Nubia).
HP, I	G. Möller, *Hieratische Paläographie*, I, 2nd ed., Leipzig, 1927 (repr. Osnabrück, 1965).
JEA	*Journal of Egyptian Archaeology*, London.
JNES	*Journal of Near Eastern Studies*, Chicago.
MDIK	*Mitteilungen des Deutschen Archäologischen Instituts, Abteilung Kairo*, now at Mainz.
MHT	W. Schenkel, *Memphis, Herakleopolis, Theben*, Wiesbaden, 1965 (*Ägyptologische Abhandlungen*, Band 12).
NARCE	*Newsletter, American Research Center in Egypt, Inc.*, Princeton and Cairo.
NIH	G. Goyon, *Nouvelles inscriptions rupestres du Wadi Hammamat*, Paris, 1957.
OLZ	*Orientalische Literaturzeitung*, Leipzig.
PM, VII	B. Porter, R.L.B. Moss, *Topographical Bibliography of Ancient Egyptian Hieroglyphic Texts, Reliefs and Paintings*, VII, Oxford, 1952 (and reprints)
PM, No...	*Ibid.*, p. 319, heavy-printed old Fakhry numbers.
PN	H. Ranke, *Die Ägyptische Personennamen*, I, II, Glückstadt & Hamburg, 1935 and 1952.
PSBA	*Proceedings of the Society of Biblical Archaeology*, London.
RdE	*Revue d'Egyptologie*, Paris.
RT	*Recueil de Travaux relatifs à la philologie et a l'archéologie égyptiennes et assyriennes*, Paris.
Sethe, *Urkunden IV*	K. Sethe, *Urkunden der 18. Dynastie*, Leipzig, 1905ff. (Urkunden des ägyptischen Altertums, Abteilung IV).
TEA	J.M.A. Janssen, *De Traditioneele Egyptische Autobiografie voor het Nieuwe Rijk*, I, II, Leiden, 1946
TR	Cairo Museum, Temporary Register.
Wb	A. Erman, H. Grapow, eds., *Wörterbuch der Aegyptischen Sprache*, I-VII, and *Belegstellen*, I-V, Leipzig & Berlin, 1926ff.
WH (No.)	The Wadi Hudi texts in the present work.
ZÄS	*Zeitschrift für ägyptische Sprache und Altertumskunde*, Leipzig & Berlin.

I dedicate this book to

Dr. LABIB HABACHI

with all my gratitude

"*Le Seigneur rend justice aux opprimés*" (Ps. 146, 7)

I: INTRODUCTION

The eastern deserts of Egypt are remarkable for their rich variety of minerals and for their scenery of desolate grandeur. Men have searched through these barren wastes to extract their hidden treasures, from remote antiquity to the present day.

The inscriptions edited in this book form a compact corpus in subject, time and space. They are the permanent memorials of ancient Egyptian expeditions sent out during the Middle Kingdom (11th, 12th, 13th Dynasties, *c.* 2000-1730 BC) to mine for amethyst in the desert hillocks of Wadi el-Hudi, some 35 km south-east of Aswan. The date of this body of texts is significant, because as a semi-precious stone amethyst was particularly favoured in the superb jewellery of the Middle Kingdom pharaohs and their queens and princesses.[1]

A branch of the Aswan to Abrak camel-caravan route runs east to join the upper or eastern part of Wadi el-Hudi, which then curves southward towards Gebel Hudi, a prominent rocky hill which is the principal landmark in that vicinity (see Map 1).

North, west and south of Gebel Hudi there is an arc of mine workings and buildings of very varied antiquity. North of both Gebel and Wadi is a barytes mine (Site 1)[2], where a Twelfth-Dynasty stela was found (WH 15). Sites 2 (a fort) and 3 (a gold mine), well north-west and just west, respectively, of Gebel Hudi, are of Roman date, as is the camp at site 4, due west of the Gebel and Site 3. These, therefore, fall outside the scope of the present study, except that some Middle Kingdom stelae were found reused as building material in the walls of the Site 4 camp. They doubtless had been taken from Sites 5 and 6.

West-south-west of Gebel Hudi and north of the traces of an ancient road (Fakhry's 'Site 7') are twin hillocks Sites 5 and 6. These were the focus of the Middle Kingdom mining activities in the area, and the sites where the overwhelming mass of Middle Kingdom inscriptions were originally located. Site 5 (the north-west hill) has remains of shelters enclosed within rough walling with entrances on the south and north sides, forming an enclosed camp-site for the Middle Kingdom miners. At the hill foot (south-west edge) was the amethyst mine of the Eleventh Dynasty whose graffiti were found nearby. Many rock-inscriptions were found on this hill,[3] also the two sandstone stelae WH 144, 145 (Rowe, II, III).[4] Site 6 (the south-east hill) bore no habitations, but instead had the greatest number of Middle Kingdom texts,[5] and apparently the great limestone stela of Hor (WH 143, Rowe I) at its summit.[6]

Not far south of Sites 5-6, close to the ancient road, was Site 9, a fort attributed by Fakhry to the Middle Kingdom, with a major amethyst mine only 100 metres from its north-east corner, and some inscribed stones near the north gate. He considered that it may have replaced the camp on Site 5. Some 7 km westward along the ancient road was Site 8, an encampment with a well, whose heaps of discarded amethyst chips suggested to Fakhry that here the amethyst spoils could be sorted and washed before return to the Nile valley.[7]

South-east from Site 9 and well south from Gebel Hudi are grouped a mica mine, Roman fort and camp (Sites 10, 11, 12 respectively). Like the late and modern gold-diggings (Sites 13, 14) to the east, across the Wadi these remains all date from long after the Middle Kingdom. Thus, of all the areas of human activity in this vicinity, Sites 5 and 6 (plus 9 and 8) represent the real scene of work done by the Egyptians who left the texts that we are concerned with.

In modern times, the history of the rediscovery and publication of the ancient mines and inscriptions of Wadi el-Hudi extends now over half a century.[8] These were first seen in 1923 by the geologist L. Nassim who unfortunately did not report their existence. Thus it was only in 1939 that members of the Egyptian Topographical Survey rediscovered the site. They, with members of the Antiquities Service, then removed the great stela WH 143 and the twin sandstone stelae (WH 144, 145), sending them on to the Egyptian Museum in Cairo, enabling Rowe and Drioton to publish them that year.[9]

Reports then came that local beduin were stealing further inscriptions and selling them to the antiquities trade; so both G.W. Murray and his Egyptian colleagues of the Topographical Survey and the Service of Antiquities removed all the inscriptions that they could to the Aswan Museum during 1939-40.

Thereafter, Mr. (later, Professor) Ahmed Fakhry decided to make a special study of the Wadi el-Hudi inscriptions. As the result of his three short expeditions to Wadi el-Hudi itself in 1944, 1945 and 1949, he managed to copy and photograph all available texts at Wadi el-Hudi and Aswan, but omitting the three Cairo stelae, for his publication issued in 1952, *The Inscriptions of the Amethyst Quarries at Wadi El Hudi*. This included facsimiles of nearly all texts, hieroglyphic transcriptions of many texts, and photographs of a good number of the texts. Brief descriptions and indexes of Egyptian names and titles accompanied these copies, but the formidable burdens of his official duties prevented Prof. Fakhry from including either translations or commentaries. As he himself remarked, his was a preliminary edition to make the texts accessible, and he looked for a fuller treatment by others in due time.

As is noted above in the Preface, I first undertook the study of the Wadi el-Hudi inscriptions as a doctoral thesis. In that connection, I visited Aswan in May 1975, recopying, checking and photographing the Wadi el-Hudi texts in the Museum there, and through the kindness of the Mines and Quarries Service was able to make three visits to Wadi el-Hudi itself. The graffiti formerly recorded there had by then disappeared or become unlocatable; however, it was possible to study and photograph the old roads, the Wadi and Gebel Hudi, a large new mine, ancient huts other building-remains and pottery fragments.

Finally, as again remarked in the Preface, this edition is divided into two parts, texts and plates, to facilitate comparison of texts with their photographs and copies, and to publish the texts promptly. The translations, notes and commentaries should, it is hoped, make these texts more fully usable than previously.

1. Examples in colour, cf. G. Brunton, *Lahun I, The Treasure,* London, 1920, pls. 1, 8; C. Aldred, *Jewels of the Pharaohs,* London 1971, pls. 36 (Middle Kingdom), 1 (Archaic Period), and 109 upper right (Tutankhamun), and pp. 174, 191f., 224, cf. pp.18, 34f., 116, 148. Also, A. Lucas, ed. J.R. Harris, *Ancient Egyptian Materials and Industries,* 4th ed., London 1962, pp.126, 388-9.
2. The site-numbers used here are those of Fakhry, for the sake of clarity. See Map 2.
3. E.g., WH 1-4, 14, 28, 41, 45, 46, 49, 144, 145, etc.
4. So Fakhry, p.2 (2), after G.W. Murray.
5. Fakhry, p.11.
6. So Fakhry, p.2. (2), Site 6/C, after G.W. Murray; the attribution to Site 5 (p.11) must be a slip of the pen. On location of WH 143 (Rowe I), cf. also A. Rowe, *ASAE* 39 (1939), p. 192, after Ibrahim Abd-el Al, with clear distinction made between the findspots of the limestone and two sandstone stelae (i.e., WH 144-5, versus 143).
7. Sites 8,9, Fakhry, pp.12-14.
8. See already Fakhry, pp.1-4, and his briefer report, *ASAE* 46 (1947), pp. 51-54.
9. A. Rowe, with contributions by E. Drioton, *ASAE* 39 (1939), pp.187-194, pls. 25-26.

II: THE INSCRIPTIONS

A. The Eleventh Dynasty: Nos. 1-5

WH, No.1. Fakhry, No. 1; Schenkel, *MHT*, No. 435; PM, No. 26 (?).
Date: Nebtawyre Mentuhotep IV, Year 1 (*c.* 1998 BC)
Bibliography: Fakhry, p.19f., fig. 14, pl. VIA; Schenkel, *MHT*, p. 260:435.
Description: Six-line text on a quartzite rock (Site 5), maximum height 45 cm; not found in 1975.

Normalised Text:

Textual Notes: 2a, 3a, 4a,b, 5a,b : hieratic forms in the original, cf. respectively *HP*, I, Nos. 317/8, 514, 511b, 263 388, 517. For 4a, a clear parallel in G. Goyon, *NIH*, p. 87, No. 64, first horizontal line, pl. 21. 3b: a poor form but usual in this group of texts. 6a: with clear head and thin neck, this bird is definitely *sꜣ* and not *w* (despite Schenkel, *MHT*, p. 260, n. *c.*). Contrast the clear *w* in WH 2:3, and the adjacent birds *w*, *sꜣ*, in WH 3:2.

Translation: (1) Year 1 (of) the King of Upper and Lower Egypt, (2) Nebtawyre, (3) The caravan leader Intef, (4) his true and favourite servitor who does (5) all that he praises. The steward Ptah-shed (wy)'s (6) son Intef.

Commentary: With year, title and cartouche, the dateline is of a relatively simple kind common also to WH 3 and 4B in the Eleventh-Dynasty group of texts here, and still to be found in the Twelfth Dynasty (e.g., WH 6, 18; 11, 15 with twin cartouches). Simpler still are those of WH 2 (omitting title), and WH 5 (omitting date), usages also found later.

The authorship of this text is clearly attributable to one man, Intef the son of a Ptah-shedwy, as this text surely conforms to common Middle Kingdom usage in employing inverted filiation, especially in the Eleventh and Twelfth Dynasties (Gardiner, § 85), and not least in our Wadi el-Hudi corpus. Therefore, Schenkel's attempt[10] to interpret this text as reading ' Ptah-shedwy son of Intef' in lines 5-6, and so to make this inscription the work of two men (Intef, the senior; Ptah-Shedwy, the junior-man-on-the-spot) must be rejected as erroneous. Thus, in turn, the suffix 'his' in lines 4-5 refers back to Intef's master the King. To this Intef must also be attributed the other texts at Wadi el-Hudi of this reign, i.e. WH 2, 3, 4, perhaps also 5, and even 26. Only in WH 3 for certain (with Khuyu) and conceivably in WH 26 (with Didiu) does he share the credit in his inscriptions. The name Intef is, of course, very common (*PN*, I, 34:1) but the name Ptah-shedwy or Shedwy-Ptah is less so (*PN*, I, 330:17, citing only New-Kingdom examples).

Of the two civil titles in this text, *ỉmy-r pr*, 'steward' is rather general. But in the light of Middle Kingdom data discussed by Helck, [11] this title can indicate the local administrator of royal property and land in a particular nome or district, being responsible to a high steward (*ỉmy-r pr wr*). The meaning and functions of *ꜥw* and *ỉmy-r ꜥw* are still uncertain. Faulkner argued for 'dragoman','caravan leader' respectively,[12] while Goedicke would render 'foreigner', 'commander of mercenaries'.[13] To this Fischer has objected, [14] preferring 'interpreter' in the broad sense, covering scouts, spies, agents, couriers and foremen of mercenaries. [15] For the honorific epithets in lines 4-5, cf. below, commentary to WH 9.

10. In *MHT*, p.260 and n.*a*.
11. W. Helck, *Zur Verwaltung des Mittleren und Neuen Reichs*, Leiden, 1958, pp.92-93, cf. 93-94.
12. In *JEA* 39 (1953), p.34, retained in his *Dictionary*, p.39.
13. *JEA* 46 (1960), pp.60-64, basing himself on A.H. Gardiner, *PSBA* 37 (1915), pp.117-125, and followed by G.E. Kadish, *JEA* 52 (1966), p.24, n.2.
14. H.G. Fischer, *Inscriptions from the Coptite Nome*, Rome, 1964, pp.28-30, 141, with reply by H. Goedicke, *JEA* 52 (1966), pp.172-4.
15. Further observations, cf. J. Yoyotte, *Orientalia NS* 35 (1966), pp.52-3, and a full study announced by L. Bell, *NARCE* 87 (1973), p.33.

WH, No. 2. Fakhry, No. 2; Schenkel, *MHT*, No. 436; PM, No. 42 (?).
Date: Nebtawyre Mentuhotep IV, Year 1 (*c.* 1998 BC)
Bibliography: Fakhry, p. 20, fig. 15, pl. VIB; Schenkel, *MHT*, p. 260f. :436.
Description: Six-line text on a quartzite rock (Site 5). Max. height, 68 cm, max. width 75 cm; not found in 1975.

Normalised Text:

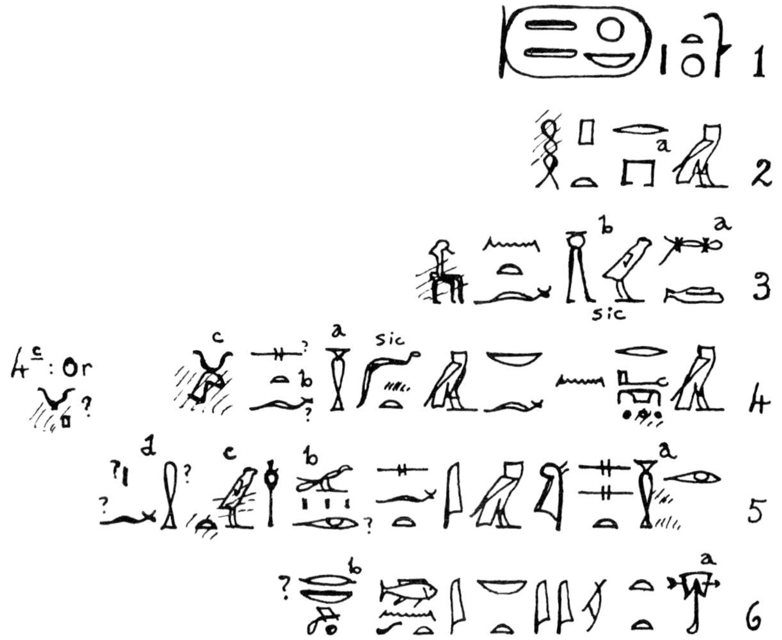

Textual Notes: 2a: *pr,* a simplified form. 3a: hieratic forms of *šd, d.* 3b: ***sꜣ*** omitted by engraver. 4a: for form of *ḥs,* cf. WH 1:5 and probably here line 5. 4b: poor form for *f*, lacking horns (as in some hieratic examples); cf. the equally poor form in *In-ỉt.f*, WH 1:6. 4c: the traces suit better the hieratic for *ssꜣ* rather than *wp* (cf. *HP*, I, Nos. 153, 155). 5a: the form would suit *ḥs* (projecting top, crude vertical body, cf. hieratic, *HP*, I, No. 502), as in line 4 and in WH 1:5, assuming accidental marks on right-hand side. 5b: perhaps hieratic form of the 'bad bird'(cf. *HP*, I, No. 197, Prisse column), of which this example may be a simplified form; otherwise, one must read the bookroll abstract determinative. Below this sign, plural strokes and *ỉr* (or *nb*), despite Blu, *Unt.*, p. 410, G. 8. 67, and n. 152 on p. 430. 5c: close scrutiny of the photo suggests a *w* (with Schenkel, *MHT*, p.260, n. *h.*) with a blotch (for a *t*?) below its tail, and not *m* despite Blu, *Unt.*, p. 410, G. 8. 67. 5d: *ḥm.f* is probable, agreeing with Fakhry, Schenkel and Blumenthal. 6a: for the hieratic form of *Stt*, cf. the close parallel in *HP*, I, No. 167 (Prisse column) 6b: either *r nb* or *r ỉr* over *ỉmꜣḫ* (and *ḫ* or stroke under this last sign. If *r ỉr* be read, a mark next to *ỉmꜣḫ* could be for a *t*.

Translation: (1) Year 1 (of) Nebtawyre. (2) The steward Ptah- (3) shedwy's <son> Intef. (4) The caravan leader of his lord, being one who says (?) what he praises, the skilled one (*or*: emissary??) (5) who does what is praised; free of falsehood; who does what His Majesty commands – (6) the beloved of Satis, Lady of the Wadi – to be (?) a revered one (*or*: possessor of revered status).

Commentary: On the type of dateline, see above under WH 1, likewise on the filiation, correcting *MHT*, p. 260. Here in line 3, the bird after the group *šd* is clearly a *w* (giving the full form *Ptḥ-šd-wỉ*), while the bird *sꜣ* must be understood as having been omitted between this name and Intef (agreeing with Schenkel).

In line 4, Schenkel's interpretation of Fakhry's readings is very ingenious but improbable (and in part, mistaken) The first group is not *ỉmy-r pr* but a badly written *ỉmy-r ꜥw*. After this, *n* is certain; *nb.f* is feasible, making more sense than *ḫ-n*. Then *ḏ* is certain, with a mark and small sign below it. What follows is certainly not *ỉn* (despite

Schenkel) which has clearly separated legs in this group of texts; thus, his reading 'Intef' must be dropped. In turn, his ingenious 'steward of the estate Khenem-djet-Intef' (which rejoices the body of Intef') must be abandoned, being at best highly unusual. The penultimate group of signs is better read *ḥst.f* (see Notes, 4a, above). Then one has an *m* of predication which confers a nuance of emphasis (Gardiner, § § 96, 2, 393, etc.), and one might emend the seeming *ḏt* to *ḏd*, the *t* being a simple slip for *d* in hieratic. The resulting phrases *m ḏd(w) ḥst.f* and *šsꜣ* (or: *wpwty*??) *ỉr ḥsst* then form a balanced pair of matching epithets, 'as one who *speaks* what he (the King) praises', and the 'skilled (envoy?) who *does* what is praised'. In the latter phrase, *šsꜣ* is preferable to *wpwty* as it features in honorific clichés in other inscriptions of this same epoch.[16]

In line 5, *ỉr ḥsst* fits the traces well (rather than Schenkel's *wꜥb* of whose determinative only two of three *n*'s could be read with any plausibility[17]). It represents the most abbreviated variant[18] in a series of clichés based on *ỉrỉ ḥsỉ*; for these, WH 9 below. Similarly, the phrase *šw m ỉsft* reflects such fuller forms as *šw m ỉrt ỉsft.*[19]

In line 6 the reading *mry Stt nbt ỉnt* is agreed also by Schenkel,[20] followed by Blumenthal.[21] Satis is no stranger to Wadi Hudi (cf. WH 22:4, 143:lunette, and probably to be restored in 20:3, 25:4). But she is usually entitled *nbt ꜣbw*, 'Lady of Elephantine', rather than as here 'Lady of the Wadi'. But such a concept is not unknown elsewhere.[22]

Dr. Blumenthal would refer this phrase *mry Stt nbt ỉnt* to the expedition leader himself, citing it as a rare example of a private official termed 'beloved' of a deity.[23] However, this is very uncertain, as the word *mry* may relate directly to *ḥm.f* – 'His Majesty, beloved of Satis'.

Finally, at the end of line 6, all authorities agree on the reading of *ỉmꜣḫ*. The two horizontal signs above it are ambiguous. The first is perhaps *r*, open as in line 2. The second may be *ỉr*, thin as in line 5 (twice). A trace at left might justify reading *r ỉrt*. But *nb* is as possible as *ỉr*, giving *r nb ỉmꜣḫ*. Either way, this adverbial phrase depends upon *ỉr wḏt ḥm.f*; obeying the king leads to becoming a revered one or to possessing revered status. This concept reappears very soon afterwards in the early Twelfth Dynasty in the famous 'Loyalist Instruction' ('Sehetepibre'), in the phrases 'attaining to the revered state' (*sbt r ỉmꜣḫ(yt)*, § 1:8) and 'whom the King has loved shall become a revered one' (*ỉw mr.n nsw r ỉmꜣḫy*, §§3:11/6:3).[24] Likewise in the Instruction of a Man for His Son, rone. §20, 'he who has no name shall become a revered one' (*šw m rn.f r ỉmꜣḫy*),[25] i.e. the small man becomes great in the context of loyalty to the throne.

16. See Janssen, *TEA*, I, p.34, Ay:1, 2-6 (Dyns. 11-13); on *wpwty* at all periods, see M. Vallogia, *Recherche sur les 'messagers' (wpwtyw) dans les sources égyptiennes profanes*, Geneva, 1976.
17. In texts of this period, *wꜥb* is not usually used on its own (as Schenkel's view requires), but as first half of a compound epithet, 'pure of . . . (offerings, altars, face, hand, fingers, etc.), cf. *TEA*, I, p.14f., Q:1-10.
18. Cf. Janssen, *TEA*, I, p.48, F:151, for this short form (Sesostris I).
19. Cf. WH 4:6, 8 (twice), and *TEA*, I, p.166, J:24.
20. In *MHT*, p.261, notes *b, c, d.*
21. Cf. Blu, *Unt.*, p.70, B.1.21, p.107, n. B 22.
22. Titles like 'Lady of the Wadi' occur with goddesses who are identified with desert-roaming fauna. So, the Hathor at Tehneh (Sethe, *Urkunden des Alten Reichs*, Leipzig, 1903, p.24:16; cf. H. Kees, *Der Götterglaube im alten Ägypten*, Berlin, 1956, p.7 and n.5): Pakhet and Sekhmet (cf. Kees, *op.cit.*, pp.7-8); Hathor at El-Kab (*ibid.*, p.10). Kees also remarks on the antelope horns of the crown of Satis (p.25), asking whether she may once have been an antelope-goddess: the title 'Lady of the (desert) Wadi' would then be very fitting.
23. Blu, *Unt.*, p.70.
24. Cf. G. Posener, *L'enseignement loyaliste*, Geneva, 1976, ad locc.
25. Cf. K.A. Kitchen, *Oriens Antiquus* 8 (1969), pp.196, 197; R.O. Faulkner, E.F. Wente, W.K. Simpson (ed.), *The Literature of Ancient Egypt*, 2nd ed., 1973, p.339.

WH, No. 3. Fakhry, No. 3; Schenkel, *MHT*, No. 437; PM, No. 49 (?).
Date: Nebtawyre Mentuhotep IV, Year 1 (*c.* 1998 BC).
Bibliography: Fakhry, p.20f., fig. 16, pl. VIIA; Schenkel, *MHT*, p. 261:437.
Description: Six-line text on a quartzite rock (Site 5, S. side); height 70 cm; width, 78 cm; not found in 1975.

Normalised Text:

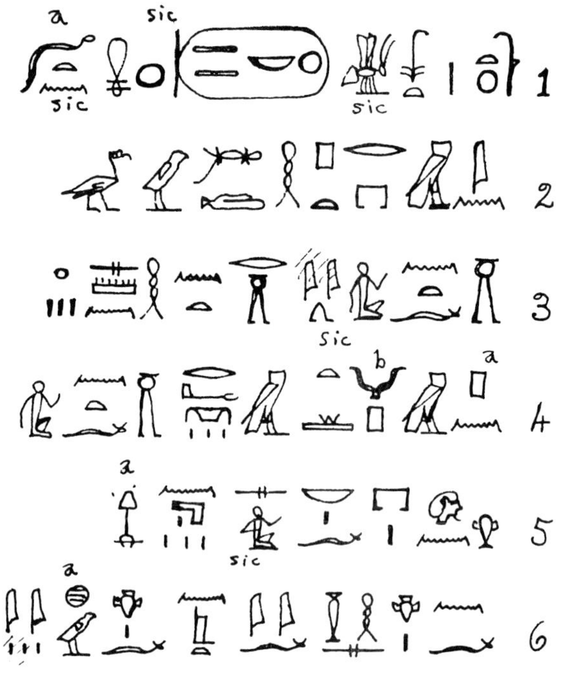

Textual Notes: 1a: *n* is wrongly written for the *tꜣ*-sign, through confusion of the similar hieratic forms (cf. *HP*, I, Nos. 317, 331). 2a, 4a,b: hieratic forms of *p*. 2b: hieratic form of *šd*. 5a: *wbꜣ*, semi-hieratic form (reading due to Fairman; independently also by Schenkel, *MHT*, p. 261, n.*g*). 6a: hieratic form of *ḫ*.

Translation: (1) Year 1 (of) the King of Upper & Lower Egypt, Nebtawyre, <living> like Re forever. (2) It is the steward Ptah-shedwy's son (3) Intef who came to obtain this (4) amethyst, on an (official) mission: – the caravan leader Intef, (5) and the superintendent of his master's house, member of the magistrates' assembly, one to whom (people) open (6) the heart, his trusted favourite Khuyu, justified.

Commentary: In line 1, after the cartouche, *mỉ Rꜥ ḏt* is an ellipsis or error for <*ꜥnḫ*> *mỉ Rꜥ ḏt* as can be seen from many parallels of Eleventh Dynasty date.[26] The solecism '*ḏtn*' for *ḏt* (*n* for *tꜣ*) is also attested in other Eleventh-Dynasty texts, at Wadi Hudi and elsewhere.[27]

Lines 2-3 exhibit the well-known construction *ỉn*+ noun[28] + participle (*ỉỉ*), 'it is *x* who came' (Gardiner, §§ 227,3; 373,1).

Lines 5-6 record the rank and style of one Khuyu, a colleague of Intef. For this name, the nearest parallel is the Khuy of *PN*, I, p. 267:13. It is not certain whether Khuyu was Intef's equal or subordinate; *nb.f* in the first case would mean the king, but in the second case Intef himself. These alternatives would make of Khuyu either an administrator like Intef (if *ḥry-tp n pr* were a variant for *ỉmy-r pr*), or a lesser steward of Intef's property. The epithet *s n ḳnbt, wbꜣ n.f ỉb* is a less usual form of a type of epithet (*s n wbꜣ n.f ỉb*) well attested in the Eleventh and Twelfth Dynasties.[29] Similarly attested by date, but less frequent is the epithet *ḥsy.f n st-ỉb.f.*[30]

The structure of this text is much like that of WH 1; in both, the principal author, Intef, is named twice over, near beginning and end. WH 2 has two series of appellatives, but names Intef only the once.

26. Cf. J.J. Clère and J. Vandier, *Textes de la première période intermédiaire et de la XIe dynastie, Bibliotheca Aegyptiaca X*, Brussels, 1948, pp.15-16, No.20:1, 12,13 (BM.614); p.22, No.26:1 (Louvre C.252); p.42, No.28: *pi*, 5,6; p.44, No.30:1-2 (Cairo TR.3/6/25/1). The *dỉ* in *op.cit.*, p.12, No.16: right of *c*, is a purely hypothetical restoration and is not required. For other examples of this reign (Nebtawyre), see: *NIH*, p.77, No.53:1; p.78, No.54:1; *CMH*, p.99, No.192:10. This Dynasty, also *CMH*, p.79, No. 112; p.81, No.114:1.
27. In WH 4:2, 11:2, 14:4 (Dyns.11 and 12); Clère & Vandier, *op.cit.*, p.22, No.26:1 (Dyn.11); *NIH*, p.87, No.64 centre-left, pl.21 (Dyn.12).
28. Or, in this case, the entire noun-phrase *ỉmy-r pr Ptḥ-sd.wy s3 'In-ỉt.f.*
29. See Janssen, *TEA*, I, p.53, R:1-10, and p.144, Ao:2,4.
30. Cf. *ibid.*, p.87, Bz:11, 12.

WH, No. 4. Fakhry, No. 4; Schenkel, *MHT*, Nos. 438 (=A), 439 (=B), 440 (=C); PM, No. 72 (?).
Date: Nebtawyre Mentuhotep IV, Years 1 and 2 (*c.* 1998, 1997 BC).
Bibliography: Fakhry, pp. 21-23, figs. 17-18, pl. VIIB; Schenkel, pp. 261-3: 438-440.
Description: Large rock-text (height, 71 cm; width, 63 cm) in fourteen lines of cursive hieroglyphs (A,B), with three more short lines (C) adjoining right-hand edge of B; Site 5, S. side. Not seen in 1975.

Normalised Text:

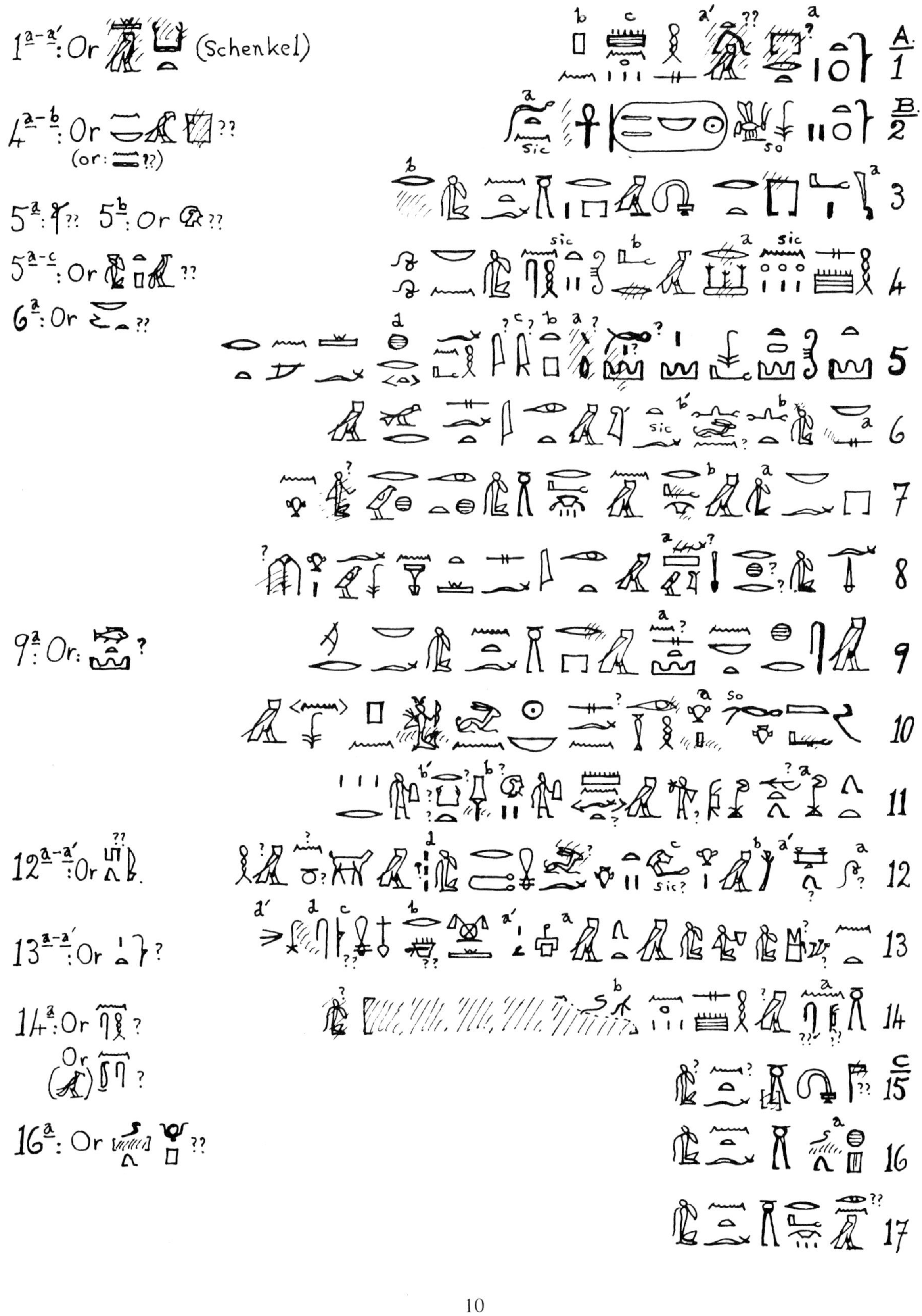

Textual Notes: 1a-a: damaged traces could suit either *prt* or Schenkel's *kꜣt* (*MHT*, p. 261, n. *i*). After this group, the uppermost trace is indefinite (bookroll or broad *t*). Below this, either a large *m*, or else a smaller *m* under a thin *ỉw*-sign. 1b: hieratic form of *pn* (cf. *HP*, I, No. 388). 1c: for the elaborate form of *mn* (also, lines 4, 14), cf. Clère & Vandier, *Textes de la première période intermédiaire*..., 1948, p. 45, No. 32:1; p. 46, No. 32: 14; p. 47, No. 33:9, 11 end, 14. 2a: *n* error for *tꜣ*, cf. above, WH 3:1, commentary. 3a: for a good hieratic parallel (Dyn. 11) for *wḥm*, cf. T.G.H. James, *The Hekanakhte Papers*, New York, 1962, palaeography section p.3, under E. 25 (162), first form (X, vs. 3). 3b: no sign appears to be lost below *r*.

4a-b: it is just possible (alternatively) to read these groups as *Ḥwt-ḥr, nb(t) Stỉ* (or: *n tꜣ Stỉ*), but the epigraphic forms that this assumes would be very poor, even for Wadi Hudi (!), and the sign above possible *nb/r/ tꜣ* can hardly be *n*. 4b: sign below ꜥ is probably *r* rather than *tꜣ* of *tꜣ -Stỉ*. For *Stỉ* used without *tꜣ* at Wadi Hudi, cf. WH 143:10. Unlike in line 5, *Stỉ* here has no determinative.

5a: only traces visible, as given; obscure. 5b: small circular sign over *p* is almost certainly *t*, in the light of other examples in this text; vertically striped *p*, cf. Clère & Vandier, *op.cit.* (n. 1c, above), p. 25, No. 27e:2; p. 30, No. 27t:2; p. 31, No. 27 phi:3; p. 45f., No. 32:1, 4, 5; p. 47, No. 33:1, 4, 5. 5c: two knobbed vertical signs, identical save for the thickened foot of the first. The context demands a verb (suffixed by *f* above a following *ḥnꜥ*), preferably of motion; and *ỉỉ* seems the only obvious candidate, despite the poor forms implied. 5d: for *r* below *ḫ* (rather than *t*), cf. the identical group in *sḫr*, line 9 below. 6a: 'bolt *s*' or *mꜣꜥt*-cubit and *t*? (cf. *HP*, I, No. 469B). 6b-b: hieratic-like forms in *ỉwt(y) wnt.f.*

7a: the seeming ꜥ*pr* (or vertical *mr*) appears, on closer inspection, to be merely a stylised seated-man determinative (as with *nb* in line 6, just above). 7b: so, rather than *mḥ* over *ỉb*. 8a: the small *f* is very doubtful (despite Schenkel, *MHT*, p. 262, n. *o*). For this and similar spellings of *šw*, cf. *TEA*, I, p. 166, J:16-18, 29; p. 167, J:42-44, 47. 9a: a line above the probable *s* could be *n*; *smt* is perhaps a safer reading than *ỉnt.*

10a: *ḥr* rather than *ḫꜣst*-sign. 10b: for forms (hieratic), cf. *HP*, I, No. 44, and Goyon, *NIH*, p. 58 top, and No. 64 (p. 87, pl. 21; second horizontal line at base). 11a: above *t* and legs, the apparent *r* is linked with further traces above it; the total sign could then be a hieratic *ḫt*-sign (*HP*, I, No. 269 and ligatures). 11b-b: readings here are uncertain.

12a-a: the *wꜣ* would be a poor form, the 'road' sign a good one; *wꜣt* is possible. Otherwise, first sign and legs might give *nmỉ* , but the sign over the legs would not be suitable as first determinative. 12b: a tall sign, *nḏm, sḫm, ỉꜣm*, or . . . ? 12c: possible hieratic form, cf. *HP*, I, No. 146. 12d: possibly a hieratic form. 13a-a: possible hieratic forms of *sꜣ* and *.ỉ* (*m-sꜣ.ỉ*); *rnpt* is also possible, but then the *t* should be over (not under) the stroke. 13b,c: highly tentative readings, but just possible (hieratic). 13d-d: totally obscure. 14a: forms ambiguous. 14b: trace of two signs largely broken away, then three or four groups are totally lost. 16a: first two signs, highly probable, for *ḫ<r>pw*, 'director'? Then traces ending in legs; perhaps a poor form for the 'striking man' determinative?

Translation: A. (1) Year 1: ⌜going forth⌝ (and) returning (??) with this amethyst (or: ⌜work (done)⌝ on this amethyst.
B. (2) Year 2 (of) the King of Upper & Lower Egypt, Nebtawyre, may he live forever. (3) Again going forth (by) the Seal-bearer and Steward Intef, for (4) the amethyst, as far as Nubia (or: of Hathor, Lady of Nubia). Every Nubian of Wawat (5), Nubia (*Stỉ*) both South and North regions . . . , each ('he') ⌜came⌝ with his necessities (?), for the sake ('love') of (6) their master (*or*: the master of Right): one without fault, innocent of doing wrong, great one in his lord's household (7), caravan-leader of caravan-leaders, In(tef); one who gets things done ('who does things'), while the knowledgeable man is in his (8) presence; one who can speak freely, innocent of doing wrong, because he has joined at council (9) with the plan(s) of the Lady of the Desert (*or*: Wadi?), the Steward Intef; one truly (10) beloved of his lord, the confidant in doing (what) he praises every day; when this expedition <of> the Southland came (11), rank upon rank (lit. 'thousand after thousand'), (each?) follower being a first (-class) warrior, while the leaders of works (??) were on (12) the road (*or*: (ready) to travel?), happy?/bold?/gracious? of countenance, heart(s) elated like men from the Residence (itself), upon (13) (my?) business. The/my (?) expedition came/returned, following me (*or*: in a year?), united completely, entirely (?) well, . . . (14) The product of the Nubians (?) /followers (?) was (*or:* The suppliers (?) brought?) amethyst, . . . [. . . for/to . . . Intef?]
C. (15) The Seal-bearer of the god (?), Intef. (16) The Director (?), Intef. (17) Made (?) by the caravan-leader, Intef.

Commentary: It must be emphasised that here (as with other WH texts), the text-readings adopted are based on repeated, intensive studies of the photographs, not simply the attempted 'facsimiles' by Fakhry; these are interpretations of what Fakhry considered that he saw, sometimes correctly, sometimes not.

TEXT A. It is unfortunate that the rock-surface in Fakhry's photograph is too damaged to arrive at a definitive reading of the two groups between 'Year 1' and 'amethyst', other than *t* and an *m*. Schenkel's reading has the attraction of simplicity and of dispensing with the rather fugitive traces possibly to be read as *ỉw*. Logically, however, the locution *wḥm-ʿ prt* that opens the Year 2 narrative (*B*, line 3), 'again going forth', would best follow a preceding, first *prt*, 'going forth', and the possible traces of *ỉwt* and a smaller *m* would fit. However, certainty is not possible.

TEXT B. In line 3, *wḥm-ʿ* is a synonym of *wḥm*, 'repeat'.[31] Here, it and *prt* are both infinitives (*wḥm-ʿ* governing *prt*), their subject being expressed by the direct genitive – lit., 'repeating going forth (of) . . . Intef' (cf. Gardiner, § § 301, 306,2). Cf. *wḥm-ʿ šmst* in WH 14:17, 'Again seeking (for amethyst . . .)'. The writing of *prt* without the legs determinative reflects older usage[32] In Year 1, Intef's only unambiguous title had been caravan-leader (*ỉmy-r pr* being possibly his father's title?), but here in Year 2 (lines 3, 9) Intef is clearly himself *ỉmy-r pr* and Seal-bearer, and so may have been promoted after his Year 1 expedition. Ptah-shedwy's name does not appear in the WH 4 text, so perhaps Intef was his father's successor. Intef otherwise boasts himself as supreme caravan-leader (line 7). The reading of the title here rendered 'Seal-bearer' (*sḏ3wty*?; *ḫtmw*?) has been open to question.[33] For the possible implications of the title *ỉmy-r pr*, see already under WH 1.

In line 4, Schenkel had read[34] *Ḥwt-ḥr nb(t) Stỉ* (cf. already the textual notes above), but close study of Fakhry's photograph (confirmed at this point by his facsimile) shows clearly a sign like *r* above and separate from a rectangular sign having three vertical elements, *k3* or *š3* (not *Ḥwt*), to which the following bird (*3*, not *ḥr*) would be phonetic complement. Again, the sign above the supposed *nb/t3* (cited also as *n*) appears in the photo and facsimile alike much more as the arm *ʿ* (with an upright projection, the 'shoulder', at its left end). The *'nb/t3'* may as easily be another *r*. These readings would produce a good version, *r-š3ʿ-r* used as equivalent of *š3 ʿr*, 'as far as'.[35] Lying as it does, south-east of Aswan and well into the desert, Wadi Hudi is in fact on the confines of Nubia, an interpretation which is explicitly supported by WH 14:8-9, 'my lord sent me to fetch amethyst from Nubia' (Ta-Seti).

In lines 4-5 we learn of the geographical origins of the manpower for Intef's expedition: 'every Nubian of Wawat, Nubia South and North'. In the Middle Kingdom (as later), Wawat was Lower Nubia extending from the First Cataract southwards to at least Korosko, and most likely as far as Buhen and the Second Cataract.[36] *Nḥsyw*, 'Nubians', was the term used basically for the inhabitants along the river-banks of the Nile in Lower Nubia,[37] besides its wider application to Nubians generally.[38] Ta-Seti, however, is ambiguous. It is at once a term for Nubia generally and also the name of the 1st Upper-Egyptian nome which included Elephantine, Aswan and Ombos.[39] The south and north regions here mentioned may be either the corresponding halves of this nome, or else a means of distinguishing between the northern Ta-Seti (1st U-Eg. nome) and the southern one (greater Nubia proper). In this connection, the foreign land determinatives to 'south' and 'north' are of special interest, being without immediate parallel,[40] and would hardly apply to Egypt proper. Hence, it is better to understand Ta-Seti as Nubia (not the 1st nome), its north and south halves being those of Wawat, or else, respectively, Wawat and the area south of Wawat.

In the middle of line 5 comes a crux, in which *ỉỉ* at least might be read, a verb in any case being needed (cf. textual notes above). In front of this, vertical traces plus *t* and *p* might just be read as *rs*, giving *rs-tp*. Depending whether the '*ỉỉ*' be read as *ỉỉ* or bad hieratic for the head-sign (*tp*), one would have *rs-tp ỉỉ.f* or *rs-tp.f* – '(every Nubian) who was active came', or simply '. . . was active'. However, *ỉỉ* is a better reading epigraphically. There is the remote possibility of reading the whole as *3tp*, with man (basket-on-head) det. instead of *ỉỉ* – '. . . was loaded with his *ḫrt*'; the *3* is possible, but the determinative is unconvincing epigraphically. As for *ḫrt.f*, it is assumed that the *t* has been omitted, while the sign above *.f* should be read as the book-roll det., not *š*; *ḫrš*, 'bundle', makes good enough sense, but is not otherwise attested so early with this meaning.[41] Thus, *ḫrt*, 'possessions/necessities', remains the more prudent reading; the workforce brought each his own weapon or tool and perhaps food.

Line 6 begins with either *nb.s(n)* or *nb m3ʿt*. Either makes good sense and is epigraphically possible. The use of *.s* for *.sn* as plural suffix is well attested, not least in the Middle Kingdom.[42] *Nb* is clear; the suffix may here precede the seated-figure determinative for better grouping, hence the rendering adopted here. However, as Schenkel suggests,[43] a mark over the seated figure's head might be the *m3ʿt*, hence *nb-m3ʿt*. This makes good sense and is a known (if rare) Eleventh Dynasty epithet,[44] followed, as here, by a negative (*ỉwty ỉsft.f*, cf. here *ỉwty wnt.f*).

The only objection (as is admitted by Schenkel) is then the apparent *s* below *nb*. The problem might be overcome by reading this horizontal sign as the *mꜣ(ꜥt)*-sickle and *t*. The epithet *ỉwty wnt.f* is well-known in both Middle and New Kingdoms.[45] For *šw m ỉrt ỉsft*, cf. above, WH 2:5, commentary.

In lines 6-7, *wr m pr nb.f* is less readily paralleled, but is very similar to such honorifics as *wr ḥs(w)t m stp-sꜣ / m pr-nsw*.[46] In line 7 after *nb.f*, one should read the seated-figure determinative, not *mr* or *ꜥpr*.[47] The following phrase 'caravan-leader of caravan-leaders' is constructed in the same way as *wr (n) wrw, ḥḳꜣ-ḥḳꜣw*, etc., cf. Gardiner, § 97. Despite Schenkel, *In* is merely a well known abbreviation for *In-ỉt.f*, 'In(tef)', one and the same man throughout this text and Nos. 1-3. In lines 7-8, the interpretation of *ỉr ḫt, rḫw n-ḫr.f* follows Schenkel,[48] as it suits the epigraphic data well.

In line 8, for *mdw r-ḫrw.f*, Schenkel's interpretation is again adopted, as it can be fitted to the admittedly difficult traces in the photograph; as often, the 'facsimile' is less helpful here. For the spelling of *šw* as diagnosed from the photograph, there are good parallels.[49] It is by no means unknown for early Middle Kingdom leaders of expeditions to repeat themselves in using honorifics in their inscriptions in the deserts.[50] The *n* in *n smꜣ.f sw* is taken here as conjunction, 'because' (Gardiner, §§ 157, 4; 164, 9). At the line-end, *ḫr* shows the same form as in line 12; *sḫ* is possible here.

In line 9, *smt* seems the likeliest reading. In lines 9-10, the honorific transposition of *mry mꜣꜥt* after *nb.f* is familiar elsewhere.[51] In lines 10/11, 13, two examples of *m* plus Infinitive (Gardiner, §§ 304, 2; 331). In line 11, *ḫt* is here understood as for *(m)-ḫt*, a known abbreviation.[52] Its use here may be deliberate, forming a punning series *ḫꜣ-ḫt-ḫꜣ*.[53] It is not clear whether the '1000s' should be taken literally. Rather, they may be understood as figurative of rank upon rank of men. *Šmsw* is not certain, but possible. *Mnt* (with warrior-determinative?) is probably a slip for *mn<f> (ꜣ/y)t*. *Ḫrp-kꜣt* is possible, if the apparent *r* is a phonetic complement to *ḫrp*.

Line 12, see textual notes above for initial sign-groups. The suggested reading *ḥꜣty* is epigraphically hazardous, but a good orthography; *wnf* would be Old Perfective ('Stative'), 'joyful/elated'. In lines 12-13, many readings are tentative but possible on photo; final traces at end of line 13 remain obscure.

In line 14, initial *ỉn* is clear, likewise *ḥsmn*. Under *n* are two vertical signs, entirely ambiguous, plus an ambiguous bird (*m, ꜣ, tyw*, or the like). Fakhry (cf. his facsimile) had favoured *nḥs(y)w*, 'Nubians'; *šmsw* would also suit very well – either would be followed by *m*. It is just possible to read *s-smn-tyw* (bird), i.e. *smntyw*, 'suppliers/ importers' (of precious stones), which would be a relatively late example of the functioning of the *smntyw*.[54] The broken traces after *ḥsmn* are obscure. The line may have ended with '(.. titles ..) Intef'.

TEXT C. Placed at the side of A/B, these three lines are almost a final, emphatic signature, with the name of Intef thrice repeated, every time with a different title. The signs in the first line (15) are badly formed, but possible. In line 16, Intef is clear, but not the title. At first it looks like [*ḥꜣt*] *-sp ꜣ* minus the year-sign plus a bird(?). But closer scrutiny shows no trace of any year-sign; the circle could be any circular hieroglyph; the strokes below it are a *p* with three vertical stripes (as in line 5, Text B, above). And the 'bird' dissolves into a squiggle, a lacuna(?) and pair of legs. This last group could be the striking-man det. to the title *ḫrp(w)*, assuming accidental omission of *r*.[55] Finally, line 17 has clear *ỉmy-r ꜥw In-ỉt.f*; above *m*, a thin *n* with a faint *ỉr* possible above it would give us *ỉr.n*, thus crediting the whole rock-text to the irrepressible Intef.

31. As established by Gardiner, *Notes on Sinuhe*, Paris, 1916, p.36 (on Sinuhe B.31), confirmed by *Wb.*, I, p.341:13, and Faulkner, *Dict.*, p.67.
32. *Wb.*, I, p.518 end.
33. Cf. latterly H.G. Fischer, *Inscriptions from the Coptite Nome*, Rome, 1964, pp.126-9, with earlier literature.
34. *MHT*, p.262 and note *e*.
35. Cf. Gardiner, §§ 179 end, 180; *Wb.*,IV, p.408:6-7.
36. As is set out by G. Posener, *Kush* 6 (1958), pp.50-55.
37. Posener, *ZÄS* 83 (1958), pp.38-43.
38. Idem, *Kush* 6 (1958), p.41.
39. Cf. G. Steindorff, in *Studies presented to F. Ll. Griffith*, Oxford, 1932, pp.361ff., and W. Helck, *Die Altägyptische Gaue*, Wiesbaden, 1974, pp.68-71.
40. Contrast *Wb.*, IV, pp.472-6, and III, pp.123-4, respectively.
41. *Wb.* (III, p.330:12) and Faulkner (*Dict.*, p.197) cite Papyrus Westcar of the Hyksos period as their earliest example. The feminine form *ḫršt* (*Wb.*, III, p.330:10-11) does go back to the Coffin Texts, but tends to be restricted to the phrase 'bundle of arrows'.

42. Cf. Gardiner, § 34 with n.12a, referring further to Gunn, *ASAE* 29 (1929), p.6; Blackman, *JEA* 16 (1930), p.64f., (5), citing six examples; and Dunham, *JEA* 24 (1938), p.6, n.15 - an Old Kingdom example.
43. *MHT*, p.262 and note *k*.
44. Janssen, *TEA*, I, p.141, Ac:15.
45. *Ibid.*, p. 153, C:18 (Dyn.12); in Dyn.18 with *wn*, cf. Sethe, *Urkunden IV*, pp.68:13, 131:10, 133:1, 414:12.
46. *TEA*, I, p.17, R:40, 42, 43, all Middle Kingdom.
47. Cf. also Schenkel, *MHT*, p.262, note *l*; for grouping, Clère & Vandier, *Textes de la première période intermédiaire...*, p.2, No.2, line 9 end.
48. *MHT*, p.262, with notes *m, n*.
49. See *TEA* reference, textual note 8a, above.
50. So in Wadi Hammamat No.199 (another Intef, under Amenemhat I), lines 3-4: *šwy m sp n mht, šwy m sp n b3gy, šwy m ist n ns* (Couyat & Montet, p.101).
51. Couyat & Montet, No.40:5 (p.47, pl.11), Goyon, *NIH*, No.84 (p.99); cf.Blu, *Unt.*, p.393, G.8.14.
52. *Wb.*, III, pp.343/4:1.
53. For an early Twelfth-Dynasty example, cf. *NIH*, No.61:8 (Sesostris I).
54. Studied by Yoyotte, *BSFE* 73 (1975), pp.44-55.
55. It is just possible to take the disc as for disc-within-horns, a sportive writing for *ḥry-tp* (cf. refs., *Wb.*, III, p.140 with *Belegstellen*, III, 140:5bis.

WH, No. 5. Fakhry, No. 5.
Date: Nebtawyre Mentuhotep IV, no year-date (*c.* 1998/1997 BC?).
Bibliography: Fakhry, p. 23, fig. 19, pl. VIIIA.
Description: Graffito (height, 14.5 cm; width, 9.5 cm) crudely engraved on the upper part of a quartzite block; Site 5.

Normalised Text:

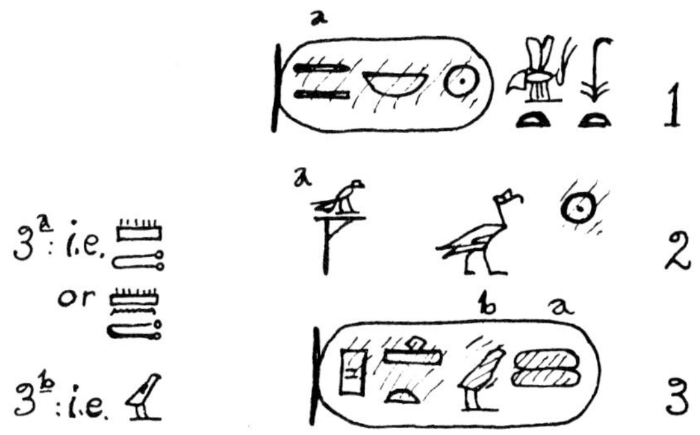

Textual Notes: 1a: either '*ḥpt*' sign, or much more likely *t3wy* as given here and as originally read by Fakhry. 2a: so, in hieratic form (cf. *HP*, I, No. 188B, especially the form from Prisse 2:8); no need to postulate an addition (as F. did). 3a: heavily worn (or erased?); read *mn* plus *ṯ* of Montu, with *n* (as normal) or without it (rarer[56]).

Translation: (1) King of Upper and Lower Egypt, Nebtawy(?)re; (2) Son of Re, (3)⌜Mentu⌝hotep (IV).

Commentary: Precisely as at Wadi Hammamat, most of the Wadi Hudi texts of this reign name the King only by his prenomen, but not exclusively. Two or three such texts have the nomen also.[57] This graffito probably dates to Years 1 or 2, as it is likely to have been cut at the same time as some of the other inscriptions of the reign.

56. Cf. Clère & Vandier, *Textes de la première période intermédiaire* . . . , p.24 middle:2; p.34 end:2.
57. So the Hammamat texts, Nos. 110, 192 and perhaps 112 (Couyat & Montet, pp.77, 98, 79, respectively).

B. The Twelfth Dynasty, I: Nos. 6-21.

WH. No. 6. Fakhry, No. 6; excavation no. 1; Aswan Museum acc. no. 1471; PM, 113.

Date: Sesostris I, Year 17 (*c.* 1955 BC).

Bibliography: Fakhry, pp. 23-4, fig. 20, pl. IX.

Description: Black granite block-stela, now 115 cm high, 52 cm wide and 38 cm thick. Three-line date over two vertical and nine horizontal lines, with two figures and two short lines below. Each man holds a baton, the first also a bow.

Normalised Text:

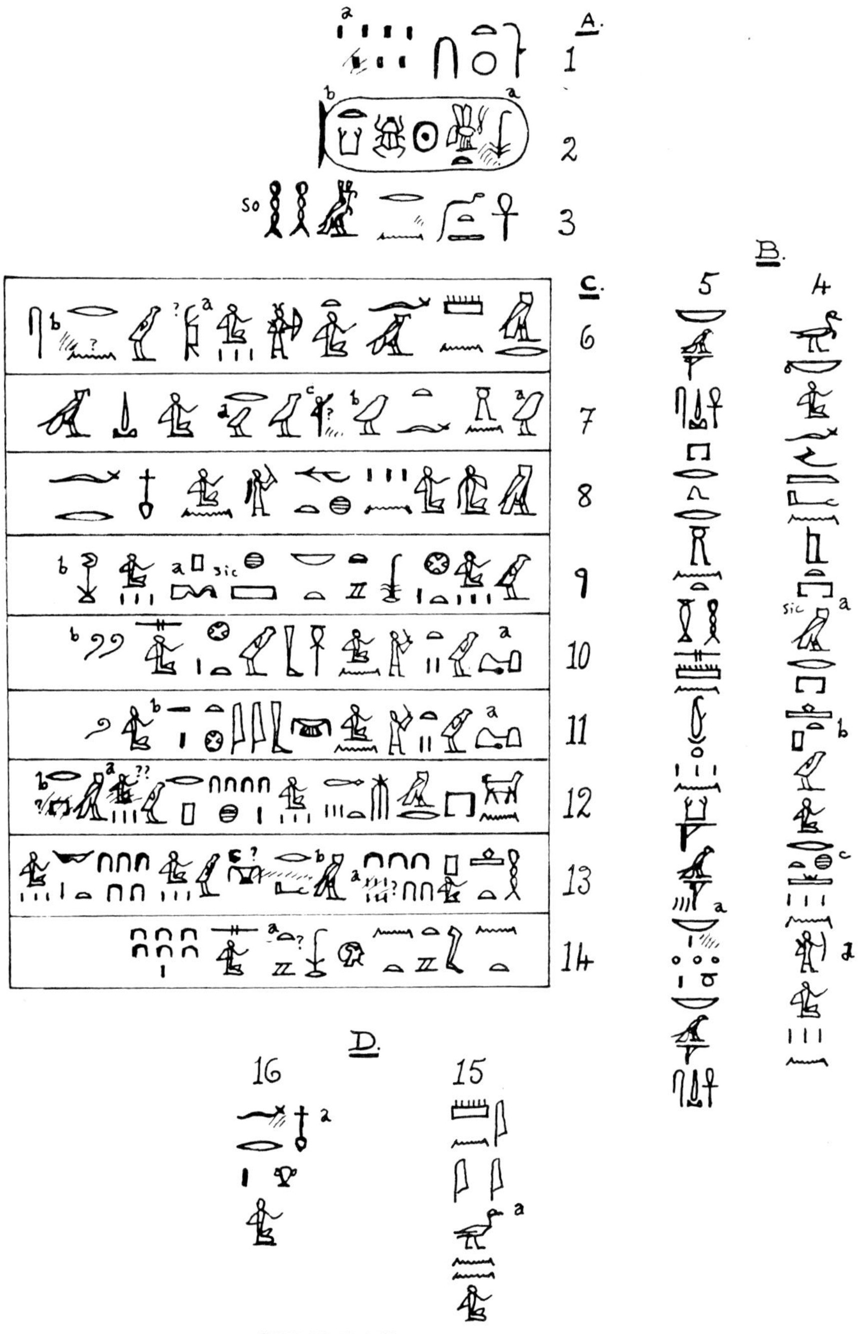

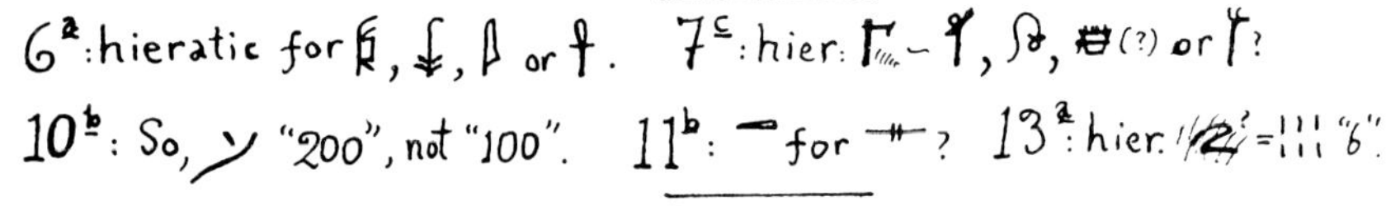

Textual Notes: 1a: a bare trace is visible of the final digit, but 17 seems certain. 2a: probably *t* lost under bee-sign. 2b: apparent *t* for *r*. 4a: *ỉb.f* omitted. 4b: hieratic group. 4c: hieratic ligature. 4d: this sign stands for *mšꜥ*, not *wr* or *sr*, (i) on context ('list of the expedition'), (ii) on form; cf. *NIH*, No. 61:1, 2, for almost identical writings of *mšꜥ*; so also, in Old-Kingdom texts, *NIH*, Nos. 36, 37. 5a: under hieratic *nb*, a vertical stroke, plural dots, then *nw*.

6a: hieratic form is ambiguous; *šmsw* or *šmꜥw* seem the likeliest readings. The former would be a second title, 'retainer'; the latter would be part of a longer military title, 'commander of troops of the South'. 6b: mark over *n* is probably accidental. 7a,b: in this text, all the bird-hieroglyphs look almost alike, regardless of whether *w, ꜣ, m,* etc., be intended. In context, these two are best read *sꜣ*. 7c-d: again the birds are indefinite in form; *w - w*, or *ꜣ - w*. The upright sign could be *wꜣ*, *ḏr*, or even *wsr*, but these readings give no proper name. Assuming damage to the foot of the sign, *rs* may be read as suggested, with *r* or 'eye' as its complement or determinative. This gives *Rsw-w(ỉ)* or even *Sꜣ-Rsw* (written *Rsw-sꜣ*, honorific transposition). 9a: hieratic forms. 9b: hieratic traces, only alternative would be '20', but less likely. 10a, 11a: the initial sign looks at first like the 'aged man' (for *ỉkw*, 'quarryman'); but it lacks the rear arm visible in (e.g.) *NIH*, Nos. 68, 69 (pp. 90, 91, pl. 17). Thus, it is more probably *ꜥḥꜣ*, giving *ꜥḥꜣwty*, showing a form half-way between the Dyn. 12 and Dyn. 18 examples in *HP*, I, No. 113 – two 'feet' like Prisse and Sinuhe, but a simpler form like Ebers. 10b: the extra mark at left (unless accidental) indicates 200, not 100. 11b: probably bolt-*s* lacking the cross-marks. 12a: possible traces. 12b: *m, r,* probable; the *pr*, very uncertain. 13a: hieratic. 13b: hieratic ligature? Reading uncertain. 13c: dubious reading. 14a: *t* or a stroke. 15a: *sꜣ* in hieratic form (*HP*, I, No. 216). 16a: *nfr* is possible, esp. as followed by *f, r.*

Translation: (1) Year 17 (2) (of) the King of Upper & Lower Egypt, Kheperkare, (3) may he live forever and ever.

(4) His true and favour<ite> servitor, the Steward Hotepu.

List of the expedition of (5) the Lord, L.P.H., that came to fetch amethyst for the sake of all the wishes of the Lord, L.P.H. (6) General of Troops and Retainer/of the South, Resuwi(?) son of (7) Intef son of Rensi. Strong troops of (8) recruits (9) of all of the Southern City, 1000 able-bodied men; (10) braves of Elephantine, 200 men; (11) braves of Ombi (Kom-Ombo), 100 men; (12) (from) the Residence: chief prospectors, 41 men; officers(?) of the Steward (?) (13) Hotepu, 56(?) men; caravan-leaders (?), 50 men; troops (14) of the Department of the Head-of-the-South, 61 men. (15) Ameny's son Neni; (16) Neferhor.

Commentary: Line 3, *nḥḥ* spelt without sun-disc determinative is the rule in Wadi Hudi texts of the Twelfth Dynasty (cf. WH 10:6; 16:2; 17:2; 20:2; 21:2; 95:2; 146:8-9), by contrast with the Thirteenth Dynasty (WH 22-25). Line 4 introduces the civilian chief of the whole expedition, the steward Hotepu. This name, *PN*, I, 257:22, and 260:8-9.

In lines 4-5, the first part of the heading ('list of the expedition . . . amethyst') is closely paralleled 21 years later in the same reign by a Hammamat text (*NIH*, No. 61:2-3): *rḫt mšꜥ* (spelt as here) *pr ḥnꜥ.ỉ r ḫꜣst tn*, 'list of the expedition that went out with me to this desert'. In both cases, *pr* is Perf. Participle qualifying *mšꜥ*. In line 5, *n kꜣw nbw nw Nb, ꜥ.w.s.* begins with a causal *n*, 'because of' (Gardiner, § 164,5), shading off into one of 'advantage' (*ibid.*, § 164,2). *Kꜣw* , a fuller form of *kꜣ*, represents the royal will, and the concept here is not dissimilar from that expressed later by Harwerre (the *bꜣw*, might, of his sovereign spurring him on).[58] The falcon-on-stand determinative to *kꜣw* and to *nb* (twice) sufficiently identifies the royal personage intended.

Line 6, for discussion of *šmsw/šmꜥw*, cf. textual notes above. In association with a relatively high title such as *ỉmy-r mnfꜣt*,[59] *šmsw* itself can be of high standing when its bearer served the king or a nomarch.[60] For the probable proper name *Rns, Rnsỉ*, cf. *PN*, I, 223:19, 224:21.

Line 7, see textual notes for (*Rnsỉ*) *sꜣ ỉn-ỉt.f sꜣ X*, where apparent readings of X as **Wꜣrw*, or **Ḏrꜣ/wrw* are discarded in favour of the altogether better **Rsw-w(ỉ)*. While not otherwise attested, such a name would be closely related to a large number of Middle Kingdom names,[61] as also would a form **Sꜣ-Rsw*.[62] Thus Resuwi is adopted here, with Sa-Resu as a second possibility.

Lines 7-9 head the list of personnel under Hotepu and Resuwi with *ḏꜣmw n nfrw*, 'troop of recruits', a term well attested in both Middle and New Kingdoms,[63] here with *nḫt* added. In WH 6 they are levied from Thebes, called here 'the Southern City'. Common in the New Kingdom, this phrase is still rare in the Middle Kingdom.[64]

But *ḫpšw*, 'strong (men)', i.e. able-bodied men (with clear determinatives) is unknown to *Wb.*[65] and Faulkner's *Dictionary* alike. *Ḫpšw* is followed by the first of a series of hieratic numerals, in this case *ḫꜣ*, 1000 (*HP*, I, Nos. 277, 641). These thousand men were evidently the main muscle-power of the expedition.

Lines 10-11 (closely parallel) introduce two allied groups of men, 200 from Elephantine[66] and 100 from Ombi (Kom-Ombo). For the reading of their function as *ꜥḥꜣwty*, not **ỉkwty*, cf. textual notes above, and the notes of Helck and Simpson.[67] *Nebuyt*, Ombi (Kom-Ombo), was situated in the northern part of the 1st Upper Egyptian nome,[68] and is not to be confused with Nubt near Tukh in the Coptite nome.[69] Thus, these two groups of men were from the same province.

Line 12 begins the next entry with the one word *ẖnw*, 'Residence', at this period, Ithet-tawy near Lisht.[70] Here it acts almost as a sub-heading, to define the place of origin of at least the next two groups of people (lines 12-13). The first group is 41 *ỉmyw-r ms-ꜥꜣt*, 'chief prospectors' (?), presumably relatively skilled men.[71] Compared to that of the whole expedition, their number is quite small, 41 out of more than 1500 men; compare 130 such men out of 9000 on Ramesses IVs great expedition eight centuries later. The second group needs care in reading the traces. *Ḫrp* can be deciphered clearly, then a poorly-formed sign or group, then *m*, then traces, followed in line 13 by *Ḥtp, 56* -'Hotepu, 56 (men)'. It seems clear that the latter name is identical with the steward Hotepu of line 4. The 56 men, therefore, are his group who came with him (as a royal official) from the Residence. From this, it is a short step to read one trace behind ***m*** **as** *r*, giving *ỉmy-r*, and so the traces below *r* as *pr* (?), hence 'steward', *ỉmy-r pr* as in line 4. The 56 men, therefore, should be *ḫrpw* of the steward Hotepu. If so, then the damaged sign(s) may be seated man det. over plural strokes; a *ḫrp* sceptre now seems less likely. *Ḫrpw* may be rendered as 'officers',[72] i.e. the staff who assisted Hotepu in running the expedition. The damaged traces below the '50' look most like a hieratic '6', hence the reading '56'.

In line 13, the next entry is 50 men whose title *may* be read (with some doubt) as *ỉmy-r ꜥw*, 'caravan-leader'. Like the following group, these probably came not from the Residence but from Upper Egypt itself, especially if they were in fact pacified or egyptianised Nubians as Dr. Lanny Bell has suggested.[73] Finally, lines 13-14 end the main list with 61 troops (*lit.*, 'bowmen, archers') of the Department of 'Head-of-the-South'. One might even prefer the literal meaning here, to contrast with the 'braves' (*ꜥḥꜣwtyw*) of lines 10-11. The 'Department' mentioned is the southernmost of the three major administrative provinces into which Egypt was divided in Middle Kingdom times,[74] and probably consisted basically of the eight southernmost nomes of Egypt (Aswan north to Abydos),[75] i.e. the nucleus-kingdom of Eleventh Dynasty Thebes prior to its reuniting Egypt. The other two provinces were then the South (other than *tp-rsy*), for the rest of Upper Egypt, and the North which would be the Delta.

In line 15, the hieratic form of *sꜣ* is one that recurs in WH 35 and 94 and at Wadi Hammamat (*NIH*, No. 82 - *Irỉ sꜣ Sbkḥtp*). The name Ameny is extremely common in the Middle Kingdom,[76] and Neni and Neferhor are well attested.[77] For wider comments, see below, Part III.

58. Sinai, No. 90:13, in Gardiner, Peet, Černý, *The Inscriptions of Sinai*, 2nd ed., I, pls. 25A, 26, II, pp. 97ff.
59. On which title, cf. Gardiner, *Ancient Egyptian Onomastica*, I, Oxford, 1947, p. 113*, No. 236 (*mnf3t*); Faulkner, *JEA* 39 (1953), p. 38; later periods, A.R. Schulman, *Military Rank, Title & Organisation, New Kingdom*, Berlin, 1964, pp. 13-14.
60. Faulkner, *op. cit.*, pp. 38-39.
61. Cf. *PN*, I, 226:18 to 227:8, especially 226:18, 29; 227:1, 3ff.
62. Cf. *PN*, I, 280:8 to 285:7, and feminines in *s3t-*, 285ff.
63. *Wb.*, V, p. 523:14.
64. E.g., only the last two out of some two dozen citations are of Middle Kingdom date in *Wb., Belegstellen*, II, p. 303 to II, 211:8.
65. III, pp. 268-270.
66. The first numeral (line 10) has a tick at left, hence '200' not '100'. Contrast W. Helck, *OLZ* 50 (1955), col. 213, and W.K. Simpson, *JNES* 18 (1959), p. 31.
67. Both of whom (*locc. citt.* first correctly diagnosed *'ḥ3wty*, here and in the Hammamat texts, e.g. *NIH*, No. 61:6, and at Sinai, in Sinai, No. 105:20 (north). In turn, these results entail reading *NIH*, No. 65:2 (p. 88, cf. pl. 19) as *'ḥ3[wty] n Gbtyw*, 'warrior of Coptos', not 'quarry man' (*ỉk(y)* . . .). Similarly (as noted by Simpson, *loc. cit.*), Couyat & Montet, No. 117:2, 3, should also be read in each case *'ḥ3wty n Gbtyw*, PN *'ḥ3wty* . . . 'warrior of Coptos, PN warrior . . . ' Contrast the phonetic writing of *ỉky* in Hammamat, No. 116. Simpson also indicates the reading *'ḥ3wty* in Couyat & Montet, No. 47:15 –'30 braves' – where the hieratic sign (barely visible, C & M, pl. 14, bottom) is similar to that in WH 6. Other examples of *'ḥ3wtyw*, cf. *NIH*, No. 64 (below):3, end, and No. 78:2. For the use of *'ḥ3wtyw* in hauling statuary from a quarry (but dressed differently from other levies), see P.E. Newberry, *El Bersheh I*, London, 1894, pl. 15, middle row, where they wear a front appendage and sometimes a feather in the hair. Other references, cf. *Wb.*, I, p. 217:8, and Faulkner, *JEA* 39 (1953), p. 40.
68. Cf. Helck, *Die altägyptische Gaue*, 1974, p.69.
69. Gardiner, *Ancient Eg. Onomastica*, II, p.5*f., No.316.
70. On which, cf. W.K. Simpson, *JARCE* 2 (1963), pp.53-59.
71. On *ms-'3t*, cf. remarks of Goyon, *NIH*, p.88, on his No.64:5.

72. Cf. *Wb.*, III, pp. 326:16-18, 328:2-6, and Faulkner, *Dict.*, p. 196, for related usages.
73. In *NARCE* 87 (1973), p.33, based on his unpublished thesis.
74. Cf. W.C. Hayes, *JNES* 12 (1953), pp. 31-33, and in summary form in his *A Papyrus of the Late Middle Kingdom*, New York, 1955, p. 138f.
75. Cf. Gardiner, *JEA* 43 (1957), pp. 6-9.
76. Cf. *PN*, I, 31:13; Couyat & Montet, Nos. 217, 225:3; Goyon, *NIH*, No. 61:2, 16; Gardiner, Peet, Černý, *op. cit.*, II, 1955, p. 223, Index (16 individuals).
77. Nen(i), cf. *PN*, I, 204:17; 205:3, 4, 26, 27. Neferhor, cf. *PN*, I, 198:6.

WH, No. 7. Fakhry, No. 7; exc. no. 2; Aswan Museum, acc. no. 1472; PM, 114.
Date: Sesostris I, Year 20 (*c.* 1952 BC).
Bibliography: Fakhry, p. 24, pl. VIIIB.
Description: Fragment of unpolished black and pink granite, max. height 34 cm, max. width 23 cm, thickness 4 cm. Nine horizontal lines of text, poorly engraved on rough surface, middle part almost effaced.

Normalised Text:

Textual Notes: 1a-a: merest traces of *ḫr* and *Ḥr*. 2a: sic! Not *tꜣwy*. 4a-a: the *r* seems clear (not a *sḏꜣwty*?), with room for *pr* before it and *t* below it. 4b-b: this first sign is more like the *kꜣt*-man (*HP*, I, No. 42) than either *ḫnt* (No, 590), *ḏbꜣ* (No. 462), or *ꜥpr* (No. 425). The book-roll over strokes compares with *HP*, I, p. 74: LXIII (Westcar col.), more than (e.g.) with *t* over *pr* (*ibid*, p. 73: LI). A second set of plural-strokes has a line across them, cancelling them? 5a-a: one might restore this whole line as [*r*] *ỉn* [*t ḥsmn pn*], cf. WH 3:3-4. 6a: end of line is blank, with no free space at start of line 7; hence, <*ỉb.f*> was forgotten by the engraver; cf. WH 6:4. 7a-a: reading is just feasible, cf. Commentary. 8a: a poor hieratic *ỉn* can appear thus, cf. *HP*, I, No. 496 (Illahun col., third example).

Translation: (1) Year 20 under: Horus, Life-of-Births, (2) the good god, Lord of the <Two> Land<s>, King of Upper & Lower Egypt, (3) Kheperkare, may he live like Re forever.

(4) [There went forth?] the Overseer of Works (?), Intef, (5) [to] fetch (?) [this amethyst?], (6) [his] true and favour<ite> [serv]itor, (7) who does all that he ever praises, (8/9) Intef, justified, son of the Director of Works (?), Didiu.

Commentary: In lines 1-3, *ꜥnḫ-mswt* is certain, and traces of *ḫr* and *Ḥr* can be made out, plus *kꜣ* and *rꜥ*. Traces between these last two signs can be taken for parts of *ḫpr*. Dating under Sesostris I is thus assured.

The restorations suggested above in lines 4-5 are conjectural, but fit context and sense perfectly, especially with WH 3 as parallel for structure. The stereotyped epithets in lines 6-7 are those common both in Wadi Hudi and other texts of the Middle Kingdom, cf. refs., WH 9 below.[78] The omission of *ỉb.f* is typical of the carelessness of this text (cf. line 2).

In line 7, if rightly read, the title *ḫrp k3t* with name *Didiw* in line 8 are together directly reminiscent of the possible *ḫrp k3t, Didiw* in WH 26:5, below, in a Year 1 of possibly Mentuhotep IV Nebtawyre. If the comparison is justified and the two men Didiu were one and the same, then the Intef of WH 7 visited Wadi Hudi on the same type of enterprise as his father Didiu had done at some 50 years' interval. This is possible, as Didiu's title may be junior to that held here by his son Intef. So, Intef may have been a senior official in his fifties or early sixties, if his father Didiu had visited Wadi Hudi in his twenties or thirties. For the name Didiu, cf. *PN*, I, 402:13.

78. This text is cited, Blu, *Unt.*, p.412, G.8.74 (*ỉr ḥsst.f nbt*).

WH, No. 8. Fakhry, No. 8; exc. no. 3; Aswan Museum, acc. no. 1473; PM 115.
Date: Sesostris I, Year 20 (*c.* 1952 BC).
Bibliography: Fakhry, pp. 24, 26-7, fig. 21, pl. XA (but caption under B); cf. PM, p. 319 under No. 115.
Description: Roughly trapezoidal piece of blackish-grey granite, with nine lines of text horizontally between ruling lines. Max. height 76 cm, max. width 40 cm, max. thickness 5cm.

Normalised Text:

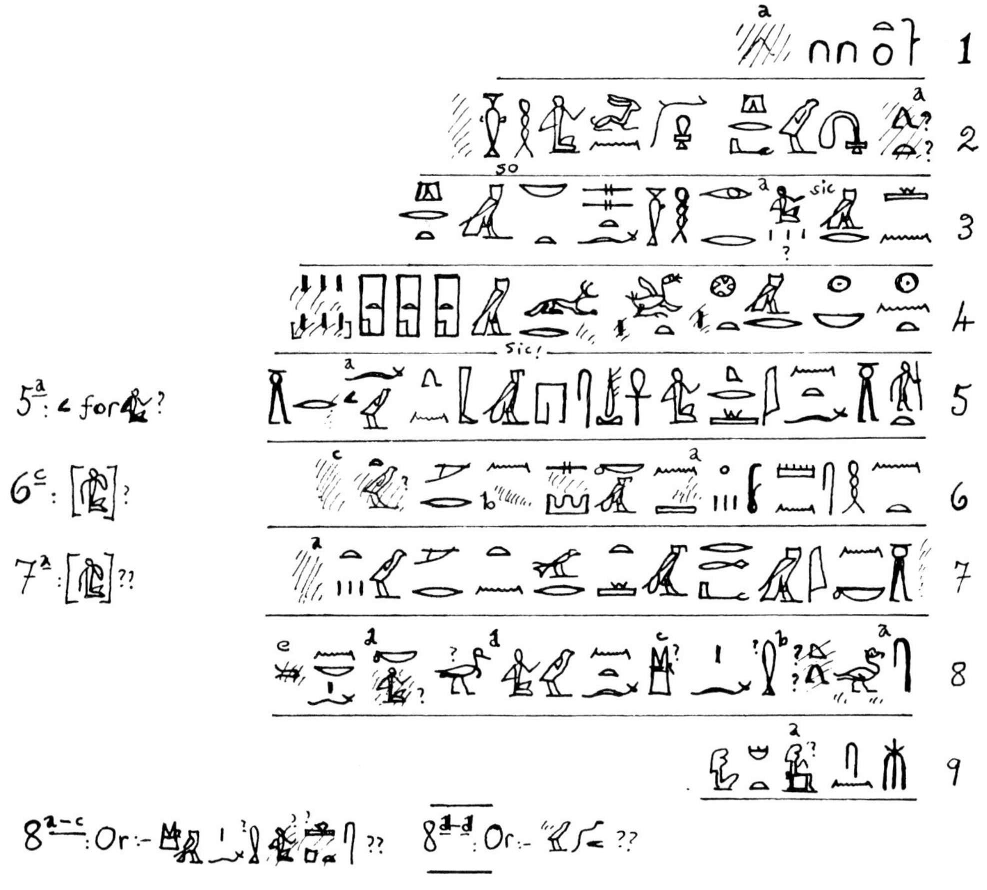

Textual Notes: 1a: no identifiable sign lost here. 2a: reading is doubtful but possible. 3a: ordinary seated man over a line, either *.f* or hieratic for plural strokes (*HP*, I, No. 561). 5a: hieratic for seated man, possible, not certain. 6a,b: apparently, accidental marks on the stone. 6c, 7a: traces doubtful but possible. 8a-c: hieratic traces, ambiguous, see figure above. 8b: difficult sign, cf. *ḥs* (*HP*, I, No. 502), *wḏ* (No. 474), or *ḥm* (No. 483) which gives best sense. 8c: difficult hieratic form, *ḫn* (*HP*, I, No. 590) rather than *ḏbꜣ* (No. 467)? 8d-d: ambiguous forms. 8e: significance of this last trace is unclear, a seated figure det. to *nb*? 9a: *šps*?

Translation: (1) Year 20: (2) There came (?) the Assistant-Treasurer to the Superintendent of the Treasury, Weni, the favourite one (3) of the army commander, one who does all that he (= the king) praises in the course (4) of every day, the city governor and Vizier, Chief of Secrets, Superintendent of the Six Great (5) Mansions, Intefoqer, L.P.H.

He sent me to fetch (6) amethyst of the land of Kas(h), so that (7) I should fetch (it) therefrom in the greatest possible quantity (*lit.*, 'very greatly'), (and) so that (8) His Majesty should present what he had charged me with (*or*: so that (8) I should please His Majesty with what he had charged me), the servitor of his lord, (9) born of a nobleman's wife (*or*: of whom is said to his lord, 'one born of a nobleman's wife').

Commentary: Line 1 gives the simple date Year 20 without specifying the king concerned, but mention of the vizier Intefoqer (lines 4-5) requires that it be attributed to Sesostris I or (less likely) to Amenemhat I, cf. on lines 3-5, 6, below. Line 2, beginning, a verb of motion (likeliest being *ỉwt*) may exist here, but the traces are uncertain;

if not, then lines 2-5 would simply present in headline form the titles and names of Weni and his high patron Intefoqer. The titles of Weni are familiar elsewhere, e.g. in the Middle Kingdom mining inscriptions at Sinai for another gemstone, i.e. turquoise.[79] His role was that of a junior representative acting for the chiefs of the royal and state treasury, to which (in principle) all precious minerals belonged.[80] Weni's name is not unparalleled.[81] In lines 2-3 remarkably, Weni denotes himself *not* as son (*ỉr.n*) of the vizier as previous interpreters have suggested, but as 'favoured one'/protégé (*ḥsỉ*) of the vizier. Usually, *ḥsỉ* expresses a relationship between an official and the King, rather than between higher and lower officials. However, the obsequious Weni treats his master the vizier almost royally, attributing to him also the tag 'Life, Prosperity, Health'. One can be *ḥsỉ* of others besides the king – of one's parents, and relations,[82] of one's nome,[83] of one's town,[84] and of 'everyone'.[85] Thus, Weni's relation to Intefoqer is striking but not anomalous.

Lines 3-5 introduce Weni's master, the vizier Intefoqer, who bears a common Middle Kingdom name.[86] This eminent personage has been long known to Egyptology.[87] His tenure of office is marked by several other monuments,[88] and it extended across the reigns of both Amenemhat I and Sesostris I, embracing their coregency. Intefoqer began his vizierate not later than Year 10 of Amenemhat I, on the evidence of a graffito in Wadi Girgawi near Korosko.[89] This confirms the previous attribution of Intefoqer's vizierate to this reign on the strength of the location of his mastaba tomb within the pyramid complex of Amenemhat I.[90] Other graffiti from Wadi Girgawi (mentioning Intefoqer) are dated to Year 19 of an unamed king, presumably still Amenemhat I.[91] But Theban Tomb No. 60, belonging to Intefoqer's wife Senet, originally had a scene showing the vizier himself in the presence of Sesostris I, (part of whose cartouche still survives). The vizier's figure was blotted out on his wife's (widow's?) orders.[92] This contemporaneity with Sesostris I was noted in one of the much later Eighteenth-Dynasty graffiti in this tomb,[93] mentioning 'this tomb of the time of Kheperkare'. It is further confirmed by the recent discovery of a stela of Intefoqer dated under Sesostris I in the vicinity of the ancient Egyptian Red Sea port at Mersa Gawasis, on which monument the vizier speaks of the king's command to fit out ships for the voyage to Punt.[94] Administrative letters of Intefoqer in Papyrus Reisner II are dated to Years 16 and 17 of an unnamed king.[95] In that same document occurs the steward Si-sopd, owner of the stela Louvre C. 166 dated explicitly to Year 17 of Sesostris I.[96] This might favour attribution of Papyrus Reisner II to Sesostris rather than to Amenemhat I, but of course is not proof. The same would apply at first sight in trying to date the Year 20 of WH 8, but here one may favour Sesostris I for reasons given below, under lines 6ff.

Among the titles and epithets accorded the vizier on WH 8 are few points of special note. Thus, *ḥry-sštȝ* is attested for other Middle Kingdom viziers.[97] The grouping of *m* and *r* in the next title (*ỉmy-r ḥwwt 6 wrt*) is most unusual (*r* before *m*), but certain. The title occurs in a variant form *ỉmy-r ḥwwt ʿȝt 6* in Senet's tomb[98] as in Papyrus Reisner II, but the form used here in WH 8 is very common with other Middle Kingdom viziers, down into the Thirteenth Dynasty.[99] The application of the tag 'L.P.H.' to a high official is paralleled by its bestowal on (e.g.) the early Middle Kingdom nomarch Neheri.[100]

In lines 6ff., Weni narrates in the first person. Of especial note is his reference to Kas (the later Kush). Epigraphically, the *k* is certain, the *alif* almost so, and the *s* and determinative fit the traces well. A convincing alternative is difficult to find. Thus, it is possible that this occurrence is an early example of the general use of the term, in contrast to its application to one limited principality. This generalising usage is already attested under Sesostris I in the inscription of Ameny at Beni Hasan,[101] as is made clear in Posener's careful study of 'Kush'.[102] Posener acutely remarks[103] that Kas (Kush) became widely known following the campaign by Sesostris I into 'Kush' in his year 18. Thus, the occurrence of Kas ('Kush') in WH 8 is readily explicable and natural if Year 20 of WH 8 is Year 20 of Sesostris I, but not if it were Year 20 of Amenemhat I, two decades before Sesostris' campaign; and it is to the reign of Sesostris I, that one may date a great expansion in Egyptian mining activities (as in other things[104]). Therefore the span from Year 10 of Amenemhat I to Year 20 of Sesostris I (including a 10-year coregency) would give a minimum tenure of office of some 30 years to Intefoqer as vizier. Intefoqer's one definitely attested son (by a wife Sit-Si-Sobek) was also called Intefoqer, occurring in the Execration Texts.[105] Arguing from this basis, Posener has recently come to a result for the vizier Intefoqer close to that adopted here.[106]

In lines 6/7, 7/8 occur two parallel clauses each governed by the compound conjunction *n-mrwt*, 'in order that' (Gardiner, § 181). The first is remarkable in having an Old Perfective ('Stative') governed in this way, but as 1st person singular of a verb of motion (Gardiner § 312, 3), this particular Old Perfective is parallel in function to a *sdm.f*. In line 7, the correct reading of the adverbial phrase *r-ʿȝt-wrt* disposes of Blumental's suggestion[107] *n wrt n-mrwt* . . . In line 8, the probable *ḥm.f* appears to be preceded by a verb beginning with *s*. Two readings of the cursive group are possible, *sʿḳ* being perhaps preferable to *sḥtp (.ỉ)* epigraphically. The hieratic form *ḫnt* (or *m ḫnt*) is uncertain but there are few convincing alternatives. Here, it would be a Perf. Relative form, 'what he (= the King) had charged me' (with/to obtain). The final groups of line 8 are also difficult. They appear to run on to line 9, as epithets of *wỉ*, 'me', i.e. Weni the speaker. *B3k n nb.f* seems preferable to *ḏdw.n nb.f* (Relative Form). In line 9, *ms* is Perf. Passive Participle, 'one born' (*n*, 'of'). The final group is best read as *ḥmt*, 'woman/wife'. The sign before it is clearly a seated human figure but not identical with the det. of *ḥmt*. The only word-sign that would fit epigraphically and orthographically would be *šps(t)*, 'nobleman/woman'. Two interpretations are then possible. The first is to take the difficult sign as the title *špst* and *ḥmt* as a proper name,[108] 'born of the noblewoman Hemet'. But as Weni does not name his father, it may be better to understand *ḥmt-šps* (with honorific transposition), 'born of a nobleman's wife,' a poetic way of claiming a good pedigree, perhaps.

79. Examples of *sḏ3wty ḫr-ʿ (n) ỉmy-r sḏ3yt* at Sinai, cf. Gardiner, Peet, Černý, *Inscriptions of Sinai,* I/II, Nos.27-8, 35, 43, 106-7, all of Amenemhat III-IV except No.43 (undated).
80. *Op.cit.*, II, p.16.
81. *Wn, PN*, I, 78:16, cf. *Wn.i, ibid.*, 79:9.
82. Especially in the Old Kingdom; *TEA*, I, p.87:21 to p.88:26.
83. In early Middle Kingdom, *ibid.*, p.88:27.
84. *Ibid.*, p.88:28.
85. *Ibid.*, p.88:29.
86. *PN*, I, 34:7.
87. Cf. A. Weil, *Die Veziere des Pharaonenreiches*, Leipzig, 1908, p.44, § 10; W.K. Simpson, *JEA* 41 (1955), p.130, and *JEA* 43 (1957), p.28.
88. Seven given in M. Valloggia, *BIFAO* 74 (1974), pp.127-8, No.6, but omitting Wadi Girgawi, see next note.
89. Cf. W.K. Simpson, *Papyrus Reisner III,* Boston, 1969, pp.10, 11; Z. Žába, publication forthcoming, 1977/8.
90. Cf. plan and references, *PM* IV, Oxford, 1934, pp.78, 79.
91. Simpson, *op.cit.* (n.89), p.10.
92. Cf. N.de G. Davies and A.H. Gardiner, *The Tomb of Antefoker,* London, 1920, Theban Tombs Series, II, pp.13-14, pl.16.
93. *Ibid.*, p.28, pl.37: No.29.
94. See Abdel Monem A.H. Sayed, *First International Congress of Egyptology, Cairo, October 2-10, 1976, Abstracts of Papers,* Munich, 1976, p.107, and in *RdE* 29 (1977), pp.169-173, pl.16. Cf. also J. Leclant, *Orientalia NS* 46 (1977), p.270, § 55, and pl.12, fig.27.
95. See W.K. Simpson, *Papyrus Reisner I,* Boston, 1963, p.20, nn.25, 26, and his *Papyrus Reisner II,* Boston 1965, pp.20-23, 40, pls.7:1, 8:1, 10:1, and *Papyrus Reisner III,* 1969, pp.10-11.
96. Cf. references, Simpson, *Papyrus Reisner I*, p.21.
97. Cf. (e.g.) Weil, *Die Veziere des Pharaonenreiches,* § 6, pp.39f. (thrice), and § 11, pp.44f.
98. See Davies and Gardiner, *op.cit.* (n.92), pp.11-12, 17, pls.6-7, 14.
99. Cf. Weil, *op.cit.*, (nn.87, 97), § 7:2 (p.42), § 14 (p.46), § 17 (p.48), § 22 (p.50), § 25 (p.51), and probably § 27.
100. Cf. R. Anthes, *Die Felseninschriften von Hatnub*, Leipzig, 1928, Unterschungen IX, p.59, No.26:1.
101. Sethe, *Urkunden des Mittleren Reichs, Urk. VII*, p.14:10, 19.
102. In *Kush* 6 (1958), pp.61-63.
103. *Op. cit.*, p.61, following on p.45.
104. As remarked by W.K. Simpson, *MDIK* 16 (1958), p.309.
105. Posener, *CdE* 14 (1939), p. 43; Valloggia, *BIFAO* 74 (1974), p.12.
106. Cf. *Annuaire du Collège de France* 76 (1977), pp.441-2.
107. Blu, *Unt.*, p.68, B.1.19. end.
108. *PN*, I, 240:11;

WH, No. 9. Fakhry, No. 9; exc. no. 4; Aswan Museum, acc. no. 1474; PM, 116.
Date: Sesostris I, Year 22 (*c.* 1950 BC).
Bibliography: Fakhry, pp. 26, 28, fig. 22, pl. XB (but caption under A).
Description: Rough grey-granite stela, well preserved, with ten lines of well cut text between ruling lines from edge to edge. Below is a man shown in pointed kilt (facing right), holding a staff and (horizontally) an *ʿb3*-sceptre. Height 68 cm, width 29 cm, thickness 23 cm.

Normalised Text:

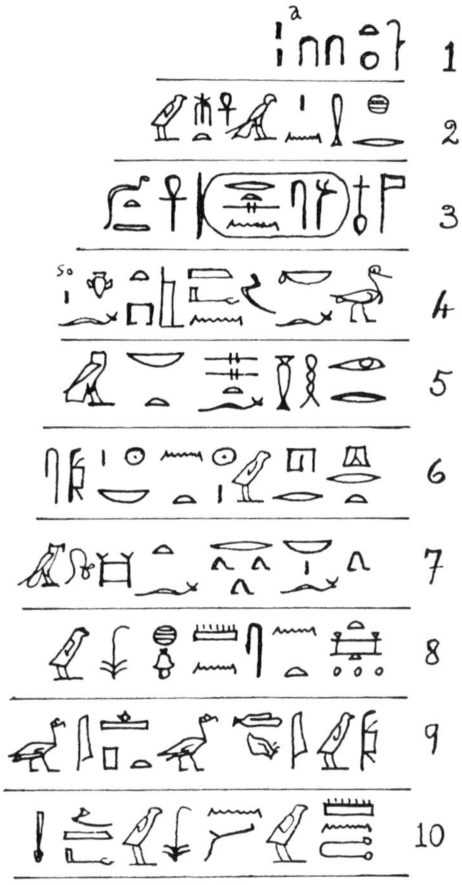

Textual Notes: 1a: Thus, two shorter strokes above one another, although the interval between them is so small as to give the appearance of just one tall stroke at first sight.

Translation: (1) Year 22 (2) under the Majesty of: Horus, Life-of-Births, (3) the good god Sesostris (I), may he live forever.

(4) His true and favourite servitor, (5) who does all that he praises (6) throughout the course of every day, one who follows (7) his master at his goings, one who sticks to the ways (8) of him who advanced him; (9/10) the retainer, Nesu-Montu, justified, son of Hetepi, son of Idi.

Commentary: Dateline and filiation apart, this text contains only three 'chains' of typical Middle Kingdom honorific epithets. The first, *b3k.f m3ʿ n st-ib.f*, is very frequently associated with the second, *ir(r) ḥsst.f nbt m ḫrt-hrw nt rʿ nb*, as is shown by other occurrences.[109] In WH 9 here, we have the most developed form of this second compound epithet.[110] In both full and abbreviated forms, it is very common in the Wadi Hudi inscriptions.[111]

The third characteristic epithet (lines 7-8), *mdd w3wt nt smnḫ sw*, was especially favoured from the early Middle Kingdom well into the Twelfth Dynasty, and occasionally much later.[112] In the earliest examples, from the Eleventh Dynasty into the reign of Sesostris I, *mdd mtn* is the preferred idiom; but from Sesostris I onwards, *w3t* tends to replace *mtn.*[113] The whole idiom recurs in other Wadi Hudi texts.[114]

The names of the dedicator and his forbears are common in the Middle Kingdom. For Nesu-Montu, cf. *PN*, I, 176:14; for Hetepi, *ibid.*, 260:3; for Idi, *ibid.*, 53:17-25. The title *šmsw*, 'retainer', is by itself too vague to fix the relative rank of its bearer.

109. Cf. Janssen, *TEA*, I, p.138, Q:3-10.
110. Cf. also *TEA*, I, p. 147f., F:147, 154.
111. See WH 1,2, 4, 7, 8, 9, 13, 14, 18, 21, 58, 144, 145, 146, 147, 149.
112. Cf. Conspectus in *TEA*, I, p. 70f., Bc:1-31, plus further refs. given by *Wb.*, II, p.192:4, 5 (*Belegstellen*) and by Blu, *Unt.*, p.341, G.5.39-41; the idiom persists down to Dyn. 18, cf. Sethe, *Urkunden IV*, p.208:7.
113. Other examples of *w3t* in plural, cf. *TEA*, I, p.71, Bc:18, 21,22, 26.
114. So in WH 18, 21.

WH, No. 10. Fakhry, No. 10; exc. no. 37; Aswan Museum, acc. no. 1507; PM, 119.
Date: Sesostris I, Year 22 (*c*. 1950 BC).
Bibliography: Fakhry, pp. 28-9, fig. 23, pl. XIIA.
Description: Granite block of elongated triangular form, bearing seven lines of horizontal text, the last being separate from the other six and just possibly by another hand. Below stands a human figure (facing right) closely similar to that on WH 9. Height 109 cm, width 36 cm, thickness 24cm.

Normalised Text:

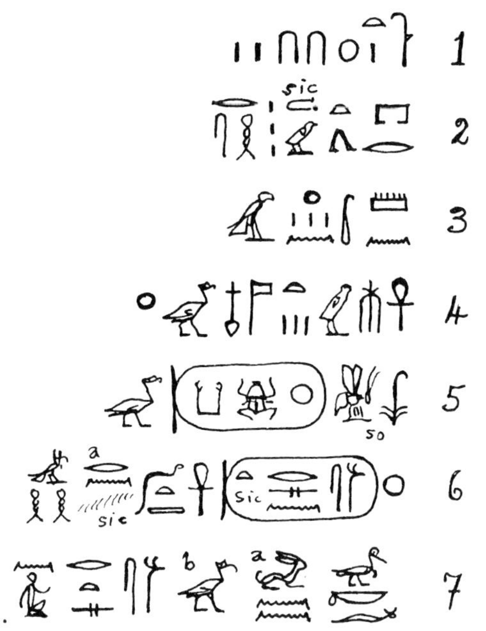

Textual Notes: 6a: *rn* has been inscribed above a space where there is a mark or flaw in the stone. 7a: the *wn*-sign is small, schematic, but clear. 7b: the bird is slightly short in the tail, but read *sꜣ*, not *w*.

Translation: (1) Year 22:

(2) People went out to (seek) (3) amethyst for: Horus, (4) Life-of-Births, the good god, Son of Re (*sic*), (5) King of Upper & Lower Egypt, Kheperkare, Son of Re, Sesostris (I), may he live for ever and ever. (7) His servitor, Senwosret son of Wenen.

Commentary: Line 1, the peculiar spelling of 'regnal year' with *t* and stroke is shared with WH 11 of the same date. Line 2 presents what appear to be two remarkable solecisms in one brief phrase (*prt.tw r ḥsmn*). *Prt* is clearly an infinitive; its subject should be expressed by *ỉn* plus noun or an independent pronoun, not by a suffix, which is normally used to express the object of an infinitive (Gardiner, § 300). But here, the indefinite suffix *.tw* appears as subject pronoun added to *prt*. And, in turn, it is misspelt, with plural strokes as a determinative, perhaps a reflex of the plurality of persons (the expedition) hidden behind the vague 'one'.

The phrase *r ḥsmn*, 'for amethyst', is an abbreviation for the fuller *r ỉnt ḥsmn* of other texts, 'to fetch amethyst'. In lines 4-5, the first occurrence of the title *Sꜣ Rʿ* is superfluous, and also misplaced when judged by customary usage. Line 7, the name Senwosret is extremely common among private individuals during the Middle Kingdom.[115] The name Wenen, as spelt here, is less easily paralleled.[116] Senwosret gives himself no functional title, but terms himself merely *bꜣk*, 'servitor', of the king.

115. See *PN*, I, 279:1.
116. But cf. similar names in *PN*, I, 78:16, 79:9, 11, 13, 21, 22.

WH, No. 11. Fakhry, No. 11; exc. no. 5; Aswan Museum, acc. no. 1475; PM, 117.
Date: Sesostris I, Year 22 (*c.* 1950 BC).
Bibliography: Fakhry, pp. 29-30, fig. 24,, pl. XIIB.
Description: Pink granite block, roughly square surface. Figure of a man as on WH 9, 10, with two vertical lines of text before him and a horizontal dateline above him. Max. height 48 cm, max. width 34 cm, thickness 12 cm.

Normalised Text:

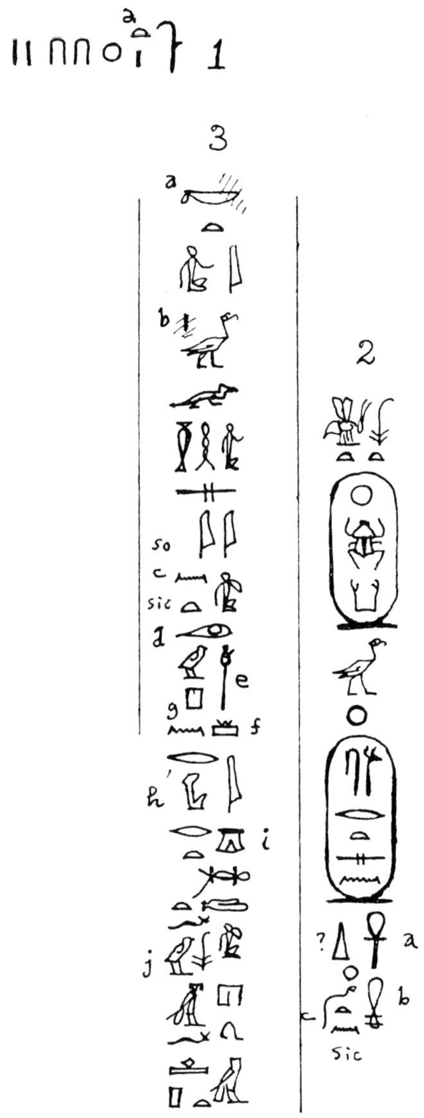

Textual Notes: 1a: this spelling, cf. WH 10:1. 2a-b: hieratic *dỉ*, then vertical sign plus *rʿ* - hence, *mỉ Rʿ*. 2c: *n* for *tꜣ* in *ḏt*. 3a: so rather than *nbw* (form different, likewise in hieratic). 3b: a stroke with transverse break across it in the stone. 3c: for *nt<y>*. 3d: *ỉr* written like *r*. 3e: hieratic for *wḏ* (*HP*, I, No. 474) but side-tick omitted, plus chick (*HP*, I, No. 200); for the forms, cf. Posener *JEA* 54 (1968), pl. IX, line 7 top (but with *ḏ*). 3f: hieratic form, very abbreviated (cf. *HP*, I, No. 538), lacking the baseline, and hence written like plural strokes. Below it, a line for *n*, at first sight like a poor *f*. 3h: poor hieratic form of the *ỉrỉ*-figure. 3i: hieratic form of *g*. 3j: hieratic *sw*, not *wḏ* (*HP*, I, No. 289 [2nd ex., Sinuhe col.], as opposed to No. 474), as its tip turns the opposite way to that of *wḏ*.

Translation: (1) Year 22: (2) King of Upper & Lower Egypt, Kheperkare, son of Re, Sesostris (I), given life like Re forever.

(3) Sobek son of Keti, the favoured one who made this stela. Now as for who (ever) reads it out, he shall return (home) safely!

Commentary: Line 1, same date in same orthography as WH 10. Line 2, *S3 Rˁ* without transposition; *di ˁnḫ* curiously reversed. Names can be found closely similar to Keti,[117] likewise Sobek as a personal name.[118]

The real significance of the second half of line 3 was first established by Posener,[119] reading *ir grt šdt(y).f(y) wḏ(.i)?, h3.f m ḥtp.* The *h3.f m htp* is clear, and the *šdt(y).f(y)* readily readable. But for *wd.i*, one should read *sw,* see textual notes above. In turn this pronoun requires an antecedent, cf. below. The *grt* offers no problem, but *ir* has the det. of *iri*, 'relating to', here superfluous. The Hatnub stela (also Year 22 of Sesostris I) published by Posener has the full expression *ir grt* [*s*] *nb, sš nb, iky nb, ḫrp nb šdt(y).f(y) wḏ pn, ḏdt(y).f(y)* . . . *iw.f r pḥ m ḥtp* . . . : 'now as for every [man], every scribe, every quarryman, every gang-controller who shall read this stela and shall say . . . (offerings), he shall reach (home) safely'.[120] This offers confirmation for WH 11:3. In mid-line 3, a badly written *wḏ pn* provides the antecedent for *sw* and object of *nty ir* (defectively spelt).[121] Blessings on readers who respect texts and curses on those who deface them occur frequently in the early Middle Kingdom graffiti at Hatnub.[122] This is the only Wadi Hudi example.

117. Cf. *PN*, I, 349:24, 25, 27, 28 (masc.), and 15, 16, 21, 23 (fem.).
118. *PN*, I, 303:20.
119. *JEA* 54 (1968), p.69, note *n.*
120. *Ibid.*, pp.67-70, pls. 8-9, completing that published by Grdseloff, *ASAE* 51 (1951), pp.143-6.
121. The defective spelling of *nt(y)* is Old Egyptian, but found still in Middle Egyptian (cf. Gardiner, § 199, p. 150, n.7, refs.); the *ir* is Perf. Active Participle.
122. Cf. R. Anthes, *Die Felseninschriften von Hatnub*, 1928, **p. 10, n.1**, for a list; a further example, W.K. Simpson, *JNES* 20 (1961), pp.25-30, completing his paper in *MDIK* 16 (1958), pp.298-309.

WH, No. 12. Fakhry, No. 12; exc. no. 6; Aswan Museum, acc. no. 1476; PM, 129.
Date: Sesostris I, Year 24 (*c.* 1948 BC).
Bibliography: Fakhry, pp. 30-31, fig. 25, pl. XIA.
Description: Roughly shaped quartzite block with four lines of irregular hieroglyphs. Max. height 34 cm, max. width 25 cm; from the valley.

Normalised Text:

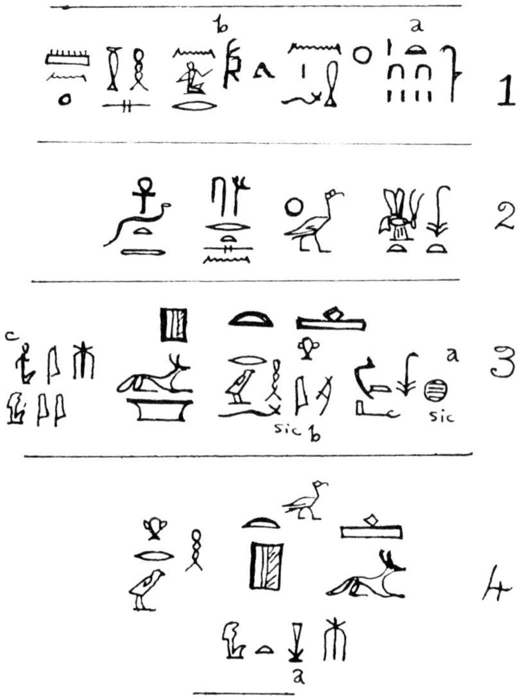

Textual Notes: 1a: 'Year' with *t* and stroke as in WH 10, 11. 1b: this sign is almost certainly *šms*, see Commentary. 3a: *r* of *rḫ-nsw* is omitted. 3b: *mrỉ* for *mry* (an *ỉ* omitted). 3c: these two signs differ slightly in form, hence read the first as seated man, hand-to-mouth. 4a: either *sn* or *smꜣ* epigraphically.

As the order of signs in this text is sometimes rather irregular, a transliteration is here appended:

(1) *ḥꜣt-sp 22 n ḥm.f; šms.n.ỉ r ḥsmn;*
(2) *nsw-bỉt, Sꜣ-Rꜥ, Snwsrt, ꜥnḫ ḏt.*
(3) *<r>ḫ-nsw mꜣꜥ, mry.f, ḥry-sštꜣ, Ḥtp-ḥrw ms Iy,*
(4) *sꜣ ḥry-sštꜣ, Ḥtp-ḥrw, ms Snt.*

Translation: (1) Year 24 of His Majesty, (when) I sought for amethyst, (2) the King of Upper & Lower Egypt, Son of Re, Sesostris, may he live for ever.

(A) (4/3) The Chief of Secrets Hetep-heru born of Senet, son of the King's real Acquaintance whom he loves, the Chief of Secrets, Hetep-heru born of Ay.

or

(B) (3/4) The King's real Acquaintance whom he loves, the Chief of Secrets, Hetep-heru born of Ay, son of the Chief of Secrets, Hetep-heru born of Senet.

Commentary: Lines 1 and 2 exhibit already the very erratic grouping and composition of this whole text. Thus, one would expect the *šms.n.ỉ r ḫsmn* of line 1 to follow, not precede, the titulary of line 2. The (at first) unusual *šms r*, 'to seek for' (object) is paralleled in WH 14:17. Attribution of this text to Year 24 of Sesostris I rather than III is made likely by the fact that its composer deemed it needless to give any further royal title to distinguish which Sesostris he served – if it were the first, no distinction was needed.

The worst orthographic confusion occurs in lines 3-4, and the safest way to proceed is by elimination. In line 3, the slightly mis-written title <r> *ḫ nsw mꜣꜥ* is clear, and with it should go the common complement *mry.f* (written *mrỉ.f*).[123] At the end of the line is *ms ꞽIy*, 'born of Ay', naming the person's mother.[124] In line 4, along the bottom, we have similarly *ms Snt*, 'born of Senet', presumably mother of the person named in this line. While the phonogram here could be read either *sn* or *smꜣ*, *sn* is preferable. *Snt* is a common feminine name in the Middle Kingdom,[125] while a **Smꜣt* seems unattested. In both lines, we are now left with (i) a group *ḥtp* in very large hieroglyphs, (ii) a group *ḥrw* below or behind *ḥtp*, and (iii) a recumbent jackal before or behind (i) plus (ii) suggests a proper name *Ḥtp-ḥrw*, and the varying position of the jackal a title – *ḥry-sštꜣ*, 'chief of secrets', being the obvious reading.[126] A personal name *Ḥtp-ḥrw*, 'Horus is contented/pacified' is not yet attested, but its close equivalent *Ḥrw-ḥtp* of similar meaning is very common in the Middle Kingdom,[127] while other names of the form *Ḥtp-x* are known.[128]

If one assumes that the *sꜣ* above *Ḥtp-ḥrw* in line 4 indicates a normal Middle Kingdom 'inverted filiation ('X's son Y'), as in the Translation (A) above, the genealogy of the like-named father and son is as follows:

Genealogy A

X = fAy
|
Hetep-heru = fSenet
|
Hetep-heru

If, however, a straight succession be assumed ('Y son of X'), the following genealogy results:

Genealogy B

X = fSenet
|
Hetep-heru = fAy
|
Hetep-heru

In this work, Geneaology and Translation A have been preferred as being more typically Middle Kingdom; but B may well prove superior in others' eyes. As for the titles of Hetep-heru son of Ay, *rḫ-nsw mꜣꜥ* is borne by other leaders and members of expeditions, both at Wadi Hudi[129] and elsewhere, e.g. at Wadi Hammamat,[130] and in a long series of texts in Sinai.[131] The title common to both Hetep-herus, 'Chief of Secrets', also recurs in both Sinai[132] and Hammamat.[133]

123. Too common to need comment; for less usual variants, cf. *TEA*, I, p.63, Aw:15, 17, 18.
124. For Ay, cf. *PN*, I, 7:17 (common for both men and women).
125. *PN*, I, 311:12.
126. This title, so spelt, cf. Gardiner, Sign-list E.15, 16; Faulkner, *Dict.*, p.249.
127. *PN*, I, 250:7.
128. E.g., *Ḥtp-ḫnmw*, *PN*, I, 426:27.
129. Cf. below, WH 16, 17, 21.
130. Goyon, *NIH*, No. 61:5, reign of Sesostris I.
131. Cf. Gardiner, Peet, Černý, *Inscriptions of Sinai*, II, p.230, Index, sub *rḫ nsw mꜣꜥ*.
132. *Ibid.*, *loc. cit.*
133. Couyat & Montet, Nos. 48:9 and 149:1, both with further qualifications.

WH, No. 13. Fakhry, No. 13; exc. no. 7; Aswan Museum acc no. 1477; PM, 120.
Date: Sesostris I, Year 28 (*c.* 1944 BC).
Bibliography: Fakhry, pp. 32-33, fig. 26, pl. XIB.
Description: Roughly trapezoidal block of granite, black flecked with pink, with ten horizontal lines of text within frame lines, in two clear sections of five lines each. Height 51 cm, width 25 cm, thickness 27 cm.

Normalised Text:

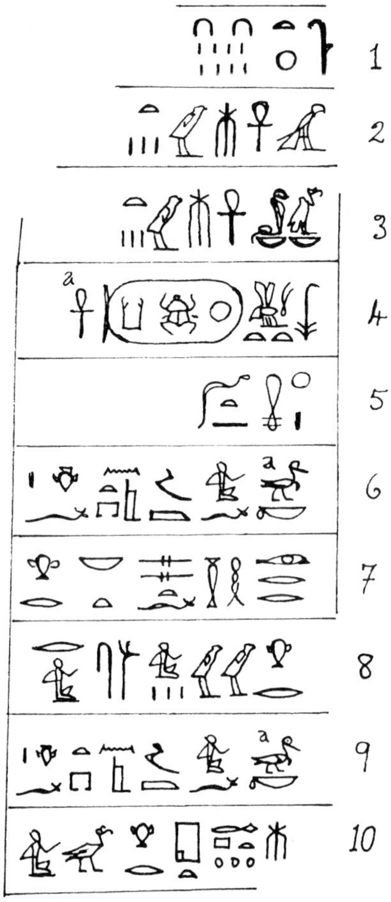

Textual Notes: 4a: hieratic form of *ʿnḫ*, cf. *HP*, I, No. 534, even more cursive than in lines 2-3. 6a, 9a: hieratic forms of *bꜣ*-bird, *HP*, I, No. 208.

Translation: (1) Year 28: (2) Horus, Life-of-Births, (3) Two-Goddesses, Life-of-Births, (4) King of Upper & Lower Egypt, Kheperkare, may he live (5) like Re forever.

(6) His true and favourite servitor (7) who does all that he praises, the supreme (8) artisan, User. (9) His true and favourite servitor, (10) the prospector Si-Hathor.

Commentary: This well articulated text divides neatly between the official dateline under Sesostris I, and the epithets, titles and names of its two dedicators. Each adopts the same posture as royal servant, the first at greater length. Both are professionally concerned with work in stone, particularly precious stones, and both bear common Middle Kingdom names. [134]

User's title *ḥr(y)-ḥrww* is securely attested in Middle Kingdom texts from other mining and quarrying districts, e.g. Sinai.[135] Among such, particularly noteworthy is Hammamat No. 40 of the late Eleventh Dynasty,[136] belonging to Ipi son of Ipi, *ḥr(y)-ḥrww m ʿꜣt nb(t) šps(t) nt pr nsw*, 'supreme artisan in every precious stone of the royal house', indicating clearly the field of activity of the *ḥry-ḥrww*.[137] Si-Hathor's title *ms-ʿꜣt*, is more commonly met with; cf. references given with the remarks on *ỉmy-r msw-ʿꜣt*, WH 6:12, above.

134. User, *PN*, I, 85:6; Si-Hathor, *PN*, I, 283:20.
135. Nos.85:N, 19, 20; 100:W, 2; cf. refs., Gardiner, Peet, Černý, *op.cit.*, p.106, note *a*.
136. Couyat & Montet, No.40, pp.46-7.
137. One may add the brief graffito, Goyon, *NIH*, No.79, p.97, pl.26, of the 'supreme artisan, Ipi-ankhu'.

WH, No. 14. Fakhry, No. 14; exc. no. 8; Aswan Museum, acc. no. 1478; PM, 118.

Date: Sesostris I, Years 20 and 24 (*c.* 1952 and 1948 BC).

Bibliography: Fakhry, pp. 33-34, fig. 27, pl. XIIIA.

Description: Vertically tapered block of porphyry, with nineteen horizontal lines of text within frame-lines. The first fourteen lines (A) are of Year 20, the last five were added (B) in Year 24. Height 78.5 cm, width 50 cm, thickness 20 to 27 cm. Found in Fakhry's Site 5 at foot of the hill.

Normalised Text:

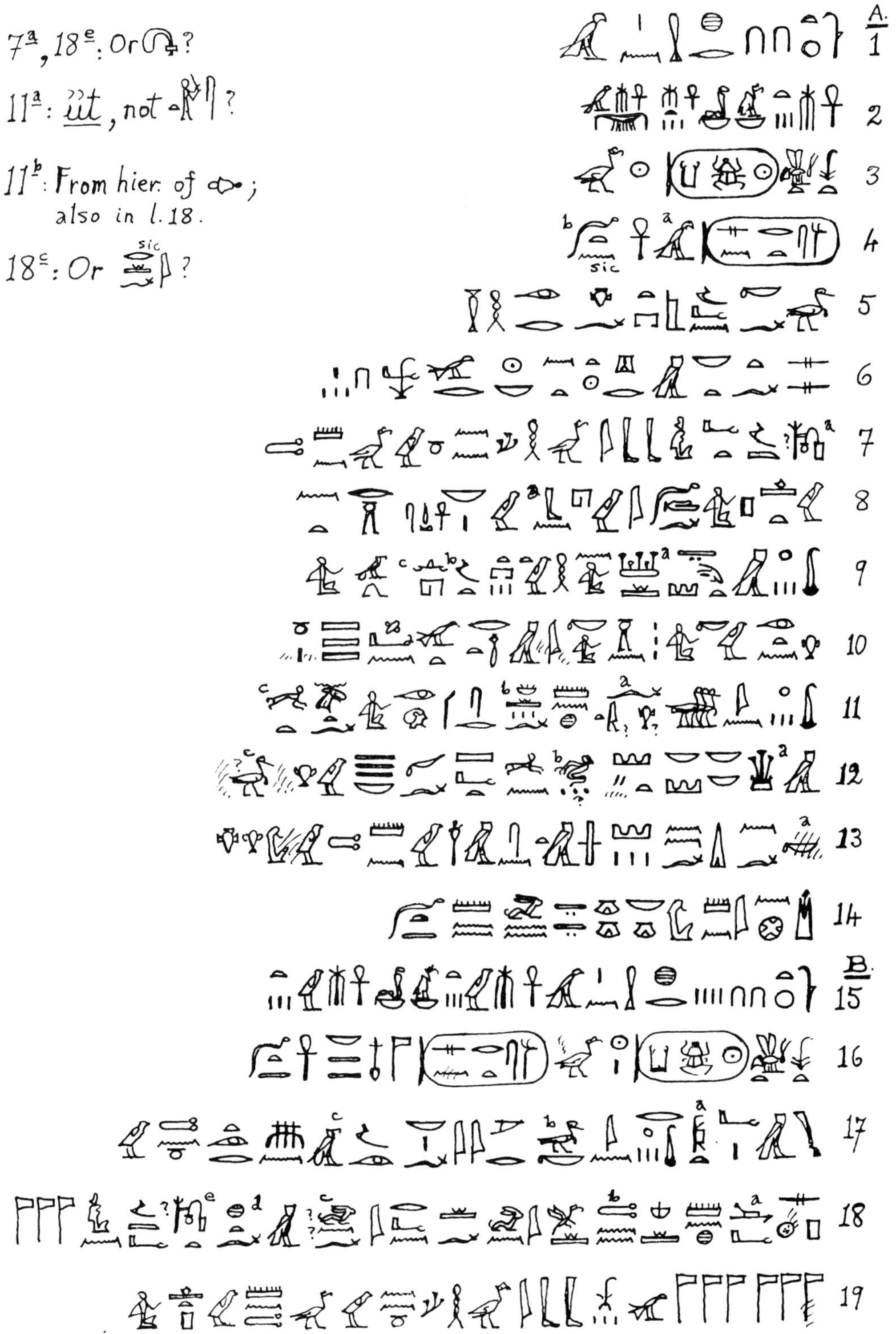

Textual Notes: 4a: falcon here is probably for falcon-on-stand. 4b: *n* for *tꜣ* in *ḏt*, as frequently in the WH texts. 7a; 18e: probably the hieratic form for *sš* (cf. *HP*, I, No. 537), rather than a summary hieroglyphic form of *sḏꜣwty*. 8a: read *h<ꜣ>b.n w(ỉ)*; *ꜣ* and legs-determinative were omitted by the scribe. 9a: hieratic form, cf. *HP*, I, No. 274. 9b: likewise, cf. *HP*, I, No. 111. 9c: likewise (*ꜣ* not *w*), *ibid.*, No. 192. 11a: traces are obscure; *ḥr ỉỉt* is epigraphically better than **snḫt*. 11b: cf. *HP*, I, No. 482, n.3, and line 18 below; other hieroglyphic exx., *TEA*, I, p. 20, Aa:5, p. 22, Aa:30, 43. 11c: semi-hieratic form of *ḫr*, *HP*, I, No. 52. 12a: hieratic form, cf. *HP*, I, No. 279. 12b: plural dots are possible. 12c: poor form of *bꜣ*? 13a: traces of *k* visible. 17a: clearly *šmst* (no det.), and not a hieratic form of *ỉỉ* or similar. 17b: hieratic for *bꜣ*. 17c: clear hieratic *ꜣ*, not *m*. 18a: hieratic *wʿ*, cf. *HP*, I, No. 461. 18b: second *n* is just visible. 18c: traces, either *ỉwn.f* or *ỉ<k>r.f*. 18d: *ḫ or* other disc possible. 18e: see above at 7a.

Translation: A. (1) Year 20 under the Majesty of: Horus, (2) Life-of-Births; Two Goddesses, Life-of-Births; Golden Horus, Life-of-Birth(s); (3) King of Upper & Lower Egypt, Kheperkare; Son of Re, Sesostris I, may he live forever.

(5) His true and favourite servitor, who does all that (6) he praises, in the course of every day, Chief of the Southern Tens, (7) Scribe (?) of Truth, Mentuhotep son of Henenu son of (8) Bebi. He says: 'My Lord, L.P.H., sent me to fetch (9) amethyst from Nubia (Ta-Seti). I ordered (excavation of) new mines. I did not fall behind (10) what others had done; I fetched therefrom in great quantity, I hewed out lumps of (11) amethyst.

It was his might which came (?)/makes strong (?), his effectiveness which kept me vigilant, his (dread) renown having fallen upon (12) the Hau-nebu, the desert-dwellers being fallen to his onset. All lands work (13) for him, the deserts yield to him what is within them, by the decree of Montu residing in (14) Armant (and) Amun, Lord of the Thrones of the Two Lands; one who abides, enduring forever!'

B. (15) Year 24 under the Majesty of: Horus, Life-of-Births; Two-Goddesses, Life-of-Births; (16) King of Upper & Lower Egypt, Kheperkare, Son of Re, Sesostris I, good god, Lord of the Two Lands, may he live forever.

(17) Again seeking for amethyst by the servitor beloved of his lord, who looks forward, who acts (on) every (18) occasion, one uniquely effective, distinguished of character, whose character (?)/excellence (?) has placed (him) in the (royal) presence; scribe (?) of Truth of the (19) Ennead, Chief of the Southern Tens, Mentuhotep son of Henenu son of Bebi.

Commentary: As comparison of lines 1 and 15 clearly shows, the main text of Year 20 and the supplementary text of Year 24 record two separate visits by the functionary Mentuhotep. This Mentuhotep (lines 7-8, 19) may possibly be identical with the father of a Henenu who visited Wadi Hudi five years later still (Year 29, cf. below, WH 144, 145). The same Henenu also left a stela under Sesostris I (no year given) at the diorite quarries west of Toshkeh in Lower Nubia.[138] In each case, Henenu bears his father's title Chief of the Southern Tens; this title is old, going back into the Old Kingdom.[139] In the Middle Kingdom it came to designate a group of officials who would be present at the official sittings of the vizier (in either Thebes or the northern Residence), in two rows on his right and left.[140] Mentuhotep's other title *x* of *mꜣʿt*, plus 'of the Ennead,' is more difficult. At first sight the sign *x* looks like *sḏꜣwty*, 'sealbearer', as is suggested for a similar loop-like sign in WH 144 by Helck.[141] This is possible. However, a title *sḏꜣwty mꜣʿt* (or plus *n psḏt*) is unparalleled, perhaps improbable. The alternative is to treat the difficult sign as hieratic *sš*, giving the well-known title *sš mꜣʿt*,[142] and a possible 'true scribe of the Ennead'. Hitherto, the earliest known examples of *sš mꜣʿt* come from the New Kingdom, but this is not a decisive objection. The Ennead mentioned is probably that of Heliopolis, the most famous of all. This would support the idea that Mentuhotep was an official not of the Southland but from the northern Residence, from which Heliopolis was not far distant.

The personal names of the family are common ones.[143] The grandfather, Bebi, might conceivably be the caravan-leader Bebi attested in Wadi Hammamat under Mentuhotep IV (Nebtawyre) about half a century earlier,[144] but of course this is beyond proof.

In line 9, Ta-Seti could in principle be either Nubia or the 1st Upper Egyptian nome; cf. already above, on WH 4:4. However, the foreign-land determinative would suggest that Nubia is intended here (rather as in WH 4).

In lines 8-11, Mentuhotep gives a brief but valuable glimpse of the activities at Wadi Hudi. The word written *'ḥwtt'* is the plural (*ḥtwt*) of 'mine, quarry'.[145] The locution *hꜣi͗ ḥr* (lines 9-10) must mean here 'to fall behind/below' (in amount) what other expeditions have achieved. It is not previously noted in *Wb.* or Faulkner, *Dict.*, in this meaning. Line 10, *kw* with plural strokes is for *k(i͗)w(y)*, 'others' (Gardiner, §98). Near the line-end is *wḥꜣ*, 'to hew' (stone, etc.); its object in the plural can be taken as *i͗nrw*, 'stones', *ꜥꜣwt*, 'gemstones', or even *ꜥrw*, 'pebbles/nodules',[146] of amethyst, *ḥsmn*.

In line 11, the next sentence is clear in outline, less so in detail (M's praise of his king). *In bꜣw.f* should introduce the well-known construction *i͗n* plus noun plus participle (Gardiner, §§ 227, 2, 373). Here, the initial *i͗n* would govern *bꜣw.f . . .*, *mnḫw.f srsi͗ (tp.i͗)*, and *šft.f ḫrt (m Ḥꜣw-nbw)*: 'it is his might which . . .s, his abilities which cause me to be vigilant, his (dread) renown which falls (upon the Hau-nebu)'.[147] However, the first of the three supposed participles is problematic. A suitable verb stem written with two vertical signs and final radical *t* does not spring to mind to fit the apparent traces. *Snḏt* (vertical *s* plus striking man) would give good sense, but does not really fit the traces. These, on the other hand, would seem to permit *ḫr i͗i͗t*; the objection here is the lack of evidence that *ḫr* plus Infinitive can substitute for a participle in this construction with *i͗n*.

Regarding the next phrase, the participle *srsi͗* by itself might mean 'who watches over' (as adopted by Posener and Blumenthal) but this does not account for *tp* (unless taken as a determinative). *Rs tp* is 'be vigilant', hence its causative form here should mean 'who makes (*.i͗* - me) vigilant'. *Ḫrt* may be a participle (like *srsi͗*), but it would be unusual in agreeing in gender with its preceding noun.[148] Therefore it may best be understood as *ḫr.ti͗*, Old Perfective (Stative), 'his renown having fallen upon . . . ' in parallel with the following clause (*ḫꜣstyw ḫrw . . .*). Lines 12-14 have been dealt with by Posener and Blumenthal.[149] Some of the phraseology here finds echoes in the stela of Hor (WH 143), e.g. *ꜥrf Ḥꜣw-nbw* and *snḏw ḫr(w) n šꜥt.f* (lines 2,4).[150] And the final phrase of WH 14:14 recurs (*wnn, mn(w) n ḏt)* in that stela, line 15 end. The *wnn* is probably a geminating participle, while *mn* is Old Perfective (Stative), in both cases, and in both cases referring to the king (see commentary on WH 143:15).

In Text B, the supplementary record of Year 24, line 17, *wḥm-ꜥ* is followed by *šmst*. As *šms* has normally a masculine infinitive, this *šmst* will be for *šms.t(w)*, unless the apparent *t* is an error for the omitted legs-determinative. *Šms r*, lit. 'to follow after', but here meaning 'to seek for', is a new idiom, so far only attested here and in WH 12:1; doubtless other examples will turn up. The main sign here can only be read *šms* (not *i͗i͗*, etc.), and therefore this determines the reading of the less definite sign in the parallel passage in WH 12:1.

Later in line 17, *mꜣ* is an active participle, followed by *ḫnt(w)*, here probably the adverb 'forward',[151] the whole probably meaning 'forward looking', applying to a man who has already foreseen situations, who plans ahead, and then acts (*i͗rr*, geminating active participle). The construction (line 18) of *wꜥ* plus epithet, 'uniquely . . . ', is attested in other Middle Kingdom texts.[152] *Ṯnn* is also a participle, and *rdi͗.n* a *sḏmw.n.f* relative form. After *rdi͗.n*, the traces may be read either *i͗wn*, 'nature, character, disposition', or as for *i͗ <ḳ>r*, with *ḳ* omitted; *m-ḫft* appears to be used like *m-bꜣḥ*.

138. R. Engelbach, *ASAE* 33 (1933), p.71:5, pl.11:3; A. Rowe, *ASAE* 39 (1939), p.193f., fig.9; Cairo, JdE.59483; cf. also Helck, *OLZ* 50 (1955), 213.
139. General discussion, cf. Helck, *Untersuchungen zu den Beamtentiteln des ägyptischen Alten Reiches,* Glückstadt, 1954, pp.18-19 (refs., n.33), 48, 112, n.5.
140. Sethe, *Urkunden IV*, p.1103:14f., 1104:8, from Dyn. 18 copy of Middle Kingdom instructions for the vizier, cf. Helck, *Zur Verwaltung des Mittleren und Neuen Reichs,* Leiden, 1958, p.2, n.1.
141. *OLZ* 50 (1955), col. 213.
142. *Wb.*, II, p.19:20.
143. Mentuhotep, cf. *PN*, I, 154:21; Henenu, *ibid.*, 245:1; Bebi, *ib.*, 95:16.
144. Goyon, *NIH*, No.60, p.81.
145. Faulkner, *Dict.*, p.179; *Wb.*, III, p.6:6.
146. Cf. Gardiner, *Grammar*, p.497, Sign-list D.39.
147. Cf. already Posener, *Littérature et politique dans l'Egypte de la XIIe Dynastie*, Paris, 1957, p.132, and E. Blumenthal, *Unt.*, p.205, F.1.1. The Hau-nebu, cf. Vercoutter, *BIFAO* 46 (1947), p.157; most recent study, L. Basch, *CRIPEL* 4 (1976), pp. 11-52.
148. An archaic usage, cf. Gardiner, § 373.
149. Posener, *loc.cit.* (n.147 above): Blu, *Unt.*, p.195, E.3.28.
150. For the parallelism of *b3w* and *mnḫ* of the king acting through lesser agents, cf. below WH 143:15.
151. Cf. Gardiner, § 205, 1; *Wb.*, III, 303:7, etc.
152. E.g. the Kahun Hymns to Sesostris III, Sethe, *Aegyptische Lesestücke,* Leipzig, 1928, pp.66:9, and 67:3.

WH, No. 15. Fakhry, No. 15; present location unknown; PM, 121??

Date: Sesostris (I, II, or III?), Year (1)6/(1)7.

Bibliography: Fakhry, p. 35, pl. XIIIB.

Description: Freestanding, well-shaped, round-topped sandstone stela with two horizontal lines of hieroglyphs over eight vertical columns of text. Almost the whole face is so badly broken and abraded that few traces of connected text can be made out. From Site 1. Height 112 cm, width 59 cm, thickness 21 cm. Not seen in 1975.

Normalised Text:

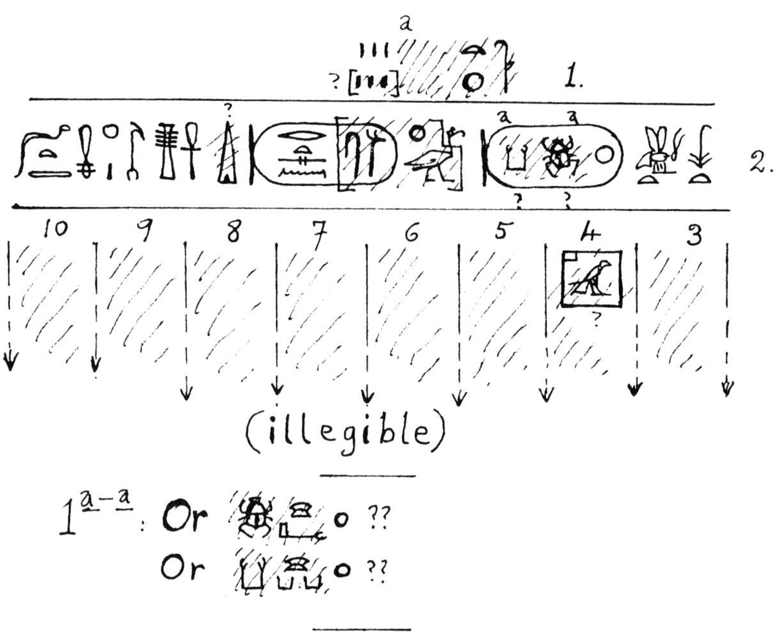

Textual Notes: 1a: three high-set units presuppose three or four below; hence, read '6' or '7'; if a ten is lost in front, then '16' or '17'. 2a-a: Fakhry confidently read this first cartouche as Khakheperre, i.e. Sesostris II. However, the published photo (admittedly poor) could be read even more easily as Kheperkare (Sesostris I), and Khakaure (Sesostris III) is not wholly excluded.

Translation: (1) Year [1?] 6/[1?] 7 (?): (2) King of Upper & Lower Egypt, Kheperkare (??)/Khakaure (??), So[n of Re], Sesostris, given life, stability and dominion like Re forever. (3) . . . .

(4) Hathor . . . . (5-10) . . [lost] . . .

Commentary: If Year 17 of Sesostris I, this goes with WH 6; if Sesostris II, it is the sole Wadi Hudi record of his reign; if of Sesostris III, this stela would belong with WH 16, 17 in both date and general arrangement.

WH, No. 16. Fakhry, No. 16; 'exc. no.' 9; Aswan Museum, acc. no. 1479; PM, 122.
Date: Sesostris III, Year 13 (*c.* 1866 BC).
Bibliography: Fakhry, p. 35, fig. 28, pl. XIVA.
Description: Pink granite stela, round-topped, with three horizontal lines over six vertical columns. Care of workmanship rivals that of WH 143. Height 42.5 cm, width 27.5 cm, average thickness 14 cm. The 'excavation no.' is a formal one, as the monument was brought in by the Frontiers Administration of Aswan (F, p. 35).

Normalised Text:

Textual Notes: 1a: *n* is an error for *t*, from misreading of a hieratic ligature by the ancient scribe; cf. similarities between *t* and *n* elements in *HP*, I, p. 73: LIII, LIV, LV - same error in WH 17:1. 1b: hieratic form (*HP*, I, No. 483). 3a: hieratic form (*HP*, I, No. 402). 6a: is clearly *š*, not *t*, and the bird rather *ꜣ* than *w*. 7a: a poor (hieratic) form of *sꜣw*. 9a: this *t*, perhaps an error (through hieratic) for the small *ỉ* of two small slanting strokes (cf. *HP*, I, Nos. 560, 575).

Translation: (1) Year 13 under the Majesty of: (2) the King of Upper & Lower Egypt, Khakaure, may he live for ever and ever, (3) beloved of Hathor, Lady of Amethyst.

(4) Real acquaintance of the King whom he loves, his favourite, firm of tread, (5) easy of gait, patient, effectual in speech, (6) possessor of respect on the day of summons; (7) Guardian of silver and gold, sealed (8) for fashioning in the workshop(s), the Chamber(9)lain, Intefoqer, begotten of Sen'ankh, possessing veneration.

Commentary: This stela and WH 17 were probably erected by members of one expedition. Lines 4-5, the sequence *mn-ṯbw, hr-nmtwt* finds ample parallel in the middle and late Twelfth Dynasty.[153] Likewise, *mnḫ-ṯsw, wꜣḥ-ỉb* and *nb-šfyt*.[154] In line 6, the word after *hrw* looks at first like *ỉ-š-w*, but the bird is more erect and has head and tail differing from those of *w*. If it is *ꜣ*, then we have *ỉꜣš*, 'to call, summon', the infinitive being here used as a noun.

Line 7 appears to begin with *sꜣw*, cf. titles such as *sꜣw prwy-ḥḏ*, and *sꜣw pr-ḥḏ*.[156] *Ḫtm(w)* may be Old Perfective ('Stative'), followed by *r ḳmꜣ.t(w)*, 'so that one may fashion (it)'; one could alternatively, take *ḳmꜣt* as a Perf. Passive Participle, 'according to (*r*) what is fashioned'. In line 8, the following phrase should be read *st-ḥmwt*, with an obscure determinative (lump of metal?). Lines 8-9, the title *ỉmy-r ꜥḫnwty* has been sufficiently studied elsewhere.[157] Line 9, both Intefoqer and Sen'ankh bear good Middle Kingdom names.[158] This Intefoqer seems to have had responsibility for precious metals used in fashioning valuable objects, whether for palace or cult.

153. Cf. Janssen, *TEA*, I, pp. 19-20, Z:9-19.
154. Cf. respectively *ibid.*, p.22, Aa:49, pp.12, 22, N:23/Aa:50, and p.142, Ac:45-47, esp. 46.
155. Sinai, Nos. 104:6, 112:E.1.
156. Gardiner, *Ancient Egyptian Onomastica*, I, pp.64-65, rt.1.
157. Cf. full survey by H. Gauthier, *BIFAO* 15 (1918), pp.169-206, critical summary by Gardiner, *Anc. Eg. Onomastica*, I, p.44*f., No.123, and subsequent notes by Posener, *RdE* 11 (1957), p.132, and J. Leclant, *Orientalia NS* 31 (1962), p.213:7, and *ibid.* 34 (1965), p.196:4.
158. Cf. respectively *PN*, I, 34:7 and 308:14.

WH, No. 17. Fakhry, No. 17; 'exc. no.' 10; Aswan Museum, acc. no. 1480; PM, 123.
Date: Sesostris III, Year 13 (*c.* 1866 BC).
Bibliography: Fakhry, pp. 35/38, fig. 29, pl. XIVB.
Description: Round-topped pink-granite stela, similar to WH 16. Below three horizontal lines at top and adjoining three vertical columns at its right is the figure of a man in a kilt, arms pendant, facing right, framed within five more lines and columns of text (two at right). Height 48.5 cm, width 32 cm, thickness 14 cm. Brought in with WH 16.

Normalised Text:

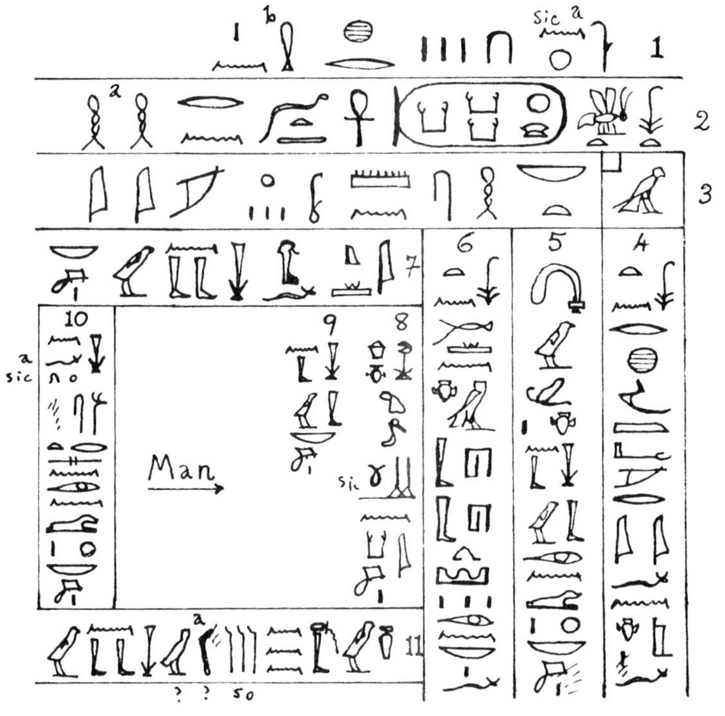

Textual Notes: 1a: *n* for *t*, cf. WH 16:1. 1b: hieratic form, cf. WH 16. 2a: no disc, so in WH 16, etc. 10a: two small marks, mere breaks in the stone? 11a: either *w* or *m* (more likely, *m*), preceded by a throwstick with a break in the stone at its upper right extremity.

Translation: (1) Year 13 under the Majesty of: (2) the King of Upper & Lower Egypt, Khakaure, may he live for ever and ever; (3) beloved of Hathor, Lady of the Amethyst.

(4) Real acquaintance of the King whom he loves, his favourite, (5) the discreet seal-bearer, Senbebu begotten by Sobek-re, possessing veneration.

(6) The King's confidant in exploring the desert territories, whose character ('nature') (7) his lord has formed, Senbebu, possessing veneration.

(8) A thousand of bread and beer, of oxen and fowl, of linen and alabaster, for the *ka* of the revered one, (9) Senbebu, possessing veneration.

(10) His brother, Senwosret begotten by Sobek-re, possessing veneration. (11) The butler pure of fingers, the Asiatic(?), Senbebu.

Commentary: Lines 1-3 are identical in date and formulation with WH 16:1-3. Line 5, the epithet *kfꜣ-ỉb*, 'discreet/careful', is applied elsewhere to seal-bearers/treasurers.[159] Both Senbebu and Senwosret are common names,[160] and Sobek-re is also attested as a personal name.[161] In line 6, *ỉb* is displaced to obtain a better grouping of the signs; read *mḥ-ỉb n nsw*. The *ỉr.n* is *sḏmw.n.f* Relative Form. In line 7, the first word is *ḳỉ*, but again grouped 'square'.[162] In line 8, *šs* is placed outside a narrow *mnḫt*-sign. Because of the entirely different and humbler title, the Senbebu of line 11 would appear to be quite distinct from the seal-bearer Senbebu, and seems to be a personal servant of Senbebu and Senwosret, as a butler.[163] The two signs before the lesser Senbebu's name offer initial difficulty in reading; but they are most probably the throw-stick plus *m*, favouring the reading *ꜥꜣm(w)*, 'Asiatic'. Thus, this butler would be an Asiatic who had been given his master's Egyptian name. A great number of Asiatics from Canaan are attested in all kinds of occupations (including butlers) in Middle Kingdom Egypt, and in some numbers as far south as the Thebaid,[164] so there is nothing specially remarkable or anomalous about an Asiatic servant here at Wadi Hudi.

159. Cf. references given by Gardiner, Peet, Černý, *Inscriptions of Sinai*, II, p.70, note *b*, plus Sinai examples, *ibid.*, p.239, Index; cf. also *TEA*, I, p.36, Bc:1-5.
160; Respectively, cf. *PN*, I, 315:6 (cf. 5), and 279:1.
161. Cf. *PN*, I, 304:19.
162. For lines 6-7 and part parallels, cf. Blu, *Unt.*, p.383, G.7.32, and p.387, G.7.48.
163. Epithet 'pure of fingers', cf. Sinai, No. 109; of a priest, *TEA*, I, p.15, Q:6. Butlers were frequently members of these desert expeditions, cf. (e.g.) Gardiner, etc., *Inscriptions, Sinai, II,* p.230, Index under *wdpw*.
164. In Thebaid, cf. W.C. Hayes, *A Papyrus of the Late Middle Kingdom,* New York, 1955, and the valuable review-study by Posener, *Syria* 34 (1957), pp.145-163, especially pp.152-3, 154.

WH, No. 18. Fakhry, No. 18; exc. no. 11; Aswan Museum, acc. no. 1481.
Date: Sesostris III(?), year 11(+x?) (*c.* 1868-x BC?).
Bibliography: Fakhry, p. 38, pl. XV.
Description: Round-topped quartzite stela with two lines of text above a man (facing left, kilted, upper half lost), framed by one column at right and two at left. Central part of this stela has been hollowed away through subsequent use as a milling-stone for quartz, damaging most of the texts. Height 79 cm, width 50 cm, thickness 19 cm.

Normalised Text:

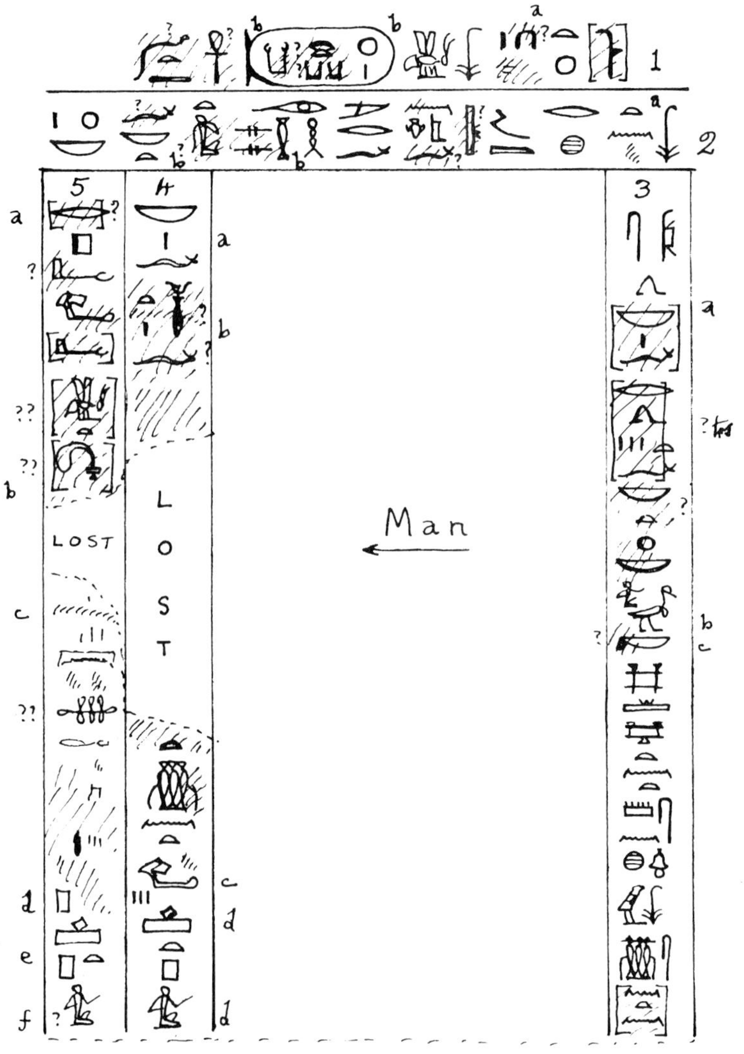

Textual Notes: 1a: the '11' seems certain, but there is no clear trace below it, just two horizontal scratches. 1b-b: cartouche is very doubtful; *ḫʿ-k3w-rʿ* would appear to suit the traces. 2a: short vertical break(?) below *t-n.* 2b-b: traces dubious but just possible. 3a-b: this number of groups, all but entirely lost; restoration given is very tentative. 3c: either *nb* or *k* (difficult to be sure of a loop for *k*). 4a: very probable. 4b: hypothetcal but possible. 4c: possible but uncertain. 4d-d: almost certain. 5a-b: highly tentative; *p* seems sure, ʿ probable, *ḥ3t(y)-*[ʿ] possible; *sḏ3wty bỉty* is conjectural. 5b-c: entirely broken away. 5c-d: traces almost totally illegible. 5e-f: name seems quite probable.

Translation: (1) Year 11 (+x?) of the King of Upper & Lower Egypt, Khakaure (?), living forever.

(2) Real acquaintance of the King, and [his] favourite whom he loves, one who does all that he praises every day, (3) one who follows [his lord (?) at all his goings (?), every day (?), a servant] who sticks to the way of him who benefited him, (4) [whose office (?)] his lord has promoted, [. . . . . .] before the chiefs (?), Hotep.

(5) [Hereditary] P [rince? and] Cou [nt?], [Seal-bearer of the King . . .??], [. . . . .], [. . *illegible*. .], Hotep(?).

Commentary: The state of this stela renders many readings uncertain, even though possible, and most inferences hypothetical. For *rḫ-nsw m3ʿ n st-ỉb.f*, compare the formulae in WH 16, 17, just above. For *ỉr ḥsst.f nbt*, cf. on WH 9, above. Well attested are such locutions as *šms nb.f r nmtwt.f (nbt)*,[165] and *sḫnt.n nb.f (st.f/ỉ3t.f*, etc.).[166] For 'chief', *ḥ3t* is possible.[167] The conjectural restorations of line 5 would accord with the relatively high rank implied by *rḫ-nsw m3ʿ* in line 2, and cf. the officials of WH 16, 17. The name Hotep, cf. above on WH 6.[168]

165. Cf. Janssen, *TEA*, I, pp.111-2, Fu:3, 4, 11-13, 17, 19; for *b3k* before *mḏd mtn/w3t* . . . , cf. *ibid.*, p.70, Bc:7, and the whole locution with *mḏd, ibid.*, p.70f., Bc:1-31.
166. Cf. *ibid.*, p.106, Ev:5, 6, 12, 13, etc. For *ḫnt* place(s) or people, cf. *ibid.*, p.134f., esp. S:3,7.
167. Cf. Faulkner, *Dict.*, p.162; *TEA*, I, p.143, Af:1, besides Fakhry's ref. to Griffith and Newberry, *El Bersheh II*, 1894, p.25 rt., line 4.
168. *PN*, I, 257:22.

WH, No. 19. Fakhry, No. 19; exc. no. 38; Aswan Museum, acc. no. 1508; PM, 124.
Date: Amenemhat III, Year 20 (*c.*1823 BC).
Bibliography: Fakhry, p. 38, fig. 30, pl. XVIB.
Description: Upper portion of a round-topped stela of quartzose sandstone, on which only the first four lines of horizontal text survive. Height 34 cm, width 35 cm, thickness 10 cm.

Normalised Text:

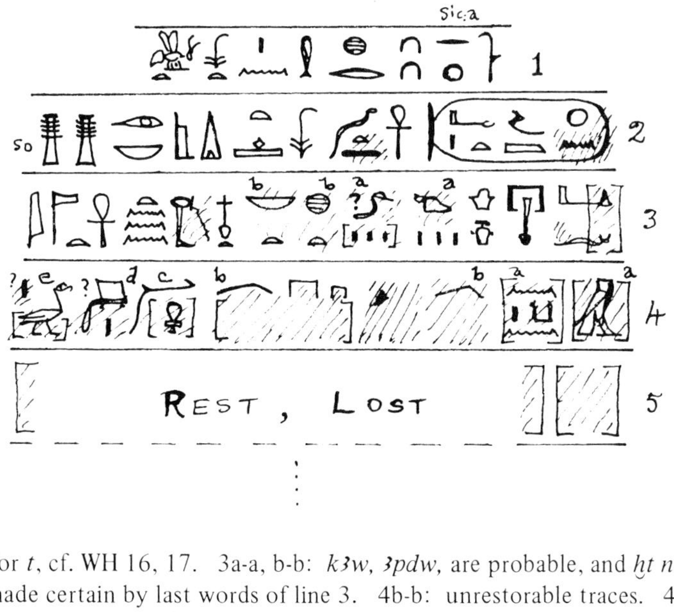

Textual Notes: 1a: *n* for *t*, cf. WH 16, 17. 3a-a, b-b: *k3w, 3pdw,* are probable, and *ḫt nbt* certain. 4a-a: conjectural restoration made certain by last words of line 3. 4b-b: unrestorable traces. 4c: curved trace below *ỉmy-r* (?) suggests *sḏ3yt*. 4d: for *ỉm3ḫ[y]*, form seems too clear to be easily dismissed. 4e: bird is certain; stroke, uncertain. A name *s3*-x is indicated.

Translation: (1) Year 20 under the Majesty of the King of Upper & Lower Egypt, (2) Nema'etre, may he live forever.

A boon which the king gives to Osiris, Lord of Busiris (3) that he may grant invocation-offerings of bread and beer, oxen and fowl, and of every good and pure thing whereon a god may live, (4) [to the *ka* of . . . . . the] Treasury Superintendent (??), the revered one, Si- (5) [. . . . *lost*].

Commentary: This reign sees the first occurrence of *ḥtp-dỉ-nsw* formulae on the Wadi Hudi stelae. WH 20, with its long list of personnel, may indicate what kind of text once occupied the now missing lower half of WH 19.

WH, No. 20. Fakhry, No. 20; 'exc. no.' 12; Aswan Museum, acc. no. 1482.

Date: Amenemhat III, Year 28 (*c.* 1815 BC).

Bibliography: Fakhry, p. 39, fig. 31.

Description: Round-topped black granite stela. Three lines of text across its entire width give place to at least eleven lines down the left side only. That nothing is lost down the right side is shown by the continuity of sense in the existing lines 4-6, directly followed by the name-list there announced. Last lines are worn away, perhaps by ore-crushing. Max. height 140 cm, width 55 cm, max. thickness 27 cm. Brought in by G.W. Murray (Fakhry, p. 39).

Normalised Text:

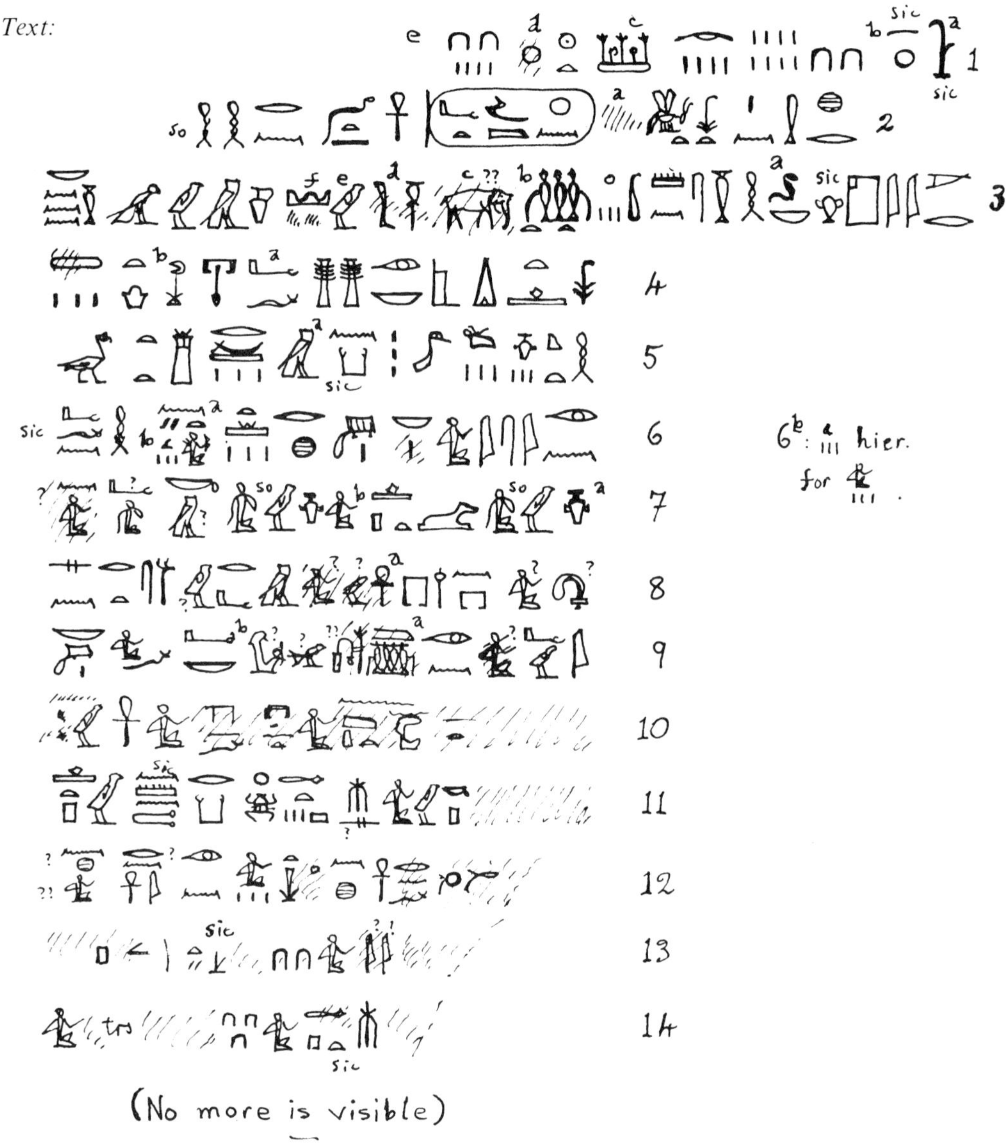

Textual Notes: 1a: hieratic form. 1b: horizontal stroke, for *t* in hieratic ligature. 1c: hieratic form of *ꜣḫt*, cf. *HP*, I, No. 274. 1d: trace visible. 1e: no further signs after '24'; line 2 immediately follows. 2a: probably only blotches on the stone; otherwise, horizontal scratches might suggest *nb-tꜣwy*. 3a: uraeus over *nb(t)*. 3b: *ḫntt* seems certain. 3c: a broad sign with curving top and vestiges below, hence suggested reading. 3d-e: *ꜣbw* is possible; a sloping horizontal gash runs across *ꜣb* and *b*. 3f: nothing below this det.? 4a: so, *'ayin* (hieratic) for *dì*. 4b: the *ḫꜣ* is pure hieratic. 5a: hieratic form. 6a: *nty* over *mšꜥ*. 6b: probably seated-man det. in hieratic. 7a: hieratic form (*HP*, I, No. 506). 7b: again, hieratic forms of *ḥtp, p*. 8a: hypothetical reading. 9a-b: highly tentative readings.

Translation: (1) Year 28, 4th month of Akhet, Day 24, (2) under the Majesty of the King of Upper & Lower Egypt, Nema'etre, may he live for ever and ever, (3) beloved of Hathor, Lady of the Amethyst, presiding in Elephantine (?), (and of) Khnum, Lord of the Cataract.

(4) A boon which the king gives to Osiris, Lord of Busiris, that he may grant invocation-offerings, (namely) a thousand (each) of bread and (5) beer, oxen and fowl, to the *ka* <of> the shipmaster Si-Bastet, (6) begotten of Isi, possessing veneration.

List of the expedition which was with him: (7) The Butler, Sobkhotep; the butler, Kema'ni (?); (8) the Seal bearer (?) of the Treasury, 'Ankhu (?); the caravan leader Senwosret-(9) -ia'u, begotten by the Chamberlain (?) and Chief Scribe (??), Iry/Sau-nebef, possessing veneration. (10) . . . . . . Khnumhotep ? . . . . .'Ankhu (??); (11) . . . . . Kapu . . ; the prospector, Kheperkare, <begotten> of Mentuhotep; (12) . . . Chief Carpenter (?). Renef-ankh-senut?, begotten of Reni-ankh; (13) . . . . . . 20 . . . . .; (14) . . . . prospectors, 30; . . . . . .

Commentary: Line 1, in year 28 of Amenemhat III, *c.* 1815 BC on accepted dates, 4th Akhet 24 would fall about mid-March. Line 2, for a similar gap between *nsw-bἰt* and the cartouche, cf. *NIH*, No. 70 of this reign.[169] Line 3, it is unusual to find *mry* written before the deities so linked to the king. Remarkable, too, is the spelling of Hathor. Line 4, the *ḥtp-dἰ-nsw* begins a new section, as in WH 19. Line 5, the title 'shipmaster' is remarkable for desert expeditions. It does occur at Sinai, which was sometimes reached by water, over the Gulf of Suez.[170] Si-Bastet is a good Middle Kingdom name.[171] For the [Ship?] master Si-Bastet in Year 11 of this reign, see below, WH 149, possibly the same man as here. If so, the two monuments combine to give his full parentage: father, Isi,[172] mother, User(et).

Line 6, end, read *rḫt ms̆ʿ nty ḥnʿ.f*; the engraver first forgot *ms̆ʿ*, then squeezed it in under *nty*, and in any case bungled *ḥnʿ.f.* For a similar heading, cf. WH 6:4. Line 7, *wdpw*, 'butler', is a function already attested in WH 17:11, see notes there. From here on, most of the names are known Middle Kingdom ones, and *PN* refs. are here given.

Sobkhotep, *PN*, I, 305:6; Kema (ʿ) ni, cf. 344:28, 345:10, 24. Line 8, Ankhu, 68:6; Senwosret-ia'u is not attested, but Senwosret compounds are, 279:2-9, and ia'u-names, 12:3ff. In line 9, Sau-nebef is not paralleled so far, but cf. similar compound, 295:16. Line 11, Kapu, cf. 339:9. On *ms-ʿȝt*, cf. above on WH 6:12. Kheperkare as a private name, *PN*, I, 269:1. The probable *n* above the *Mn* of Mentuhotep suggests the emendation <*ἰr.*>*n*, 'begotten of'. Line 12, for Reni-ankh, cf. *PN*, I, 222:24, and the commoner Renef-ankh, 223:6.

169. Goyon, *NIH*, p.91, pl. 20 below.
170. Cf. Sinai, Nos. 47:6, 48 (left), 77, 92:W.4, and Gardiner, Peet, Černý, *Inscriptions of Sinai,* II, pp. 12, 16, 18.
171. *PN*, I, 281:19.
172. *Ibid.*, 46:7.

WH, No. 21. Fakhry, No. 21; exc. no. 13; Aswan Museum, acc. no. 1483.
Date: Amenemhat IV, Year 2, (*c.* 1797 BC).
Bibliography: Fakhry, pp. 39-40, fig. 32.
Description: Round-topped, black-granite stela, ten of eleven lines inscribed. Height 38 cm, width 22 cm, thickness 15 cm.

Normalised Text:

Textual Notes: 2a, 3a, 4a: hieratic forms. 8a: determinative omitted. 8b: a poor hieratic form, identity uncertain. 9a: below *pr*, either *r* or *t* with either *t* or *r* and det. omitted. 9b: the foreign-land det., a poor hieratic form. 9c: below *n*, either *t* or *r*. 9d: hieratic form, probably *š3* with Fakhry (cf. *HP*, I, No. 274), otherwise possibly the *bi3* sign (*ib.*, No. 489). 10: signs at end, very doubtful.

Translation: (1) Year 2 under the Majesty of: (2) the King of Upper & Lower Egypt, Ma'etkherure, may he live for ever and ever.

(3) Real acquaintance of the King, whom he loves, his favourite, (4) who does all that he praises throughout the course of every day, (5) firm of tread, easy of step, one who sticks to the way of (6) him who has advanced him, the Assistant Treasurer of (7) the Superintendent of the Treasury, Si-Hat<hor>, born of Mereryt.

(8) He went out to survey the amethyst desert, (9) according to His Majesty's command. He went out to the desert land of Shau/the mining region, (10) the Seal-bearer and Ship<master?>, Men-tjebet (??) (11) <being with him?>.

Commentary: Line 1, the date given here for Year 2 of Amenemhat IV is a conventional one; his probable co-regency with Amenemhat III and the scope of its length (which affects the dating of year-dates) has been reviewed latterly by Murnane.[173] Line 3, *rḫ-nsw m3 ʿ*, etc., cf. on WH 149 below. *Mn-ṯbt*, 'firm of tread', occurs in this and similar sequences elsewhere,[174] likewise *ḥr-nmt(w)t.*[175] For *mdd w3t* . . , cf. already on WH 9 above.[176] The title of Assistant to the Superintendent of the Treasury (lines 6-7) recurs in the texts of Sinai expeditions.[177]

Line 7, the element Hor has been omitted from the common name Si-Hathor;[178] the name Mereryt is also a known one.[179]

In lines 8 and 9, *prt* is a narrative infinitive, each time introducing a new section (Gardiner, § 306, 2). Line 8, in its context *ḫꜣ* should be a verb, 'he went to *ḫꜣ* the desert . . '; Blumenthal's ingenious suggestion 'Kharu' (Syria) is excluded on multiple grounds.[180] Rather, we need something like the verb *ḫꜣ*, 'examine, measure', i.e., to survey the district for new lodes of amethyst. Line 9, Shau might just possibly be an Egyptian name for the Wadi Hudi mining-district, but should not be confused with the different Ro-Sha'awet mentioned by Fakhry (p.40, n.1).[181] The latter produced turquoise (cf. Sinai). But if one reads here *bỉꜣ* instead of *šꜣ(w)*, then we have a general term for mining-district applied to Wadi Hudi. The personal name *Mn-ṯbt* is not too well paralleled.[182] At the beginning of the blank line 11, one should perhaps understand an uninscribed **<hnꜥ.f>* or **<ỉw ḥnꜥ.f>*.

173. See W.J. Murnane, *Ancient Egyptian Coregencies,* Chicago, 1977, pp. 13-20, 26-29, for fresh suggestions on this theme.
174. Cf. exx. in Janssen, *TEA*, I, p.19f., Z:9-22, esp. 11-13, 15, 17, with same sequence of epithets as here.
175. *Ibid.*, p.29, Ak:19-32.
176. This example (WH 21) is cited by Blu, *Unt.*, p.341, G.5.41.
177. E.g., Sinai No. 105:N.1, cf. Gardiner, Peet, Černý, *Inscriptions of Sinai,* II, pp.16, 109.
178. *PN*, I, 283:20.
179. *Ibid.*, 162:25.
180. Blu, *Unt.*, p.398, G.8.31. Thus, reading *ir* is unlikely, and the det. is impossible; the amethyst-district of Wadi Hudi (dependent on Aswan) is in Nubia, not conceivably Syria, and Kharu came into use in the New Kingdom.
181. And cf. Helck, *OLZ* 50 (1955), cols. 213-4.
182. For an Old Kingdom analogy, cf. *PN*, I, 150:26 (*Mn-ṯbwt*).

C. The Thirteenth Dynasty: Nos. 22-25.

WH, No. 22. Fakhry, No. 22; exc. no. 14; Aswan Museum, acc. no. 1484; PM, 127.
Date: Sobkhotep IV (Khaneferre), Year 6 (*c.* 1720 BC).
Bibliography: Fakhry, p. 40 (no figure or plate).
Description: Remains (in five pieces) of a quartzose sandstone stela, probably round-topped (cf. WH 21), perhaps originally about 52 cm wide. Parts of five or six lines of text survive, lightly engraved.

Normalised Text:

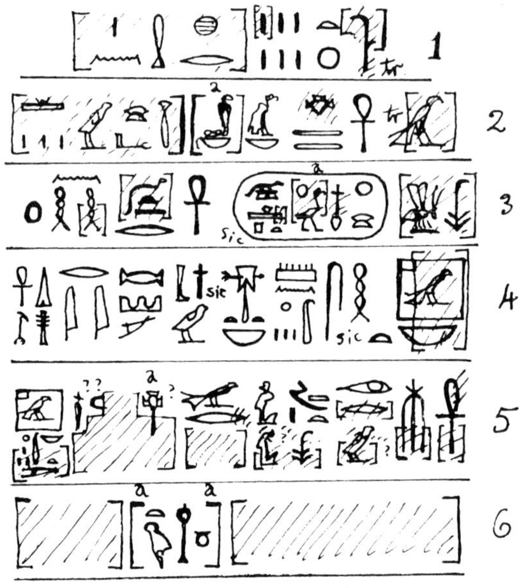

(Rest lost)

Textual Notes: 2a: after Fakhry, now lost. 3a: trace of legs and lower body of *sꜣ*. 5a: hieratic form. 6a-a: after Fakhry, now lost.

Translation: (1) Year 6 [under the Majesty of:] (2) [the Hor]us, Life-of-the-heart-of-the-Two-Lands; Two Goddesses,[Flourishing-of-Epiphanies], (3) [King of Upper & Lower Egypt], Khaneferre, Son [of Re], Sobekhotep IV, may he live for ever and ever, (4) beloved of Hathor, Lady of Amethyst, and Satis, Lady of Elephantine, (being) given life, stability and dominion;

(5) the 'Life-of-Births', one who performs truth, a king (?) great in [. . . .], protector [of . . .], [. . . .], [beloved of] Hathor, Lady of Amethyst, (6) [. . . . united with] the White Crown, [. . *rest lost* . .] .

Commentary: The lesser length of line 1 suggests that this stela had a rounded top. For Year 6, see also WH 24 below. Khaneferre Sobkhotep should in fact be numbered 'III', not 'IV', because the supposed Sobkhotep 'II' (von Beckerath's 'I') does not exist, but is a king Sobkhotepre, attested by his own monuments as well as the Turin Canon.[183] The real Sobkhoteps I and II are Sekhemre-Khutawy Sobkhotep I (von Beckerath's 'II') and Sekhemre-Sewadjtawy Sobkhotep II (von Beckerath's 'III'), leaving Khaneferre as the true Sobkhotep III (not 'IV'). Kha'ankhre Sobkhotep is probably later (V), and is certainly not to be confused with the earlier king Sobkhotepre.[184] However, in this book, to avoid confusion, the erroneous numbering by Hayes and von Beckerath is retained simply to avoid confusion until the real numbering is finally accepted generally.

Line 5 contains a series of damaged phrases that do not seem to be the titles or name of any expeditionary official, unlike WH 23-25 for example. Rather, these phrases seem much more like continuing epithets of the king himself: 'life-of-births' would re-echo the titles of the redoubtable Sesostris I of the previous Dynasty, while *ỉrw m3ʿt* and *nsw wr-* [. . .] would virtually clinch this explanation. If so, Hathor *nbt-ḥsmn* at the line-end must relate in some way to the king, hence the suggested restoration [*mr(y)*]. The one trace of line 6, seen only by Fakhry, suggests further royal epithets there. In short, this stela appears to be a 'royal' stela in this group of four (WH 22-25), lauding the king, while the other three commemorate the principal officers of the expedition sent by this king.

183. Turin Canon, Col. VI.13, original monument, E. Naville, *XIth Dynasty Temple at Deir el-Bahari*, II, 1910, pp. 11, 21, pl.X(H).

184. As is done by J. von Beckerath, *Untersuchungen zur politische Geschichte der zweiten Zwischenzeit in Ägypten*, Glückstadt, 1965, pp.42f., 233f.

WH, No. 23. Fakhry, no. 23; exc. no. 15; Aswan Museum, acc. no. 1485; PM, 128.

Date: Sobkhotep IV (Khaneferre), no year-date (*c.* 1720 BC).

Bibliography: Fakhry, pp. 40/42, fig. 33.

Description: Fine sandstone stela (round top, broken away), with two officials at right honouring a king at left (who holds *wꜣs*-sceptre and mace) and a prince named but not shown. Below are six horizontal lines of text, the signs being grouped vertically within these. Present height 116 cm, width 56 cm, thickness 30 cm.

Normalised Text:

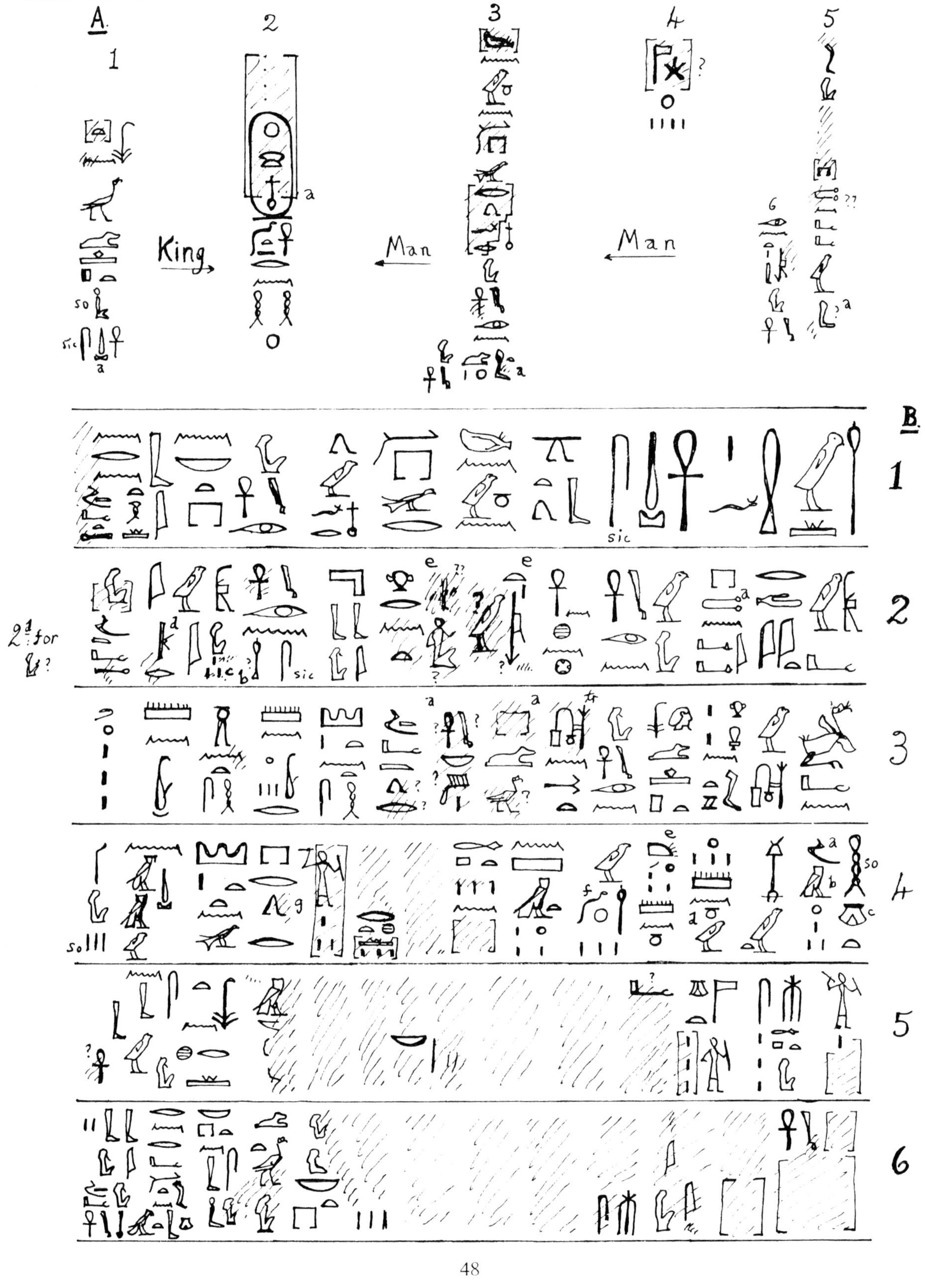

Textual Notes:

A. *Scene.*

1a: hieratic form of *(w)ḏꜣ*, cf. *HP*, I, No. 391. 2a: read base of *nfr* at lower end of cartouche, hence restore [*Ḫꜥ*-] *nfr*-[*rꜥ*]. 3a: poor form, part like *wꜥr*-leg, part like a seated figure, perhaps the former. 5a: possibly a seated figure?

B. *Main Text.*

2a: simplified hieratic ligature, *ṯ* over *n*. 2b: poor hieratic form for *ḥḏ*? 2c: plural strokes with cross-scratches, which confuse the reading. 2d: hieratic for *iri*-figure? 2e-e: traces uncertain. 3a-a: not certain but probable. 4a-f: all hieratic forms in the original. 4g: no *t*.

Translation:

A. *Scene.*

(1) The King's Son, Sobkhotep, L.P.H. (2) [The King . . . ,] [Kha]nefer[re], may he live for ever and ever. (3) Deputy of the High Steward, [Iu]nefer, repeating life, begotten by the District Officer (?), Sobek-re, repeating life. (4) [Adoring the god], four times. (5) The officer? . . . Didiu-tjeni (?), (6) begotten of Wa'ati (?), repeating life.

B. *Main Text:*

(1) His Majesty, L.P.H., commanded the sending of: the Deputy of the High Steward, Iunefer, repeating life, born of the lady of the house, Benrit;
(2) the Retainer of the Judgement-hall, Didiu-tjeni, repeating life, begotten of the citizen Wa'u . . (?); the Chief of the *tm*, Bebi, repeating life, begotten by the Inspector of Retainers, Rehu-iri, justified;
(3) the *tꜣw-n-sš*, holding the seal of the Region 'Head-of-the-South', Sobkhotep, repeating life, begotten by the Scribe (?) of the Prison/Harim, Si-Sobek, repeating life (?), possessing veneration (?).
Proceeding to the amethyst-desert, to fetch: amethyst; (4) garnet; greenstone (?); black quartz; white quartz; green felspar - the precious stones of [. . . . . .] .

List (?) of the expedition that went out to this desert land: Chief of recruits of (5) the expedition, one; [. . .]; prospectors, stonemasons (?), [. .]; [. . . . . *(much lost)* . . . . . .] .

The King's acquaintance, Senbebu-ankh; (6) [. . . . . . title?, PN?], repeating life; [. . . . .] *mes* [. . . . . . . PN]; lady of the house, Sit-Sobek; lady of the house, Sonb (Senbeb?), ... the District Superintendent of Koptos, Bebiy, justified, repeating life.

Commentary:

A. *Scene.*

The king and a prince are honoured by two officials, authors of the stela and probably leaders of the expedition. The frequent use of the epithet *wḥm-ꜥnḫ*, 'repeating life', links this stela with the other Thirteenth-Dynasty stelae from Wadi Hudi (WH 22,24,25), a date indicated also by the presence of a 'King's Son Sobkhotep'. The restoration of the cartouche (line 2) as Khaneferre (trace of *nfr*) at once fits this period as required and links this stela directly with the other three of this Dynasty. The prince named is otherwise unknown. As a son of Sobkhotep IV, he may eventually have succeeded his father as Khahotepre Sobkhotep V.[185]

Two additional fragments from the top of the stela (not in Fakhry's edition) help to restore the legends accompanying the two officials. They are the same Iunefer and Didiu-tjeni of the Main Text (*q.v.*). They render virtually divine honours to their sovereign - 'adoring the god four times', as is done for deities.[186]

B. *Main Text.*

Line 1, Iunefer[187] was a middle-rank official, 'Deputy' of the High Steward - not himself high steward as previously thought.[188] The pleonastic spelling of Benrit, his mother's name, is known in other cases.[189] The legends in the scene appear to name his father as Sobek-re.[190]

In line 2, the title and name of Iunefer's main colleague offer some problems. The spelling *ʿrdyt* is, surely, a slip for *ʿrryt*, 'judgement hall',[191] through the easy confusion of *r* with *d* in hieratic. The proper name is patently a compound *Ddw-X*, where X is a divine name or epithet, in this case ending in *nỉ*. The first sign is a simplified hieratic form of *ṯ* as written in ligatures - hence, *ṯnỉ*, 'the Exalted One' in the name Didiu-tjeni, known elsewhere.[192] His parentage is in part obscured by damage to the stone; the title *ʿnḫ-n-nỉwt* seems probable, but the name is broken both here and in the scene-legends - *Wʿwt* . . is highly tentative, but of a known type.[193] Of the third personage, both the name[194] and the title[195] are (severally) known elsewhere. For the retainer, the name *Rḥw-ỉrỉ* here proposed is not directly paralleled, but it has sufficiently good analogies.[196]

In line 3, the title *ṯ3w n sš* remains obscure; on the Department 'Head-of-the-South', cf. above, WH 6. The presence of a Scribe of the Prison would not be untoward, given that one role (among others) of ancient Egyptian prisons was to act as a forced labour pool.[197]

Then we are told the objectives of the expedition - not only amethyst, but a whole range of semi-precious and allied stones.[198] Thereafter (line 4, end), a fresh section of the text, best restored as a heading - 'List of the expedition that went out . . . ', an interpretation which is supported by the fact that the rest of lines 4 (end) - 6 is just that, i.e. a list of personnel. Unfortunately, no statistics are given, unless they are now lost in the damaged part of lines 5 and 6. At the end of line 5, the list begins a new series of people, seemingly with a man of relatively high rank, the royal acquaintance bearing the good Middle-Kingdom name Senbebu-ankh,[199] and reference to two women in close succession, Sonb and Sit-Sobek.[200] After Sonb occurs a group whose real meaning remains obscure, but the last man's title is quite clear if perhaps unusual.

185. Possible sequence Khaneferre, Khahotepre, cf. von Beckerath, *op.cit.*, p.58.
186. See, e.g., a stela of Sobkhotep 'III', showing two princesses adoring Min-Horus with this formula (W.M.F. Petrie, *A History of Egypt,* I, 6th ed., London, 1907, p.211, fig.121).
187. *PN*, I, 15:21.
188. E.g. Helck, *OLZ* 50 (1955), col.213.
189. *PN*, I, 97:17.
190. *PN*, I, 304:19.
191. E.g., Faulkner, *Dict.*, p.45.
192. *PN*, I, 403:2, cf. 20.
193. Cf. *PN*, I, 76:14, 18-21.
194. *PN*, I, 95:16.
195. *ZÄS* 40 (1907), p.96.
196. *PN*, I, 225 19, 20, 24ff., and cf. WH 24:5 below.
197. Cf. W.C. Hayes, *A Papyrus of the Late Middle Kingdom,* New York, 1955, pp. 37-8, 39 and n.134 (prison scribes); Kitchen, *Tyndale House Bulletin* No.2 (1957), pp.1-2. The name Si-Sobek, cf. *PN*, I, 284:11.
198. These are discussed in J.R. Harris, *Lexicographical Studies in Ancient Egyptian Minerals,* Berlin, 1961 ('Harris', below), and in A. Lucas, ed. J.R. Harris, *Ancient Egyptian Materials and Industries,* 4th ed., London, 1962 ('Lucas' below). The detailed references are: *ḥsmn*, 'amethyst' - Harris, 121-2, Lucas, 388-9; *ḥm3gt*, probably (not certainly) garnet, found in Nubia and Aswan area - Harris, 118-120, Lucas, 394-5; *ḥmwt* (prob. *ḥmt* of other texts) is a green mineral, possibly an artificial frit (Harris, 117-8), its natural eqivalent sought in the eastern desert might then be beryl just conceivably (on which, cf. Lucas, 389-390), perhaps differently named in later times (Harris, 102, 103, 105). *Mnw km, ḥḏ*, 'black, white, quartz' (Harris, 110-111, Lucas, 402-3) could certainly be found in the Aswan deserts. *Nšmt*, 'green felspar', is again a product of the Egyptian deserts (Harris, 115-6, Lucas, 393-4).
199. *PN*, I, 315:1-12, Senbebu and compounds.
200. *PN*, I, 312:15 (Sonb), and 293:9 (Sit-Sobek).

WH, No. 24. Fakhry, No. 24; exc. no. 16; Aswan Museum, acc. no. 1486.
Date: Sobkhotep IV (Khaneferre), Year 6 (*c.* 1720 BC).
Bibliography: Fakhry, p. 42, pl. XVIA.
Description: Black granite stela, roughly rectangular, eight horizontal lines of sometimes cursive hieroglyphs, slightly damaged at the beginnings. Height 32 cm, width 20 cm, thickness 7 cm.

Normalised Text:

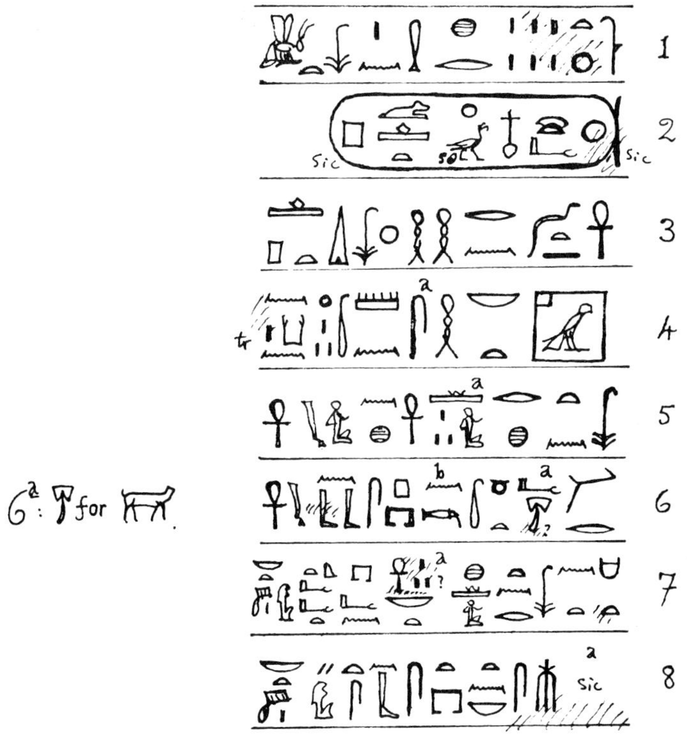

Textual Notes: 4a: here and throughout this text, *s* is reversed. 5a: here and throughout, the seated man is shown almost without arms. 6a: remarkably, the 'skin' sign is substituted for normal *ḫn*. 6b: hieratic form of *k3p*, followed by flattish rounded sign for *p*. 7a: unsatisfactory group, but this reading is possible despite horizontal mark below plural (?) and *ʿnḫ* (?). 8a: no signs lost.

Translation: (1) Year 6 under the Majesty of the King of Upper & Lower Egypt, (2) Khaneferre, Son of Re, Sobkhotep IV, (3) may he live for ever and ever.

A boon which the king gives to (4) Hathor, Lady of Amethyst, for the *ka* of (5) the King's acquaintance, Rehu-ankh, repeating life; (6) the palace-chamberlain, Senbeb, repeating life; (7) the wife of the King's acquaintance, Rehu-ankh, the lady of the house, Didit-Anuqet, possessing veneration, (8) born of the lady of the house, Senebtisi, possessing veneration.

Commentary: Lines 1-3, this text dates to the same year (and doubtless the same expedition) as WH 22 and 25. It shares the use of the *ḥtp-dỉ-nsw* formula with WH 25 of the same date, as well as WH 19 of about a century earlier. In lines 5 and 7, the principal official has the common name Rehu-ankh[201] and one respectable court title.

His companion (line 6) bears a title which, from Helck's discussion,[202] seems to belong to a class of official normally attached to the administration of the royal palace, subject to orders of superiors (e.g., the vizier), and passing these on to appropriate subordinates for execution. However, as in WH 24, such officials could be employed far from the Residence - one that Helck cites had to transport a sacred image from Thebes elsewhere. Senbeb's name is common[203] as are those such as the two ladies mentioned.[204]

201. *PN*, I, 225:19-20, cf. 21, and other *rḥw*-names 22ff.
202. *Zur Verwaltung des Mittleren und Neuen Reichs,* Leiden, 1958, p.252.
203. *PN*, I, 315:1, cf. 2-8.
204. Didi-Anuqet, cf. *PN*, I, 403:9, and Senebtisi, 314:25.

WH, No. 25. Fakhry, No. 25; exc. no. 17; Aswan Museum acc. no. 1487; PM, 126.
Date: Sobkhotep IV (Khaneferre), [Year 6] (*c.* 1720 BC).
Bibliography: Fakhry, p. 42, fig. 34, pl. XVIIB.
Description: Black granite stela with six lines of text, incomplete at top and down right hand side. Height 28.5 cm, width 17 cm, thickness 5 cm.
Normalised Text:

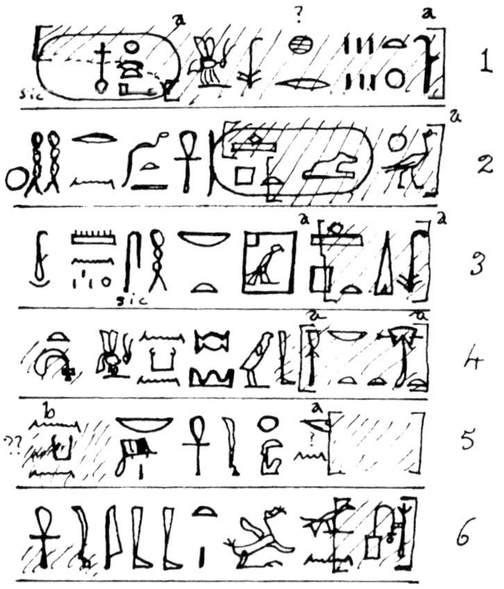

Textual Notes: 1a-a: from the restoration of line 3 (*q.v.*), four groups will have been lost before the cartouche; *ḥ3t-sp 6 ḫr nsw-bît* will just neatly fill this lacuna. For grouping of *Ḫ*ʿ*-nfr-r*ʿ, cf. WH 22. 2a-a: two groups lost before *ḥtp, s3-R*ʿ *Sbk-* just fits. 3a-a: in line 4, *n k3 n* implies a *ḥtp-dî-nsw* formula (cf. WH 24), and before *Ḥtḥr* of line 3 is the *p* of *ḥtp*; hence restore *ḥtp-dî-nsw* which then fixes the line-length of this stela. 4a-a: restored on parallels, see below. 5a: either *îr* or *nb*. 5b: reading rather hypothetical apart from upper *n*. 6a: room for [*sš*] and just possibly one more sign.

Translation: (1) [Year 6 under the King of Upper & Lower Egypt], Khanefer[re], (2) [Son of Re, Sobkhot] ep IV, may he live for ever and ever.

(3) [A boon which the king giv]es to Hathor, Lady of Amethyst, (4) [and to Satis, Lady of Elephant] ine, for the *ka* of the Seal-bearer of the King of Lower Egypt, (5) [. . . .] Ir/Neb-en-Re, repeating life, possessing veneration; and for the *ka* of (6) the Chief Scribe of the Vizier, Bebi, repeating life.

Commentary: Line 1, the lacuna is too long to be filled only with *nsw-bît, nb-t3wy,* and hence restore year-date (cf. WH 22, 24) and *ḫr* - probably not room for *ḥm n* also. Line 4, for the restoration of Satis in this text, cf. as parallels WH 2 and 22 above. Line 5, the final group may have been a final title of Ir/Neb-en-Re. The name Ir-en-Re is attested in the Old Kingdom,[205] but *Neb-en-Re is not so readily paralleled. At the end of this line is a group very difficult to interpret, but *n k3 n*, which is possible, would fittingly precede the next name. In line 6, restoring *sš* provides a well-attested title.

205. *PN*, I, 39:26.

D. Undated Inscriptions, I: Nos. 26-100

WH. No. 26. Fakhry, No. 26.
Date: Unknown King (Mentuhotep IV?), Year 1 (*c.* 1998 BC?).
Bibliography: Fakhry, p. 44, pl. XVIIA.
Description: Graffito (or, graffiti) on roughly rectangular sandstone block; not seen in 1975, because it has probably been destroyed by quarrying done since Fakhry's expeditions.

Normalised Text:

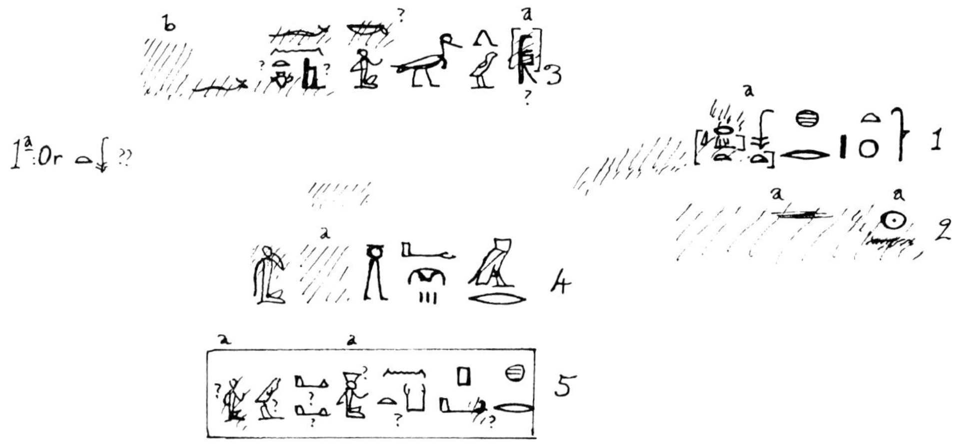

Textual Notes: 1a: if *nsw-bỉt* was here, only the body of the bee-sign can be seen, with what may be the faintest shadow of its wings. 2a-a: apart from a roughly circular sign (*Rʿ*), only vague traces. 3a: traces of what is either lower part of *šms* or simple legs *ỉw*. After *b3k*, traces are very faint. 3b: possibly a group or word lost from here, but not necessarily. It is uncertain whether any further line of signs once existed between the present lines 3 and 4. 4a: possibly *n-t-f* now lost from here? Certainly so, if det. is correctly read. 5a-a: these readings are hypothetical but just possible.

Translation: (1) Year 1 under the King of Upper [& Lower?] Egypt , . . . (2) [Nebtawy?] re, ...

(3) The retainer?/There came? his favourite servitor . . . , (4) the caravan-leader, In[tef]. (5) Director of Works, Didiu(?).

Commentary: The date of this inscription is uncertain. The combination of 'Year 1' and mention of the caravan-leader In[tef] points with greatest likelihood to Year 1 of Nebtawyre Mentuhotep IV. This inscription would then belong with WH 1-3 above. The mention of a possible colleague of Intef would be paralleled by his joint text with Khuyu (WH 3). Again, either version of Intef's name - In or Intef - can be found also in WH 4, of Year 2. If rightly read, Didiu may even be the father of a later Intef who visited Wadi Hudi in Year 20 of Sesostris I (see under WH 7). Finally, Mentuhotep IV is the only king (so far) whose Year 1 is attested at Wadi Hudi. These several converging lines of evidence fall short of certainty in dating WH 26 to this king, but they do lend considerable support to the suggestion.

WH, No. 27. Fakhry, No. 27. exc. no. 18. Aswan Museum acc. no. 1488.
Bibliography: Fakhry, p. 44, fig. 35, pl. XVIIIA.
Description: Bottom left-hand corner from a black-granite block used as a rough stela; part of three lines of text are visible. Max. height 16.5 cm, max, width 27 cm, thickness 15 cm.

Normalised Text:

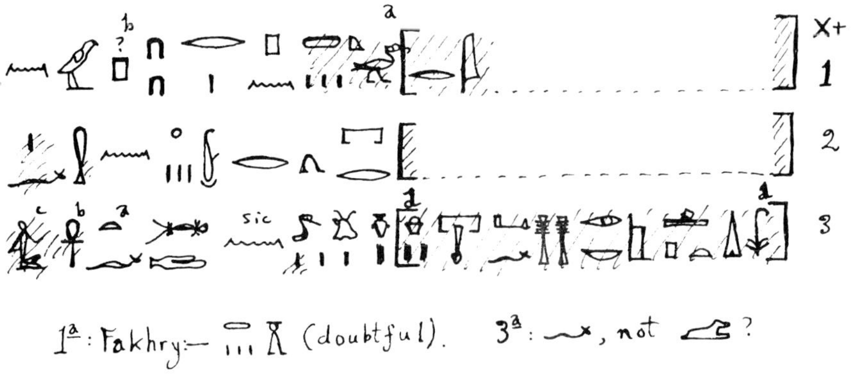

Textual Notes: 1a: traces obscure, but legs on low body would suit *ʿḳ* rather than *ỉn*. 1b: *p*, or a pot (*nw*?). 3a: *.f* rather than Sobek. 3b,c: possible traces. 3d-d: conjectural restoration.

Translation: (x+1) [. . . . . as for] this provision (?), it is the 20th part of/for (x+2) [each man of the expedition? who] went out for amethyst on behalf of His Majesty. (x+3) [A boon which the king gives to Osiris, Lord of Busiris, that he may grant invocation-offerings of bread and] beer, oxen and fowl, for <the *ka* of> Shed-iotef-ankh.

Commentary: Several lines are probably lost before the three surviving ones, besides the right half of each of these latter. One might conjecture the loss of a dateline, titles and name(s) of the leadership, then note of the provisions for the expedition-members where our fragment begins. Finally, an offering-formula for a leader.

Line 1, for *ʿḳw* in such texts, cf. Goyon, *NIH*, No. 61:16; the translation given here assumes that a numerical amount of food was given, of which the ordinary members had 1/20th each. Line 2, *pr* is probably a Perf. Active Participle, implying a missing antecedent like *mšʿ*; otherwise, simply a 'heading' infinitive with *t* omitted. The mention of 'His Majesty' should imply a year-date and royal name in the lost beginning of the text.

Line 3, one should probably restore a *ḥtp-dỉ-nsw* formula, as in WH 19, 20, 24, 25, but in this case at the end of the main text instead of following the datelines directly. The *n* appears to be a slip for *n kꜣ n*. For the name, rather than *Šdty-Sbk-ʿnḫ* or *Sbk-šdty-ʿnḫ*, one should read *Šd-ỉt.f-ʿnḫ*. None of these *ʿankh*-forms are directly paralleled, but they are legitimate formations from such as *Sbk-šdty* and *Šd-ỉt.f*, which are well paralleled.[206] The lack of title before this man's name may indicate lesser status in the expedition-leadership, or is merely because his full titles had already been given in the now missing beginning of the text.

206. For *Sbk-šdty*, cf. *PN*, I, 305:14, and *Šd-ỉt.f*, *ibid.*, 330:13 (for Hildesheim 1884, cf. H. Sternberg, *Göttinger Miszellen* 28 (1978), pp.45-54, esp. p.48b).

WH. No. 28. Fakhry, No. 28; exc. no. 19; Aswan Museum, acc. no. 1489; PM, 130.
Bibliography: Fakhry, p. 44, fig. 36.
Description: Bottom left-hand corner (broken in two) of a grey-granite stela, with last five lines of text, incomplete at right; from western side of Site 5. Max. height. 36 cm, max. width 23 cm, thickness 19.5 cm.

Normalised Text:

Textual Notes: 2a: obscure traces, hieratic .ỉ not certain. 3a: *wr* or *sꜣ*, possible trace of cartouche favours latter; long-bodied bird, head lost.

Translation: (x+1) [. . . . . god X], (and) Hat[hor? . . . . . .] (x+2) [. . .] my (?) equals, [. . . . .], (x+3) [. . . b]efore him. As lives for me the Son [of Re, *Royal Name*], (x+4) [I have spoken] in truth. The revered one, Chief of the Southern Tens, Sobek-re's (x+5) son, Intef, justified.

Commentary: Line 1, squarish trace behind divine figure could be base of *ḥwt* of 'Hathor'. Line 3, *ꜥnḫ n.ỉ* may be part of a well-known type of oath-formula,[207] with which the interpretation *sꜣ Rꜥ* plus royal name would fit very well. Then a restoration in line 4 of [*ḏd.n.ỉ*] *m mꜣꜥt* would follow perfectly. For the title 'Chief of the Southern Tens', cf. above under WH 14.

207. Cf. J.A. Wilson, *JNES* 7 (1948), p.131:I.A.1-4; Gardiner, § 218.

WH, No. 29. Fakhry, No. 29; exc. no. 20; Aswan Museum, acc. no. 1490; PM, 135.
Bibliography: Fakhry, p. 45, fig. 37, pl. XVIIIB.
Description: Column of text (height 24 cm) on pink granite block, height 42 cm, width 29 cm, thickness 51 cm.

Normalised Text:

Textual Note: 1a: stroke not certain, probably accidental.

Translation: The Count, Overseer of Prophets, Nakht-ankh, born of Kama‘.

Commentary: The titles are those proper to a nomarch; cf. (e.g.) those of Hapdjefi of Siut.[208] Unfortunately, Nakht-ankh gives no clue to which nome he hailed from. His and his mother's names are common in the Middle Kingdom.[209]

208. As in Sethe, *Aegyptische Lesestücke,* Leipzig, 1928, pp.92ff.
209. Nakht-ankh, *PN*, I, 210:1; Kama‘, *ibid.*, 344:28.

WH, No. 30. Fakhry, No. 30; exc. no. 21; Aswan Museum acc. no. 1491.
Bibliography: Fakhry, p. 45, fig. 38, pl. XIXA.
Description: Large lump of pink granite, with an archer and 3 columns of text.

Normalised Text:

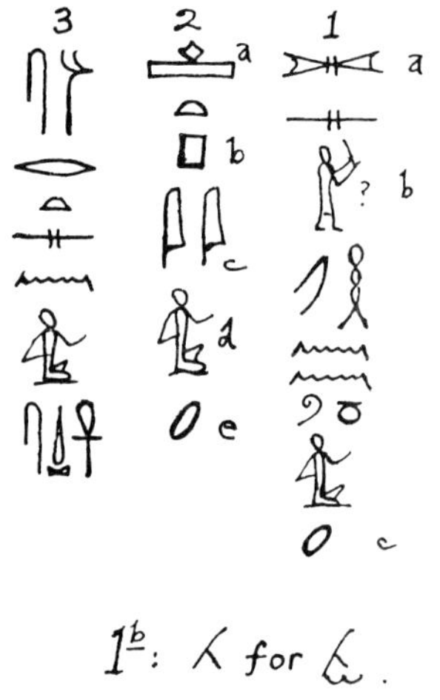

Textual Notes: 1a: hieratic form, cf. *HP*, I, No. 535. 1b: simplified hieratic form? 1c, 2e: simplified hieratic form of *s3*, 'son', cf. *HP*, I, No. 216B, and Goyon, *NIH,* No. 82, p. 98. 2a-d: all hieratic forms.

Translation: (1) The commander, Henenu's son (2) Hetepy's son (3) Senwosret, L.P.H.

Commentary: Graffito with lineage of one man; his and his forbears' names are good Middle Kingdom ones, already met with.[210]

210. *PN*, I, 279:1, 260:7, and 245:1, respectively.

WH, No. 31. Fakhry, No. 31; exc. no. 22; Aswan Museum, acc. no. 1492; PM, 132.
Bibliography: Fakhry, p. 46, fig. 39, pl. XIXB.
Description : On a black granite boulder, figure of a striding man (facing right) grasping another by the neck. Max. height 38 cm, max. width 55 cm, max. thickness 30 cm.

Normalised Text:

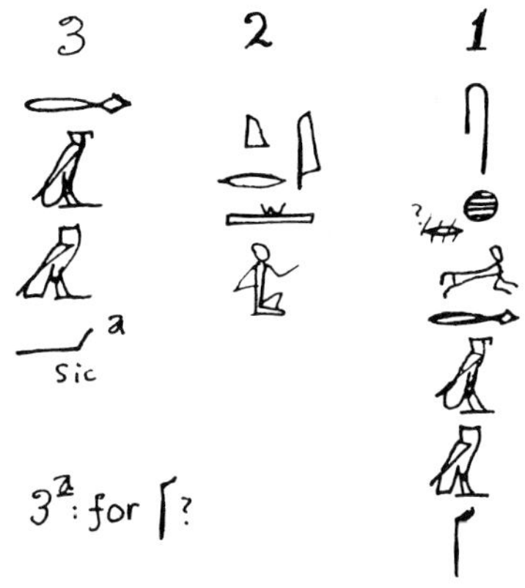

Textual Notes: 1a: possibly trace of a small, faint *r*. 3a: uncertain sign, see above figure.

Translation: (1) Overthrowing the Asiatic; (2) Iqer; (3) Asiatic.

Commentary: Iqer is a common name.[211] This graffito may reflect clashes between Egyptian expeditionaries and the desert-dwellers, as *Aamu* can cover E. - desert nomads as well as inhabitants of Canaan.[212]

211. *PN*, I, 47:16.
212. On Aamu, 'Asiatics', cf. latterly Couroyer, *Revue Biblique* 81 (1974), pp.321-354, 481-523.

WH, No. 32. Fakhry, No. 32; exc. no. 23; Aswan Museum, acc. no. 1493.
Bibliography: Fakhry, pp. 46-7. fig. 40, pl. XXA.
Description: Pink granite boulder as a roughly triangular stela. At right, a man (facing left), holding staff, sceptre and *ankh*. Below him, a rectangle (dais?). At left, three columns of signs. Height 88 cm, width 50 cm, thickness 19 cm.

Normalised Text:

Textual Notes: 1a: cursive *w*. 1b: hieratic seated man, lacking centre stroke. 2a: apparently just a vertical scratch. 2b: possibly *nw*-adze in one group with *nw*-pot and cursive *w*. 2c: cursive hieratic form?

Translation: (1) Kamose. (2) Overseer of Hunter(s), Kamose. (3) Messenger, Kamose.

Commentary: The name Kamose goes back to Middle Kingdom times,[213] although it is more familiar later. Chief hunters occur in other desert mining areas, e.g. Hammamat.[214]

213. *PN*, I, 338:5.
214. Cf. (e.g.) Goyon, *NIH*, Nos. 29, 55, 93, and Couyat & Montet, No. 126. On *ỉmy-r nww*, cf, further Erman & Grapow, *Wörterbuch*, II, 218:21, Newberry, *Beni Hasan I*, pl.30, Gardiner, *Anc. Egyp. Onomastica*, I, 188*, 189*, and *ZÄS* 65, 108ff., Gardiner & Weigall, *Topographical Catalogue of the Private Tombs of Thebes*, 1913, No. 149, among others.

WH, No. 33. Fakhry, No. 33; exc. no. 24; Aswan Museum, acc. no. 1494.
Bibliography: Fakhry, p. 48, fig. 41, pl. XXB.
Description: Column of signs (height 27 cm) on pink granite block, height now 45 cm, width now 25 cm, thickness 36 cm.

Normalised Text:

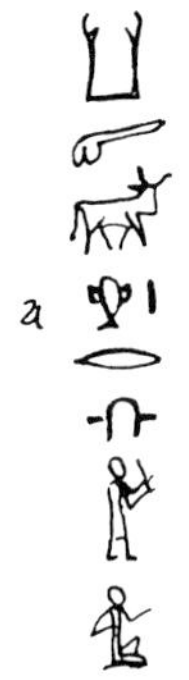

Textual Note: 1a: hieratic form of *ḥr*, cf. *HP*, I, No. 80c.

Translation: Ka-her(it).

Commentary: A known name, cf. *PN*, II, 321:21.

WH, No. 34. Fakhry, No. 34; exc. no. 25; Aswan Museum, acc. no. 1495.
Bibliography: Fakhry, p. 48, fig. 42, pl. XXIB.
Description: Line of text down a pink granite block, height 33 cm, width 9 cm, thickness 17 cm.

Normalised Text:

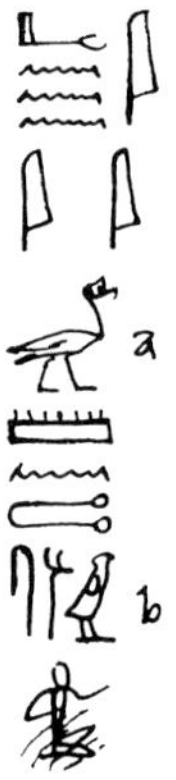

Textual Notes: 1a,b: hieratic forms.

Translation: Ia'y's son Montuwoser.

Commentary: Known names, cf. *PN*, I, 12:2 and 153:27, respectively.

WH, No. 35. Fakhry No. 35; exc. no. 26; Aswan Museum, acc. no. 1496.
Bibliography: Fakhry, p. 48, fig. 43, pl. XXIA.
Description: Roughly rectangular pink granite block with a column of signs; height now 40 cm, width 25 cm, thickness 5 cm.

Normalised Text:

Translation: Si-Ipu.

Commentary: A known name, cf. *PN*, I, 280:17 (cf. 18-20).

WH, No. 36. Fakhry, No. 36; exc. no. 27; Aswan Museum acc. no. 1497.
Bibliography: Fakhry, p. 49, fig. 44, pl. XXIC.
Description: Irregular, lozenge-shaped pink-granite block with one line of text; height 14 cm, length 34 cm, thickness 14 cm.

Normalised Text:

Textual Note: 1a: reading not certain but possible.

Translation: The supreme artisan, Wenen's son Senwosret.

Commentary: For the title, see above on WH 13; for the names Wenen and Senwosret, cf. *PN*, I, 79:21-22 (*Wnn.ỉ/y*), and 279:1.

WH, No. 37. Fakhry, No. 37; exc. no. 28; Aswan Museum, acc. no. 1498.
Bibliography: Fakhry, p. 49, pl. XXIIB.
Description: Grey-granite trapezoidal block with figure of an archer wielding also a mace; line of signs above him. Height 60 cm, width 21 cm, thickness 32 cm.

Normalised Text:

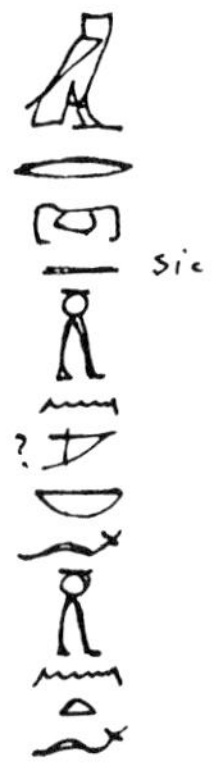

Translation: The caravan-leader who brings what his lord desires, Intef.

Commentary: The *ʿw* sign is formed almost like a *pr*; cf. WH 88 below.

WH, No. 38. Fakhry, No. 38; exc. no. 29; Aswan Museum acc. no. 1499.
Bibliography: Fakhry, p. 49, fig. 45, pl. XXIIA.
Description: Pink granite boulder with a line of signs; height 54 cm, width 41 cm, thickness 32 cm.

Normalised Text:

Translation: The Scribe, Intef-ʿo.

Commentary: This name, *PN*, I, 34:10.

WH, No. 39. Fakhry, No. 39; exc. no. 30; Aswan Museum, acc. no. 1500.
Bibliography: Fakhry, pp. 49-50, fig. 46, pl. XXIIC.
Description: Black granite block, man with staff next to text; on protrusion at left, two more men (one in a square). Height 20 cm, max. length 67 cm, thickness 28 cm.

Normalised Text:

Translation: Nakht.

Commentary: This name, cf. *PN*, I, 209:16; the 'dog' in Fakhry's facsimile is more likely the traces of the dets.

WH, No. 40. Fakhry, No. 40; present location, unknown.
Bibliography: Fakhry, p. 50, fig. 47.
Description: Irregular quartzite block; two columns of signs.

Normalised Text:

Translation: (1) The revered one, Ankhu born of Hetepi; (2) the revered one, Intef, justified.

Commentary: Common names, *PN*, I, 68:6, 260:3 (or 13, if *Ḥtpt*), 34:1.

WH, Nos. 41, 42, 43/44. Fakhry, Nos. 41, 42, 43/44; present location, unknown.
Bibliography: Fakhry, p. 50, fig. 53 (on p.54).
Description: A boulder seen at Site 5, with these graffiti.

Normalised Texts: 43/44 42 41

Translations: **41**: (Obscure).
42: One offering-slab.
43/44: The stonemason, Intef (?), justified (?).

WH, No. 45. Fakhry, No. 45; present location, unknown.
Bibliography: Fakhry, p. 51, fig. 53 (p.54), pl. XXIXA.
Description: Three signs in rectangle, with man at left side, one hand to mouth, the other with a dagger. On path up to top of Site 5 hill.

Normalised Text:

Translation: The sandalmaker, Hesi.

Commentary: For the possible hieratic forms, see respectively *HP*, I, Nos. 433, 502, 432. Names of type *Ḥsỉ*, cf. *PN*, I, 254:13, cf. 28, 29.

WH, No. 46. Fakhry, No. 46; present location, unknown.
Bibliography: Fakhry, p. 51, fig. 48.
Description: Irregular rock., three columns of signs; originally Site 5.

Normalised Text:

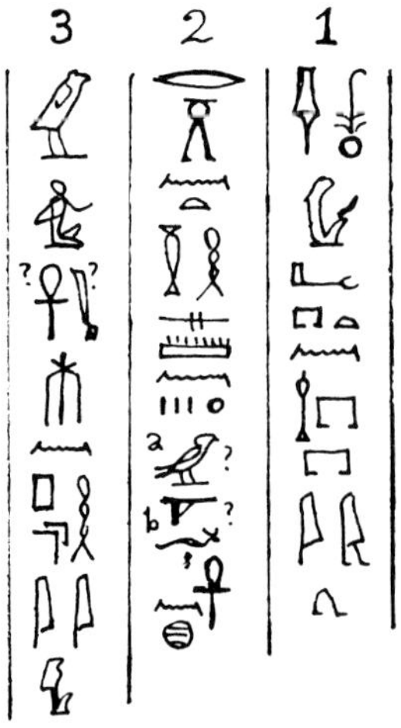

Textual Notes: 2a: for falcon? 2b: hieratic ligature of stand over *.f*?

Translation: (1) Director of Royal Property (??), petty official of the Treasury, who came (2) to fetch amethyst <for> his lord (!), Ankhu (3), repeating life (?), born of Hepy.

Commentary: These names, cf. *PN*, I, 68:6 and 238:6. The fuller title, *ỉry-ʿt n pr-ḥḏ*, is familiar.[215] The first compound sign before it could stand for *(r)ḫ-nsw*, but this title hardly suits a minor official, and takes no account of the *sḫm/ḫrp*. Nor is there ready parallel for **ḫrp šmʿw/rsw*, in which transposition would be needless. Hence, perhaps read as *ḫrp ḫ(t) nsw*. In line 2, if one reads 'falcon-on-stand' plus *f*, to give *nb.f*, then the omitted dative is easily understood as phonetically merged into the *n* of *nb.f*, and hence not written out.

215. Cf. Helck, *Zur Verwaltung des Mittleren und Neuen Reichs*, 1958, p.181.

WH, Nos. 47, 48. Fakhry, Nos. 47, 48; present location, unknown.
Bibliography: Fakhry, p. 51, fig 49 (p.52), pl. XXIXB.
Description: Two adjacent blocks, each with a column of text.

Normalised Text:

48

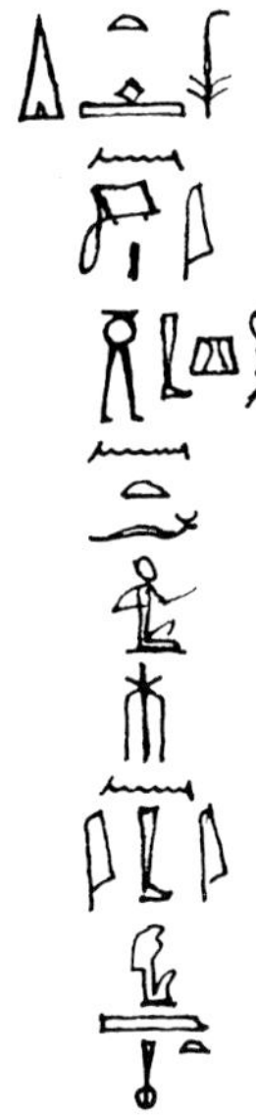

47

Translation: 47: Nesu born of Idi, justified.
48: A boon which the king gives, for (the benefit of) the revered one, the lector-priest Intef, born of Ibi, justified.

Commentary: No. 47: the names, see *PN*, I, 173:12 and 53:22, 23, respectively. No. 48: the introductory formula is unusual, perhaps heavily abbreviated, since no deity acting for the *ka* of . . . is included. Ibi, cf. *PN*, I, 20:10.

WH, No. 49. Fakhry, No. 49; present location unknown, was on South of Site 5.
Bibliography: Fakhry, p. 51, pl. XXXB.
Description: Large boulder with two columns of hieroglyphs.

Normalised Text:

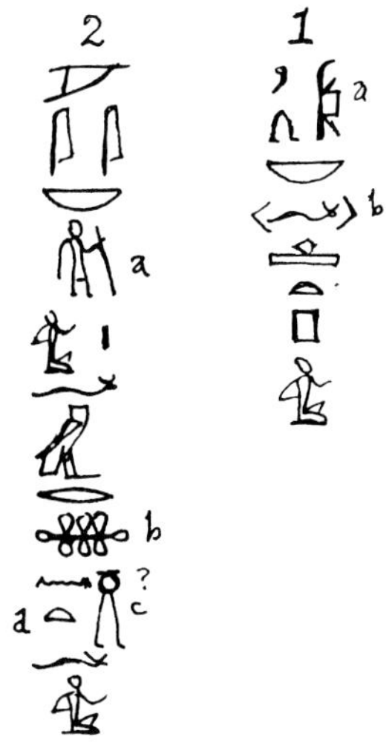

Textual Notes: 1a: hieratic form, cf. *HP*, I, No. 443. 1b: *.f* omitted. 2a: cf. *HP*, I, No. 11. 2b: hieratic form, identical with 'bolt-*s*', cf. *HP*, I, p. 51, n.2. 2c: ligature of *ỉn* plus *n*? 2d: hieratic form of *t*, *HP*, I, No. 575.

Translation: (1) Follower of <his> lord, Hotep. (2) Beloved of his lord, Superintendent of a Contingent, Intef.

Commentary: For Hotep, cf. *PN*, I, 257:22. Line 2, for spelling of *nb*, probably cf. WH 51:2. The title *ỉmy-r sꜣ*, cf. also WH 148 (esp. line 10), plus Hammamat (*NIH*), Nos. 68, 69, for parallels.[216] The reading of Intef here is just possible; convincing alternatives seem few.

216. Cf. Goyon, *NIH*, pp.90-91; and on titles with *sꜣ*, the remarks of W.K. Simpson, *JNES* 18 (1959), p.32.

WH, No. 50. Fakhry, No. 50; present location, unknown.
Bibliography: Fakhry, p. 52, fig. 53 (p. 54).
Description: Groups of signs on a boulder.

Normalised Text:

Translation: Amethyst.

Commentary: No photo is available to check the fascimile; allowing for rough cutting on the stone, the above reading is offered with due reserve.

WH, No. 51. Fakhry, No. 51; present location, unknown.
Bibliography: Fakhry, p. 52, fig. 50, pl. XXXA.
Description: Rock-face with three columns of hieroglyphs.

Normalised Text:

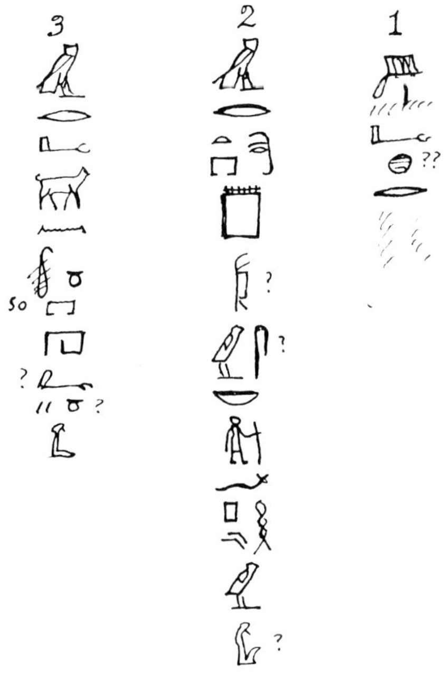

Textual Notes: Some signs dubious, but readings are possible.

Translation: (1) Gifts for/by: (2) Superintendent of the Council - chamber (?) of the palace (?), follower of his Lord, Hepu. (3) Superintendent of the Audience-chamber, Hanui (?).

Commentary: Line 2, *ḫnrt* in itself is ambiguous; 'prison', 'fortress', 'audience-chamber', are all possible (cf. Faulkner, *Dict.*, p. 193, refs). For spelling of *nb*, cf. WH 49:2. For Hepu, cf. *PN*, I, 238:14. Line 3, no name *ḥnwy* in Ranke, but cf. *PN*, I, 229:28-32, for possibly related names and forms.

WH, No. 52. Fakhry, No. 52; present location, unknown.
Bibliography: Fakhry, p. 53, fig. 51, pl. XXXIB.
Description: Mark and two lines of signs on a boulder, formerly 'near the middle path leading up the hillside' (Fakhry).

Normalised Text:

Translation: (1) . . ? . . (2) The Warrior, In(tef)oqer; the warrior, Heqaib; (3) Iqu.

Commentary: The first sign remains obscure. Line 2, the repeated title appears to be a hieratic form of *ꜥḥꜣ(wty)*, cf. *HP*, I, No. 113, and at Hammamat.[217] As for the names, In-oqer is transparently an abbreviation of Intefoqer (*PN*, I, 34:7), Heqaib is very common (*PN*, I, 256:3), but Iqu is not readily paralleled in this simple form. Compare however, Didi-iqu (*PN*, I, 401:10); it is possible that 'Iqu' is a graphic error for Iqeru (*PN*, I, 47:25). It is written in a rougher style than line 2, and without title.

217. Goyon, *NIH*, Index, p.180, right, for his No. 61:1, 19, to which add his No.64.

WH, No. 53. Fakhry, No. 53; present location unknown; was near WH 52; PM, 29 (?).
Bibliography: Fakhry, p. 53, fig. 54 (p.55), pl. XXXIA.
Description: Boulder on whose smoother face is scratched four lines of cursive text. Height 78 cm, width 47 cm.

Normalised Text:

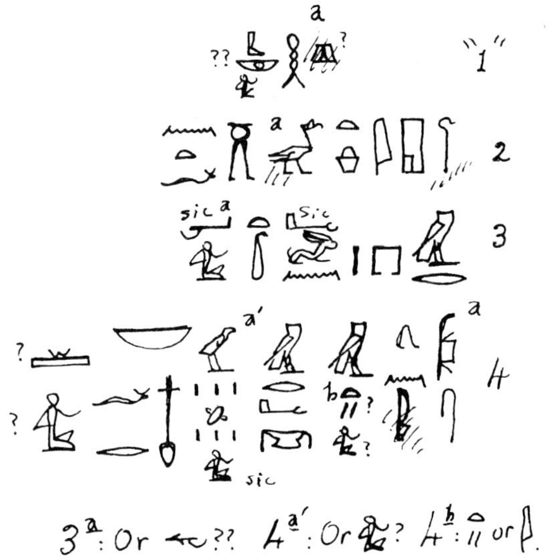

Textual Notes: 1a: this group probably belongs before 'Intef' in line 2; for the group *ḥb*, cf. *HP*, I, p. 48, n.5. 2a: abbreviated, hieratic form. 3a: this sign seems clear, but superfluous. 4a-a: all hieratic forms, *nm* (*HP*, I, No. 585), *tỉ* (*ibid.*, IXL), det. (*ibid.*, No. 33B, very reduced forms).

Translation: (2) Ruler of a Domain, Ita's son (1) the lector-priest, (2) Intef. (3) The Steward 'Awenti (?). (4) The retainer, Nemti. The caravan-leader of the workforce (?), Nebnufer.

Commentary: For *ḥry-ḥ(ꜣ)b* between *sꜣ* and 'Intef', cf. WH 54 below; the title was evidently omitted and thus added in over the main line of text. The title *ḥḳꜣ ḥwt* is known for other Middle Kingdom expeditionaries.[218] The name Ita is familiar (*PN*, I, 49:3), but not so 'Awenti; if the determinative were the stick-sign (rather than reversed *ʿayin*), it would at least be related to the word for 'stave'. Nemti, cf. *PN*, I, 204:13, cf. 14, 15. The term *ḥsbw* is known for manual labour, virtually slaves.[219] Added to the title *ỉmy-r ʿw*, it here clearly defines the people under his command. Nebnufer, cf. *PN*, I, 185:18, cf. 19-21. The occurrence of older titles together here – Lector, Ruler of a Domain, Caravan-leader – might suggest an Eleventh-Dynasty date for this text and the related WH 54, etc.

218. Cf. Goyon, *NIH*, No. 53 (p.77) of the Eleventh Dynasty.
219. Goyon, *NIH*, No.61:8, etc. and W.K. Simpson, *JNES* 18 (1959), p.31f.

WH, No. 54. Fakhry, No. 54; present location unknown; PM, 38 (?).
Bibliography: Fakhry, p. 53, fig. 52.
Description: Line of text on a rock near WH 52, 53.

Normalised Text:

Textual Note: 1a: conjectural restorations, based on WH 53.

Translation: Ruler of a Domain, It[a's son], the Lector Intef.

Commentary: This text was probably written by (or, for) the same man named in WH 53, *q.v.*

WH, Nos. 55, 56A/B. Fakhry, Nos. 55, 56A/B; present location unknown.
Bibliography: Fakhry, p. 53 end, fig. 53 (p.54).
Description: Three lines of text on same boulders as WH 52-54.

Normalised Text:

56B 56A 55

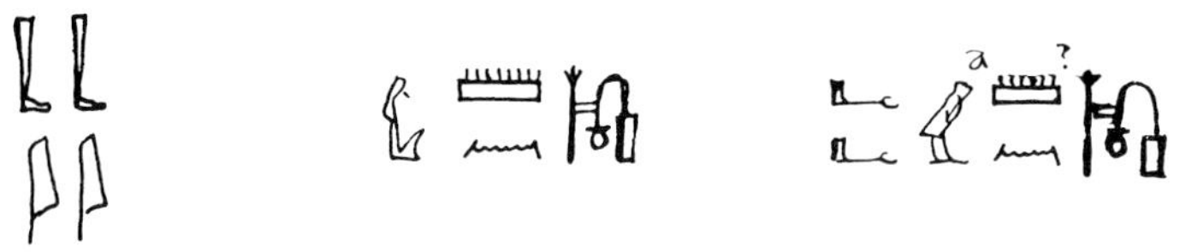

Textual Note: (55) 1a: probably $\underline{t}$ has been omitted.

Translations: **55**: The Scribe, Didi-Mon<t>u (?)
56A: The Scribe, Meni. **B**: Bebi.

Commentary: For these three names see *PN*, I, 402:19, 149:29, and 95:16.

WH, No. 57. Fakhry, No. 57; present location unknown; was near WH 3.
Bibliography: Fakhry, p. 56, fig. 55, pl. XXXIIA.
Description: Four-line graffito on boulder, under a rough mark.

Normalised Text:

Translation: (1) In(tef) oqer. (2) Henenu. (3/4) The prospector, Ipi.

Commentary: The names, *PN*, I, 34:7, 245:1, 22:15. 'Prospector', cf. WH 6.

WH, No. 58. Fakhry, No. 58; present location unknown; was near WH 57.
Bibliography: Fakhry, p. 56 end, pl. XXXIIB.
Description: Five-columned text on a boulder.

Normalised Text:

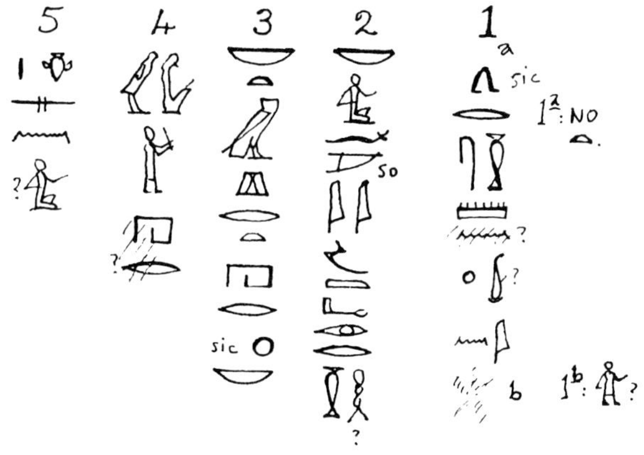

Translation: (1) Coming for amethyst by (2) the truly beloved of his lord, who does all (3) that is praised throughout the course of every day, (4) the Guardian, (5) Heribsen (?).

Commentary: Transposition in *mry nb.f mꜣʿ* (line 2) is known.[220] For the cliché after it, cf. above, WH 9. The name Her(ib)sen is not directly paralleled, but cf. *PN*, I, 230:5ff. The readings here adopted are likely but not certain.

220. Cf. Janssen, *TEA*, I, p.63, 7, 16.

WH, No. 59. Fakhry, No. 59; present location unknown; was East face of rock with No. 58 (F).
Bibliography: Fakhry, p. 57, fig. 56, pl. XXXIIIA.
Description: One line of text near WH 58.

Normalised Text:

Textual Notes: 1a: small, vague sign between *w* and *ḥry-sštꜣ*. 1b: hieratic form possible. 1c: either ʿ or *n*.

Translation: The retainer Inpu's son, the Chief of Secrets, Thuty-wedja-ef.

Commentary: For Inpu ('Anubis') as a personal name, cf. *PN*, I, 37:4. For *Ḏḥwty-wḏʿ.f* as a known Middle Kingdom name, cf. *PN*, I, 407:21. The readings adopted here result from repeated scrutiny of the published photo, as against Fakhry's facsimile.

WH, No. 60. Fakhry, No. 60; present location, unknown.
Bibliography: Fakhry, p. 57, fig. 57.
Description: Two vertical columns of signs, same rock as WH 49.

Normalised Text:

Translation: (1) Caravaneer for the Count[s], one [who] follows (?) (2) his lord, P[. .] tiu (?).

Commentary: Fakhry's copy (no photo) gives little sense as it stands; the above version attemps to utilise his copy by offering slightly different interpretations of some signs and traces.

WH, No. 61. Fakhry, No. 61; present location unknown; was near previous ones.
Bibliography: Fakhry, p. 57, fig. 58 (p. 58).
Description: Four-column text between figures of two men in long kilts. Man at left, one hand raised, *ankh* in other; man at right, one hand raised, horizontal sceptre in other. Height 14 cm, width 14.5 cm.

Normalised Text:

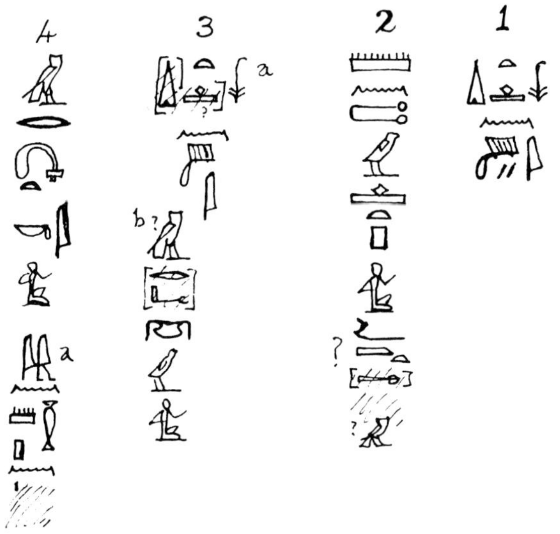

Textual Notes: 3a: traces of *dỉ* and *ḥtp*, same formula as in line 1. 3b: *m* rather than F's seeming *w*? 4a: just possible; if it were a *p*, it would differ entirely from either of two possible forms (here taken as *mn* and *p*) just below.

Translation: (1) A boon which the king gives, for the revered one, (2) Mentuhotep, justified (?) . . . . .

(3) A boon which the king gives, for the revered one, the caravan-leader, (4) the Superintendent of the Seal, Iku, who came (?) on account of this amethyst. . . .

Commentary: Lines 1, 3, for a similarly-abbreviated *ḥtp-dỉ-nsw*, see above WH 48. For the names, cf. *PN*, I, 154:21, and 48:9-10. At the end of line 4, *pn . . . pn* makes no sense, but *ỉỉ n ḥsmn pn* seems possible. In this context, *n* is not dative (one uses *r ḥsmn*) but gives cause (Gardiner § 164, 5). One might also amend the text to read *ỉỉ.n(.ỉ) r ḥsmn*, 'I came for amethyst . . ', but this seems needless.

WH, No. 62. Fakhry, No. 62; present location unknown; was next to WH 61.
Bibliography: Fakhry, p. 57, fig. 59 (p. 58), pl. XXXIIIB.
Description: Two figures of men, identically with one arm raised, facing right; the smaller (at right) is in a rectangle, with text before and beneath him. He may be looking behind him.

Normalised Text:

Translation: (1) The retainer, Iqeri (?) (2) born (of) Sit-Re (?).

Commentary: For the names as read, cf. *PN*, I, 47:22-23, 290:21. For the mother's name one alternative is *S3t-tnỉ*, cf. *PN*, I, 294:22. The theoretical alternatives for Iqeri are unparalleled and less convincing.

WH, No. 63. Fakhry, No. 63; present location unknown; was in hut on hill.
Bibliography: Fakhry, p. 57, fig. 60, pl. XXXIVA.
Description: Four lines of text on stone in ruined hut.

Normalised Text:

Translation: (1) Dependant of the Ruler's Table, (2) Hor, L.P.H. Henenu's (3) son Bebi, (4) L.P.H.

Commentary: For the three names, cf. *PN*, I, 245:18, 245:1, and 95:16. Hor's title is a known one of especially the Middle Kingdom.[221]

221. Cf. Gardiner, *JEA* 24 (1938), p.88, n.5, and (on *ṯt*) pp.171, 179.

WH, No. 64. Fakhry, No. 64; present location unknown.
Bibliography: Fakhry, p. 59, fig. 61, pl. XXXVB.
Description: Group of signs on a hillside boulder.

Normalised Text:

Translation: (1) Mimi. (2) Si-Mut (?).

Commentary: For possible parallels to Mimi, cf. *PN*, I, 146:14 (cf. 15), and 149:18. For Si-Mut, *ibid.*, 282:3.

WH, No. 65. Fakhry, No. 65; present location unknown.
Bibliography: Fakhry, p. 60, fig. 61 (p. 59), pl. XXXVB.
Description: Three columns of signs on a hillside boulder.

Normalised Text:

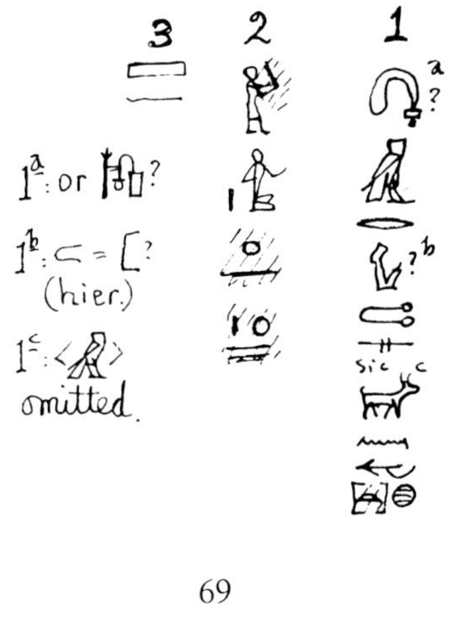

Translation: (1) The Seal-bearer/Scribe, Superintendent of Dog-handlers, Nakht. (2,3) . . . (illegible). .

Commentary: The first sign is ambiguous, and the notes in the above figure are merely an attempt to extract likely sense from what may be a poor facsimile of a slovenly scrawl, not clearly identifiable in Fakhry's plate XXXVB. For other 'doggy' personnel, see WH 93.

WH, No. 66. Fakhry, No. 66; present location unknown.
Bibliography: Fakhry, p. 60, fig. 62, pl. XXXIVB.
Description: Four columns of hieroglyphs, originally on interior of the rock wall of a hut, 'in the middle of the southern side of the hill' (F).

Normalised Text:

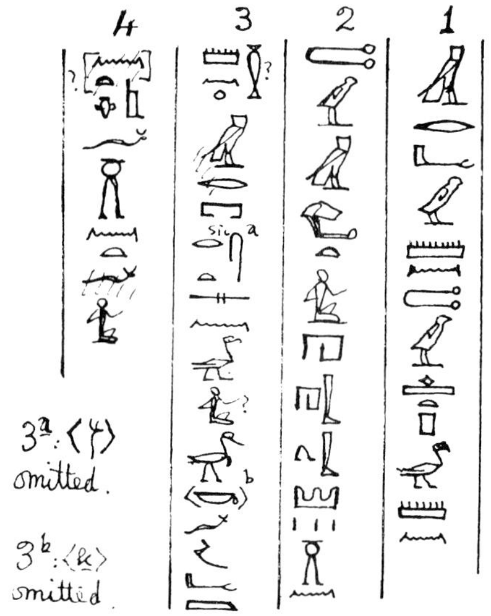

Translation: (1) The caravan-leader, Mentuhotep's son (2) Montemhat, who travels the deserts, who brings (3) amethyst (?); the Steward, Sen<wos>ret's son, his true and (4) favourite servitor, Intef.

Commentary: For Mentuhotep, Montemhat, cf. *PN*, I, 154:21, 7. For the idiom *hbhb ḫ3swt,* cf. references, WH 149:9-11 below; *hbhb* and *ìn* will be participles, the latter requiring an object. Here, *ḥsmn* is proposed, based on scrutiny of the photograph (with due reserve), like most of the readings that follow. *Wsr* and *k* appear to have been omitted from the name Senwosret (*PN*, I, 279:1) and term *b3k*, respectively.

WH, Nos. 67-72. Fakhry, Nos. 67-72; present location unknown.
Bibliography: Fakhry, p. 60, fig. 63, pl. XXXVB.
Description: Six short columns of hieroglyphs on a single rock, originally 'in the valley leading from the amethyst quarry, Site 5, to the amethyst quarry, Site 6' (F).

Normalised Text:

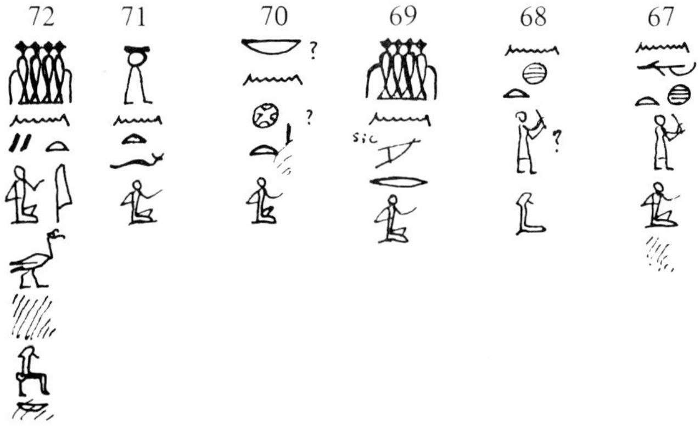

Translation: **67**: Nakht. **68**: Nakht (?). **69**: Meri-Khen<ty>.
70: Nebenniut. **71**: Intef. **72**: Khenty's son [. . . .] .

Commentary: Nos. 67, 68: cf. *PN*, I, 209:16; visible on F's pl. XXXVB, left half (right side). No. 69: cf. *PN*, I, 159:9 for feminine equivalent. No. 70: cf. *Nb-nỉwt, PN,* I, 185:16. No. 72: *Ḫntỉ*, cf. *PN*, I, 271:19-20, and 272:1-2; rest is illegible.

WH, Nos. 73-78. Fakhry, Nos. 73-78; present location unknown, cf. WH 67-72.
Bibliography: Fakhry, p. 60, fig. 63, pl. XXXVB.
Description: Five columns of signs, then two in a *hwt* rectangle.

Normalised Text:

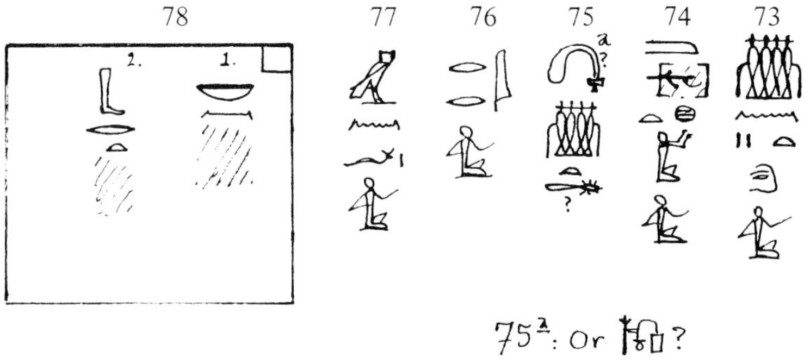

Translation: **73**: Khenti. **74**: The follower, Dwa/Sba. **75**: The Seal-bearer/Scribe, Khenty-kheti (?).
76: Irer. **77**: Menef. **78**: Neben . . , Beret . . .

Commentary: No. 74: title *ỉmy-ḫt*, cf. Faulkner, *Dict.*, p. 19 and refs. For Dwa, cf. *PN*, I, 398:21 (fem.). No. 75: title, ambiguous writing; name, cf. *PN*, I, 272:15. No. 76: cf. *PN*, I, 43:13. No. 77: obscure, but a reading as 'Intef' would be difficult to sustain. No. 78: mere traces.

WH, Nos. 79, 80. Fakhry, Nos. 79, 80; present location unknown.
Bibliography: Fakhry, p. 60, fig. 63, pl. XXXVB.
Description: No. 79 is a rectangle containing the figure of a man facing right, with two columns of signs before him. No. 80 is a single line of signs. No. 79 was near Nos. 67-78, with No. 80 on another rock lower down.

Normalised Text:

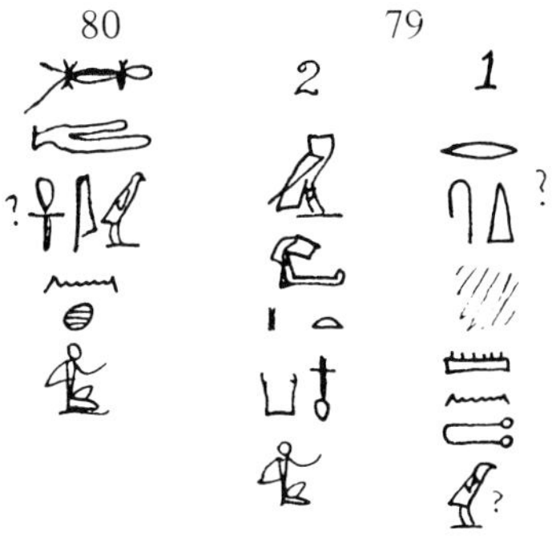

Translation: **79**: (1) . . . . , Montem- (2) hat's (son) Kanufer. **80**: Shedwi-ankh.

Commentary: No. 79: The initial group in line 1 makes no clear sense as copied by F. A filiation is perhaps to be understood between the two apparently contiguous names. Montemhat, *PN*, I, 154:7. Neferka and Kanufer, cf. *PN*, I, 200:16, 340:10.

No. 80: The reading adopted here assumes a name related to either Shedwi (*PN*, I, 331:19, Middle Kingdom), 'Shedwi lives', or else the type Shed-wi-DEITY (cf. *PN*, I, 330:16-19), here 'the living one rescues me'.

WH, No. 81. Fakhry, No. 81; present location unknown.
Bibliography: Fakhry, p. 60, fig. 64 (p.62), pl. XXXVIB.
Description: Two columns of signs, seen on block on South side of summit of southern hill (F), i.e. Site 6.

Normalised Text:

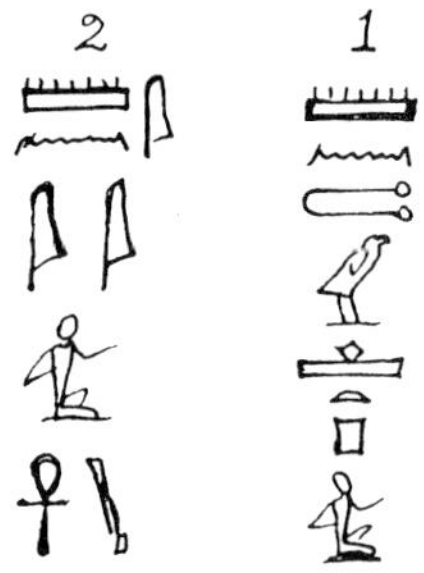

Translation: (1) Mentuhotep. (2) Ameny, repeating life.

Commentary: The *n* of Ameny is visible in the photo, not in F's sketch.

WH, Nos. 82, 83. Fakhry, Nos. 82, 83; present location unknown.
Bibliography: Fakhry, p. 62, figs. 65, 66; pl. XXXVIA (No. 83).
Description: No. 82, a rectangle containing two lines of text; a man is shown outside at right (facing right).
No. 83 is a column of text.

Normalised Text:

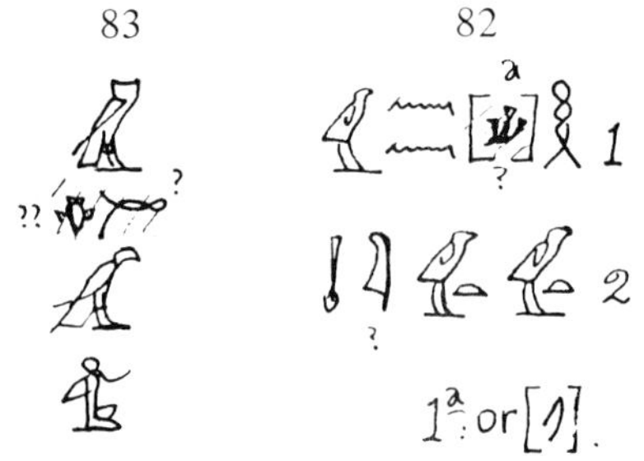

Textual Note: **82**: 1a: One may here restore either plant or hoe *ḥn*-sign.

Translation: **82**: (1) Henenu. (2) Tutu, justified.
83: Meh-ib-Hor.

Commentary: No. 82, the names, *PN*, I, 245:1 and 385:24-27, 386:1. No. 83, for names *mḥ-ỉb*-DEITY, cf. *PN*, I, 163:15-17, esp. 17.

WH, No. 84. Fakhry, No. 84; present location unknown; was near WH 82/83.
Bibliography: Fakhry, p. 62, fig. 67, pl. XXXVIIA.
Description: Crudely drawn figure of a man, facing left, with text before him.

Normalised Text:

Textual Notes: 2a: cf. *HP*, I, No. 318. 2b: cf. *HP*, I, No. 294 (semi-hieratic form, in WH 84).

Translation: (1) The warrior Mimi, of the City: (2) 'I am one praised (of) the whole land, (3) whom his entire city loves'.

Commentary: Line 1, *ʿḥꜣwty* is read on basis of studying photo besides the facsimile. Name, cf. WH 64 and *PN*,I, 146:13-15. The City may be Thebes, a harbinger of New-Kingdom usage. Line 2, an irregular writing of the 1st person singular Independent Pronoun, but the photo is clear, and the form not unknown (*Wb.*, I, p. 101). In *ḥsw* the 'plural' dots serve to express the *w*. Line 3, Imperf. Relative Form *mrrw*; the *twt* is probably for *twt.tỉ*, Old Perfective ('Stative'), with assimilation of two *t*'s.

WH, No. 85. Fakhry, No. 85; present location unknown.
Bibliography: Fakhry, p. 62 (no illustration).
Description: A line of text (28 cm.) on block near WH 81-84.

Normalised Text:

Translation: The retainer, Nesu-Montu.

Commentary: This name, cf. *PN*, I, 176.14.

WH, Nos. 86-88. Fakhry, Nos. 86-88; present location unknown.
Bibliography: Fakhry, p. 62f., figs. 68-70, pls. XXVIIIB, D, XXXVIIB.
Description: Three single columns of text; a *ḥn*-sign beside No. 86, the figure of a walking man with staff in front of No. 88.

Normalised Text:

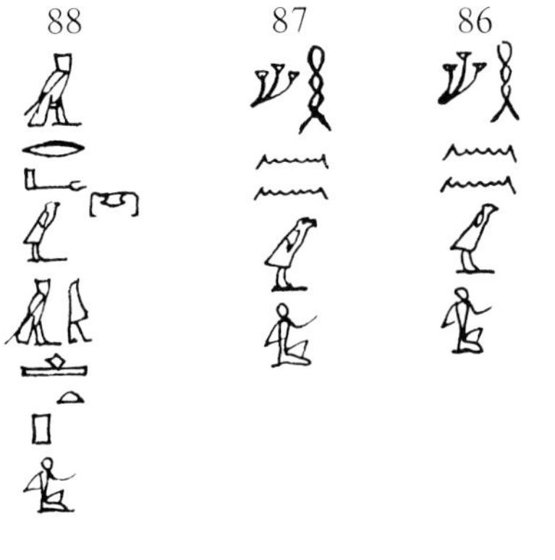

Translations: **86**: Henenu. **87**: Henenu. **88**: Caravan-leader, Iyemhotep.

Commentary: Nos. 86, 87, are a pair of scrawls, probably by the same man. No. 88, at first sight, seems to begin with *ỉmy-r pr*, 'steward', but the *ʿw* indicates the true reading; Iyemhotep, cf. *PN*, I, 9:1.

WH, No. 89. Fakhry, No. 89; present location unknown.
Bibliography: Fakhry, p. 64, without any reproduction.
Description: A very rough sketch of a man with his name before him, on a block of stone rolled to the side of the hill.

Normalised Text:

Translation: Montuwoser.

Commentary: The orthography offered is theoretical, lacking a copy.

WH, No. 90. Fakhry, No. 90, A/B; present location unknown, was near No. 89.
Bibliography: Fakhry, p. 64, fig. 70, pls. XXXVIIIC (90A), A (90B).
Description: No. 90A, two men walking to right (one partly above the other), with text before them; No. 90B, a line of text with trace at right.

Normalised Text:

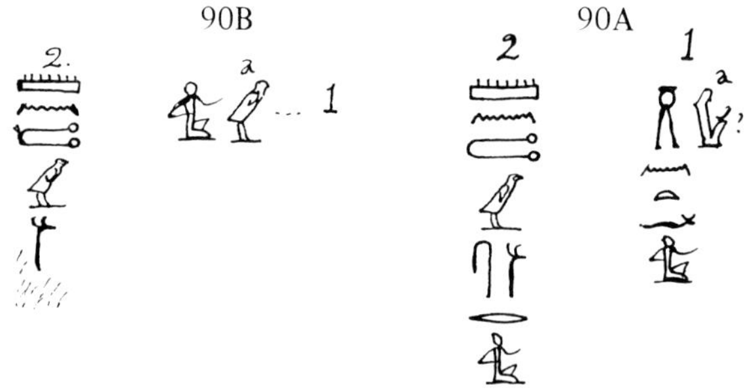

Textual Notes: 90A, 1a, 90B, 1a: traces visible on photo, omitted from the facsimile.

Translation: **90A**: (1) The Guardian, Intef; (2) Montuwoser.
90B: (1) The . . . . . . , (2) Montuwoser.

Commentary: It is possible that these men were in reality *mnỉw-(ṯsmw)*, 'dog-handlers', cf. WH 93 below.

WH, No. 91. Fakhry, No. 91; present location unknown, near No. 90.
Bibliography: Fakhry, p. 65, fig. 71, pl. XXIIIA.
Description: Figure of a man (facing right) carrying a baton and vertical staff. Above and behind him, four columns of hieroglyphs.

Normalised Text:

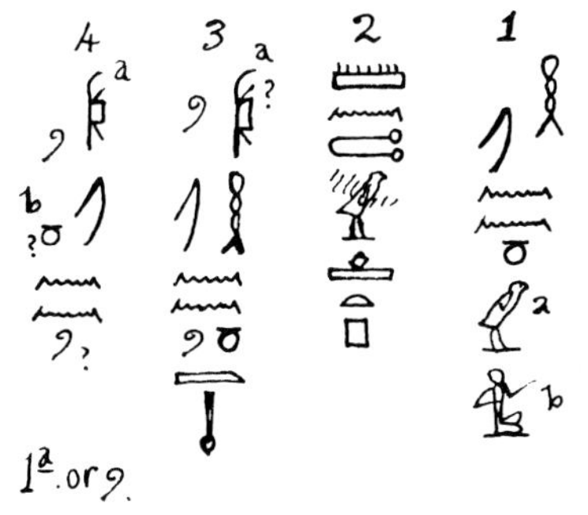

Textual Notes: 1a: here (as in lines 3, 4) the *w* is very cursive. 1b: very cursive form. 3a, 4a: abnormal form for *šms*. 4b: The *nw* may be only an accidental scratch; no *ḥ* before *ḥn*.

Translation: (1) Henenu. (2) Mentuhotep. (3) The retainer, Henenu, justified. (4) The retainer, Henenu.

WH, No. 92. Fakhry, No. 92; present location unknown.
Bibliography: Fakhry, p. 65, fig. 72 (p. 66), pl. XXIIIC.
Description: Figure of an ibex, with two (three?) other animals and a column of rough signs before it; was near No. 91.

Normalised Text:

Translation: The chamberlain, Tjebuy.

Commentary: For similar names, cf. *PN*, I, 390:17, 18; this text is so badly written that almost any interpretation is distinctly theoretical.

WH, No. 93. Fakhry, No. 93; present location unknown.
Bibliography: Fakhry, p. 67, fig. 73, pl. XXIVA, cf. XXVA.
Description: Above a long rock-fault, large figure of a man (facing right), mace upraised in his right hand to strike an animal held out in his left hand. Above him at left, a small figure walks to left. Before him, two men approach, the first with fists clenched on chest, the second with arms pendent. Over main man, one line of text, a column being beyond the two. Below the rock-fault, one archer-figure at right, drawing bow and arrow, another in centre holding bow and arrow in separate hands, and seven groupings of signs.

Normalised Text:

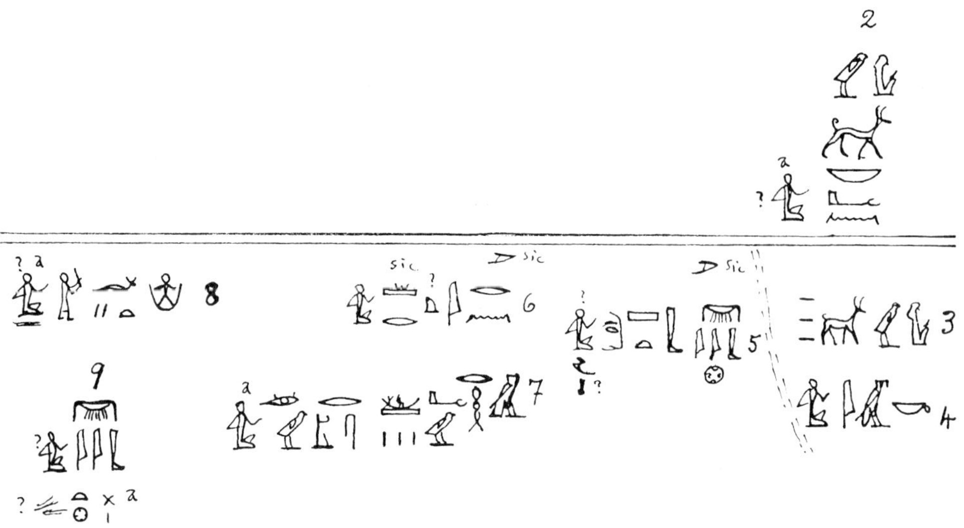

Textual Notes: 2a, 7a, 8a: all these appear to be idiosyncratic variants of the seated-man determinative. Several handwritings seem to be represented in this group of graffiti. 9a: the last few signs are obscure.

Translation: (1) The dog-handler, Nakht; (2) the dog-handler, Neb-ʿan. (3) The dog-handler, (4) Kai; (5) the Ombite, Beshet; (6) Ren-oqer; (7) the Shipmaster, Resu; (8) the brewer, (9) Nuby, ...

Commentary: The title here translated 'dog-handler' should be transliterated *mniw-tsmw* (cf. *Wb.*, V, p. 409:22), as is shown by (i) the *-w* ending of the first element, and (ii) by full writings like that on Florence stela 1539 (Inv. 2517),[222] of an officer (*wʿrtw*) of dog-handlers, a title attested also in Papyrus Boulaq 18, the palace accounts of the Thirteenth Dynasty.[223] The reading *iry-ṯsmw*[224] is excluded by the *-w* ending, and by this fuller evidence. On names, for Neb-ʿan, cf. *PN*, I, 183:24; for Kai, *ibid.*, 341:15; for Beshet, *ib.*, 98:23-24; for Ren-oqer, *ib.*, 222:23; for Resu, *ib.*, 227:1; for Nuby, *ib.*, 192:13. Line 8, for *ʿfty*, 'brewer', on these desert expeditions, cf. also Hammamat, *NIH*, No. 61:8. The last traces in line 9 are illegible.

222. Cf. S. Bosticco, *Museo Archeologico di Firenze, Le Stele Egiziane*, I, Rome, 1959, p.54, pl.54.
223. Cf. Scharff, *ZÄS* 57 (1922), p.66 and p.18**, § XXXVIII, 6-8.
224. Goyon, *NIH*, p.80 (on No.58).

WH, No. 94. Fakhry, No. 94; present location unknown.
Bibliography: Fakhry, p. 67, fig. 74, pl. XXVII.
Description: At top left, a man on a canopied stool, facing right; below him, a man with hoe (bow??), facing left; texts, to right of both. Max. height 63 cm, max. width 52 cm.

Normalised Text:

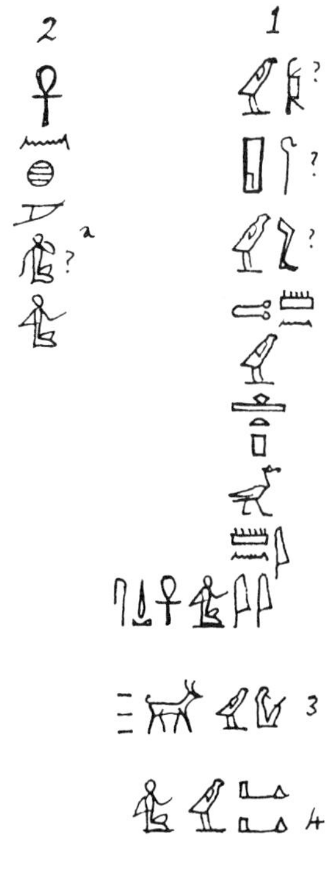

Textual Note: 2a: a rather dubious reading (with others in line 1).

Translation: (1) The retainer, Ruler of a Domain, officer (?), Mentuhotep's son Ameny, L.P.H. (2) Mer-ankh (?). (3) The dog-handler, (4) Didiu.

Commentary: The titles in line 1 are of uncertain reading. For *mniw-tsmw,* see WH 93. For the apparent *ʿnḫ-mr (.ỉ?),* cf. *ʿnḫ-mr.s* in *PN*, I, 64:17, but perhaps *Mr-ʿnḫ* is intended (*PN*, I, 155:28).

WH, No. 95. Fakhry, No. 95; present location unknown.
Bibliography: Fakhry, p. 69, fig. 75.
Description: 'On a small block of stone are a few signs which appear to have been part of a larger text' (F). Height 6 cm, width 7 cm.

Normalised Text:

Translation: (1) .... (titles, lost) ... , Sen[wos]ret, may he live for ever (2) and ever.

Commentary: The tag suggests that a king is here named (but without use of cartouche); if so, perhaps this is a poor graffito from some expedition under Sesostris I of the Twelfth Dynasty.

WH, No. 96. Fakhry, No. 96; present location unknown.
Bibliography: Fakhry, p. 69, fig. 76, pl. XXVIIID (cf. XLIVB).
Description: A line and group of signs, with figure of a dog at left; was on a rock at hill-summit.

Normalised Text:

Translation: (1) Mentuhotep's son Amennakht, born of Sobk (?) hotep, (2) L.P.H.

Commentary: These names, *PN*, I, 154:21, 29:21, 305:6, respectively.

WH, No. 97. Fakhry, No. 97; present location unknown.
Bibliography: Fakhry, p. 69, fig. 77 (p. 70), pl. XXVIA.
Description: Two lines of text over figures of four men (facing right), the last being smaller in size. The first has bow, arrow and baton; the second, arms pendent; the third, a staff, long triangle, and plume in his hair; the fourth, a staff in one hand and bag (?) in the other. Found near WH 96.

Normalised Text:

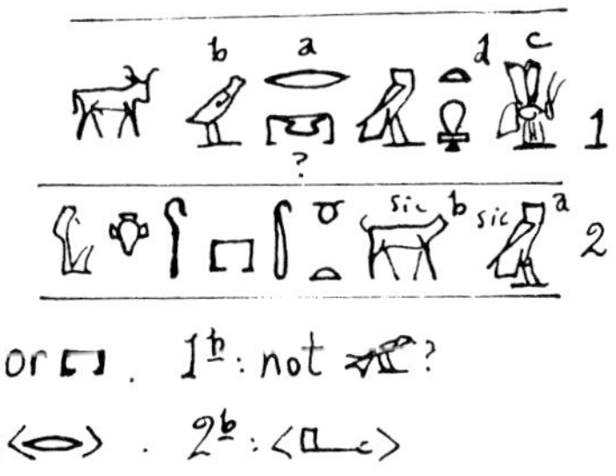

Textual Notes: 1a: under *r*, a *pr* or ʿ*w*. 1b: *w* not *wr*, hence read *i̓my-r* ʿ*w*, not *i̓my-r pr wr*. 1c: hieratic form, cf. *HP*, I, No. 260. 1d: hieratic form, *ibid.*, No. 422. 2a,b: the engraver appears to have omitted *r* and ʿ.

Translation: (1) Seal-bearer of the King of Lower Egypt, caravan-leader, Ka; (2) Chamberlain, Heqaib.

Commentary: Mention of two men, not four, may suggest that the scene below illustrates two 'great men' each with his attendant. For the names, cf. *PN*, I, 337:21 and 256:3.

WH, No. 98. Fakhry, No. 98; present location unknown.
Bibliography: Fakhry, p. 70, fig. 78, pl. XXVIB.
Description: Row of signs over a man facing right, arms pendent; was on East side of hill.

Normalised Text:

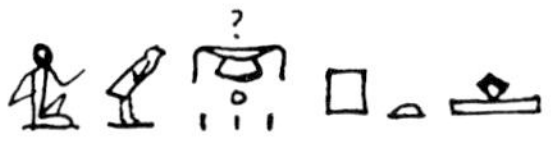

Translation: Hotep-nubu.

Commentary: Sign(s) between hotep and *w*, uncertain; for *ḥtp-nbw*, see *PN*, I, 258:19.

WH, No. 99. Fakhry, No. 99; present location unknown; was near 96-98.
Bibliography: Fakhry, p. 70, fig. 79, pl. XXVIIIB.
Description: A column of text, turning left at base.

Normalised Text:

Translation: (1) The revered one, Keri's son Mentuhotep's son Iqeru, (2) born of Sobk-em-sa-es.

Commentary: All these names are attested ones, cf. *PN*, I, 346:25, 154:21, 47:25, and 304:8, respectively.

WH, No. 100. Fakhry, No. 100; exc. no. 38; Aswan Museum, acc. no. 1501.
Bibliography: Fakhry, p. 71, fig. 80, pl. XXXIXA.
Description: Crude figure of a man (facing right), holding baton (?). Before him, an offering-table and two loaves (?); above the former, the 'text'. Height 17 cm, width 62 cm, thickness 38 cm.

Normalised Text:

Translation: Offerings . . .

Commentary: These 'signs' may, in fact, be simply representations of a *ḥtp* slab and of objects as seen on top of such an offering-slab.

E. Non-inscriptional Graffiti: Nos. 101-142.

WH, No. 101. Fakhry, No. 101, p. 71, fig. 81 (p. 72), pl. XLB. Man walking to right, carrying staff and mace; mark or 'head' at front of mace is probably only a flaking of the rock-surface.

WH, No. 102. Fakhry, No. 102, p. 71, fig. 82 (p. 72), pl. XLIA. Man walking to right with long staff. Height 55 cm. Cf. Hellström, *Rock Drawings,* A 266 - 157.C26, A 286 - 157.C27.

WH, No. 103. Fakhry, No. 103, p. 71, fig. 83 (p. 72). Man, kilted, facing right, holding *wꜣs*-sceptre and mace, with plume on head, standing within a tall rectangle open at top. On block of reddish gneiss, height 37 cm, width 25 cm; figure, height 23 cm, width 11 cm. Cf. Hellström, A 279 - 378.G5?, A 368 - 287.1. Aswan Museum, acc. no. 1502; exc. no. 32.

WH, No. 104. Fakhry, No. 104, p. 72, fig. 84, pl. XXVA. On summit of South hill (i.e., Site 6). Two men, one (facing right) with *wꜣs*(?) and club, the other with hands spread out horizontally. Height 19 cm, width 27 cm. Cf. Hellström, A 47 - 169.J30, A 314 - 378.G49.

WH, No. 105. Fakhry, No. 105, p. 73, fig. 85. Man walking to right, kilted, holding staff. Height 19 cm. Cf. Hellström, A 286 - 157.C27.

WH, No. 106. Fakhry, No. 106, p. 73, fig. 86, pl. XLA. Man, kilted, walking to left (unusual in these figurations), holding long staff. Before his head, a circular mark and the hieroglyphic numeral '22'. The number of men or the regnal year of an expedition? Near No. 105. Cf. Hellström, A 280 - 157.K27; A 270 - 388.M8; A 267 - 157.C26.

WH, No. 107. Fakhry, No. 107, p. 73, fig. 87. Man walking to right, with a baton and one arm outstretched. Cf. Hellström, A 278 - 378.G.5 (which are plumed).

WH, No. 108. Fakhry, No. 108, p. 73, fig. 88. Man walking to right, with a *wꜣs* sceptre. Cf. Hellström, A 295 - 154.MI.

WH, No. 109. Fakhry, No. 109, p. 74, fig. 89, pl. XLIVA. Archer (facing right) shooting an arrow. At Aswan, acc. no. 1505, exc. no. 33; height 60 cm, width 44 cm, thickness 19 cm. Cf. Hellström, A 193 - A 263.

WH, No. 110. Fakhry, No. 110, p. 74, fig. 90. An archer facing right, height 18 cm. On large stone, summit of South Hill. Cf. Hellström, A 193 - A 263.

WH, No. 111. Fakhry, No. 111, p. 74, fig. 91, pl. XLIIIA. A warrior facing left, plume or foliage on head; holds shield and bow or club or possibly an axe (fenestré type); height 49 cm. Cf. Hellström, A 193 - A 263.

WH, No. 112. Fakhry, No. 112, p. 75, fig. 92. A dignitary, facing right, in a long robe, perhaps a waterskin slung from the shoulder and a handkerchief in his right hand. Block, height 67 cm, width 38 cm.; figure, height 28 cm. Aswan, acc. no. 1504, exc. no. 34.

WH, No. 113. Fakhry, No. 113, p. 75, fig. 93, pl. XLIB. Small figure of an archer shooting (facing right); height 19 cm, width 14cm. Cf. Hellström, A 193 - A 263.

WH, No. 114. Fakhry, No. 114, p. 76, fig. 94, pl. XLIIB. Crude figure of archer running to right, shooting; block, height 38 cm, width 14 cm. Cf. Hellström, A 193 - A 263. At Aswan.

WH, No. 115. Fakhry, No. 115, p. 76, fig. 95; near cairn, hill-summit. Two men, facing right; the upper left one with arms outspread, holding a stick (?). Height 30 cm. Cf. Hellström, A 193 - A 263.

WH, No. 116. Fakhry, No. 116, p. 76, fig. 96. An archer, facing right; height 21 cm. Cf. Hellström, A 193 - A 263. On block near WH 115.

WH, No. 117. Fakhry, No. 117, p. 76, fig. 97. Man walking to right, with bag or pot in right hand, the left upraised; height 23.5 cm. On same block as No. 116. Cf. Hellström, *loc. cit.*

WH, No. 118. Fakhry, No. 118, p. 76, fig. 98. Unfinished figure of a man, in double outline, facing right; height 31 cm. On same rock as WH 93, 96, etc. Cf. Hellström, A 92 - 377.F1, A 100 - 159.F2.

WH, No. 119. Fakhry, No. 119, p. 76, fig. 99. A man, kilted, walking right, holding a stick or bow (?); height 22 cm. On same rock as WH 116. Cf. Hellström, A 282 - 386.D1.

WH, No. 120. Fakhry, No. 120, p. 77, fig. 100. A kilted man, facing right, near and above WH 99; height 48 cm. Cf. Hellström, A 280 - 257.K27.

WH, No. 121. Fakhry, No. 121, p. 77, fig. 101, pl. XLIIA. Man leaning on stick, facing right; height 23 cm. Cf. Hellström, A 266 - 157.C26, A 367 - 359.38.

WH, No. 122. Fakhry, No. 122, p. 77, fig. 102. Kilted man, walking to left; height 25 cm.; on boulder in the valley. Cf. Hellström, A 109 - 157.M173.

WH, No. 123. Fakhry, No. 123, p. 77. fig. 103. Kilted man, arms up level, walking to left; height 38 cm. Cf. Hellström, A 280 - 157.K27 (but has baton).

WH, No. 124. Fakhry, No. 124, p. 77, fig. 104. Man in long kilt walking to right, tress of hair hanging at rear of head - a foreigner? Height 40 cm. Cf. Hellström, A 34 - 381. A10.

WH, No. 125. Fakhry, No. 125, p. 77, fig. 105. Robed man walking to left; height 29 cm. Cf. Hellström, A 26 - 159.A16, A 27 - 378.K2, A 20 160.K10, A 39 - 152.A17, A 51 - 379.B56.

WH, No. 126. Fakhry, No. 126, p. 78, fig. 106, pl. XLIIIB. Kilted man with staff, walking to right; height 40 cm. (In detail, fig. and pl. differ). Cf. Hellström, A 260 - 157.C26.

WH, No. 127. Fakhry, No. 127, fig. 107. Man walking to right, carrying a mace head downward, on rock-fragment; height 6 cm. Cf. Hellström, *loc.cit.*

WH, No. 128. Fakhry, No. 128, p. 78, fig. 108. Man walking to right with staff. Cf. Hellström, *loc. cit.*

WH, No. 129. Fakhry, No. 129, p. 78, fig. 109, pl. XLIID. Kilted, plumed man facing right grasps head of another (facing left), to smite him with a mace - a 'victory scene'. Cf. Hellström, A 213 - 157.M219, A 228 - A 229. 160.S5, also Quibell, *Hierakonpolis II*, pl. XXVI.

WH, No. 130. Fakhry, No. 130, p. 78, fig. 110. Unfinished male figure, facing right; height 33 cm. Cf. Hellström, A 107 - 160.H3, A 92 - 377.F1.

WH, No. 131. Fakhry, No. 131, p. 78, fig. 111. Man walking to right, with a staff and baton; height 26 cm.

WH, No. 132. Fakhry, No. 132, p. 79, pl. XLIIC. Man walking to right, with *wꜣs* sceptre and ankh-sign.

WH, No. 133. Fakhry, No. 133, p. 79, fig. 112, pl. XLVC. A quadruped facing left, perhaps a sheep (taken as an elephant by Fakhry). Block in Aswan; height 73 cm, width 43 cm, thickness 18 cm, animal nose to tail 26 cm, height 25 cm. Cf. Hellström, G 14 - 152.B68. Exc. no. 39.

WH, No. 134. Fakhry, No. 134, p. 79, fig. 113, pl. XLIVA (upper). Sacred cow facing to right before an offering table; with a sun-disc between her horns, she may stand for Hathor, patroness of desert enterprises. Now at Aswan Museum, acc. no. 1505, exc. no. 33. Height 71 cm, width 45 cm, thickness 22 cm. Same block as 109.

WH, No. 135. Fakhry, No. 135, p. 79, fig. 114 (p. 80), pl. XXXIXB. Figure of a bull or cow with large horns; above, heavier cut, a warrior, plumed, with staff and knife (?); both face right. Animal, cf. Hellström, C 1 - 553.

WH, No. 136. Fakhry, No. 136, p. 79, fig. 115 (p. 80). Bull or cow running to right; boulder on hill-summit. Cf. Hellström, *loc. cit.*

WH, No. 137. Fakhry, No. 137, p. 80, fig. 116. Bull/cow facing right. Cf. Hellström, *loc. cit.*

WH, No. 138. Fakhry, No. 138, p. 80, fig. 117, pls. XLIVC plus XLVC. A long-horned bull facing right; an angular sign before it might be *Mr-wr,* i.e., the Mnevis-bull (so Fakhry). Cf. Hellstrom, *loc. cit.*

WH, No. 139. Fakhry, No. 139, p. 80, fig. 118. A pair of oxen facing right, on same boulder as WH 138. Cf. Hellström, *loc. cit.*

WH, No. 140. Fakhry, No. 140, p. 81, fig. 119, pl. XLVB. A mountain goat, with curving, chamois-like horns, 25 x 20 cm, on block of height 56 cm,width 30 cm, thickness 32 cm. Now at Aswan Museum; exc. no. 35. Cf. Hellström, D 7 - 378.J4, D 13 - 160.J10.

WH, No. 141. Fakhry, No. 141, p. 81, fig. 120. Dog, facing right; cf. Hellström, E - Dogs, E.1 - 59.

WH, No. 142. Fakhry, No. 142, p. 81, fig. 121, pl. XLVA. A mountain goat with prominent back curving horns, facing right; above WH 97. Cf. Hellström, D 22 - 376.C5.

F. The Twelfth Dynasty, II: Nos. 143-149.

WH, No. 143. Rowe, I; Cairo Museum JdE. 71901; PM, 110.
Date: Sesostris I, no year (*c.* 1971/1926 BC).
Bibliography: A. Rowe (with E. Drioton), *ASAE* 39 (1939), pp. 187-191, pl. 25.
Description: Round-topped limestone stela, height 93.5 cm., width 49.5 cm. Very well carved, found at Site C (Site 6); broken in two places.

Normalised Text:

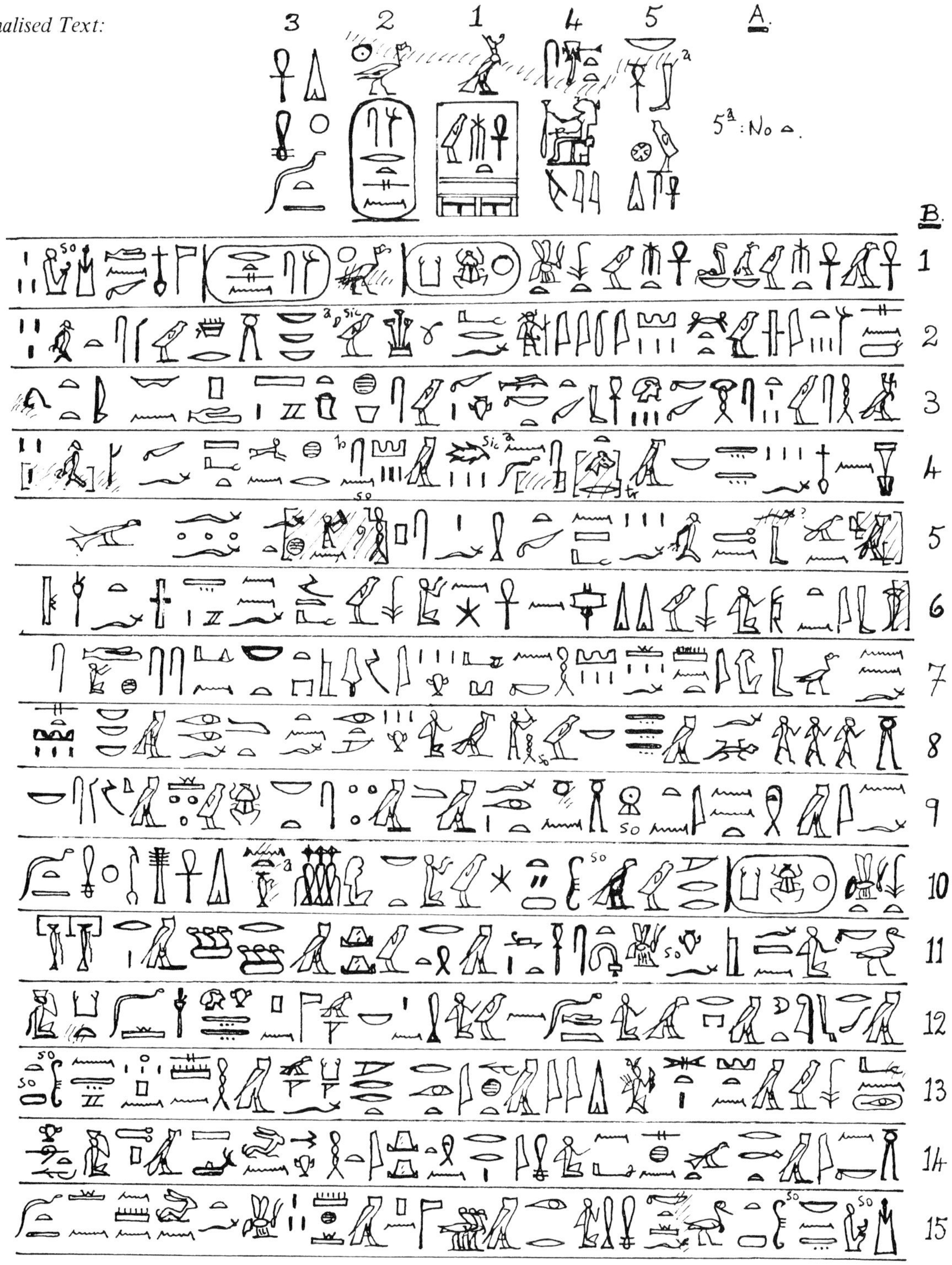

Textual Notes: (Main Text) 2a: small, egg-shaped cut. 4a: head of *snḏ*-duck is omitted. 4b: this *n* is clear, although accidentally omitted from Rowe's printed text, *ASAE* 39, p. 189. 10a: after *ḫnt*, trace of horizontal signs (*nt* or *tꜣ*) and of vertical sign below (*ḳbḥ*?).

Translation:

A. *Top.*

(1) Horus, 'Life-of-Births', (2) Son of Re, Sesostris (I), (3) given life like Re forever, (4) beloved of Satis, (5) Lady of Elephantine, may she grant life.

B. *Main Text.*

(1) Horus, 'Life-of-Births', Two-Goddesses, 'Life-of-Births', King of Upper & Lower Egypt, Kheperkare, Son of Re, Sesostris I.

The good god who slays the tribesfolk, (2) who slits the throats of the Asiatics; Sovereign who hems in the Hau-nebu, who makes an end of Nubian (3) hordes, who lops off heads of disaffected tribes; broad of boundary, wide of step; (4) whose goodness has united the Two Lands, master of striking-power [against]? the fearful in their countries, (they) falling to his slaughtering/sword, the rebels (5) perishing because of him (?); those who defy him are (doomed) to the slaughtering/sword of His Majesty, who has rounded-up ('lassoed') his enemies.

The great one, (6) sweet-natured to whoso follows him, who grants the breath of life to him that adores him. The land has produced for him what is in it, Geb has (7) decreed for him his secret treasures; the deserts make offering, the hills show favour, every place has yielded up what it conceals. (8) His emissaries abound in all lands, messengers doing what he has desired, what is in his sight, in coastlands and deserts (alike). (9) To him belongs what the sun-disc encircles, what (?) the Eye brings for him from what is in her, the Lady of forms, from her every creation (?).

(10) The King of Upper & Lower Egypt, Kheperkare, the beloved of Horus of Nubia (*Stỉ*), one praised of the Lady who presides over [the Cataract (?)], may he be granted life, stability and dominion like Re forever.

(11) His true and favourite servitor, the Seal-bearer of the King of Lower Egypt, Sole Companion, Superintendent of the Department of Wildfowl pools, Superintendent of the Department of Waterfowl, (12) Superintendent ent of horn, hoof, feather and scale, the Steward Hor says:

'The Majesty of my lord sent me out, this god ruling over the Two Lands, who decreed the work – (13) beautiful is he, (even) in this desert! – a force being put in my charge to perform what his Will (*kꜣ*) desired in (regard to) this amethyst of Nubia (*Tꜣ-Stỉ*). (14) I brought (it) from there in great quantity, when I collected (it) just like at the door of a granary, (it) being dragged away by sledge, loaded into pallets. (15) (As for) every native of Nubia (*Tꜣ-Stỉ*), his impost (?)/wages (?) (shall be) like (that of) a (my?) servant who acts by the power of this god, by the effectiveness of his Sovereign, one who abides enduring forever!'

Commentary:

A. *Top.*

Of interest is the fact that the King, and this stela, are put under the aegis of Satis, Lady of Elephantine, cf. line 10 below.

B. *Main Text:*

Line 1 end, *dn* is the first of a series of seven or eight Perfective Active Participles in a stream of epithets glorifying the pharaoh (*dn, sn, ʿrf, ỉn, sk, ꜣbt?, wsḫ, pḏ*). *Dn* may here mean 'to behead', as in the New Kingdom.[225] Line 2, *sn-wsrt* is literally 'to cut necks'.[226] *Imyw* plus place-name = the people of that place, cf. Sinuhe, R.14. See above on WH 14 for the Hau-nebu.[227] Probably *ỉn-ḏrw* should be understood as the idiom 'vanquish', 'bring to an end'.[228] *Rswt* remains an obscure word; Faulkner's recent rendering (*Dict.*, p. 152 end) as 'sacrificial victims' does not fit here. Vercoutter had suggested 'rebels',[229] but best is perhaps 'hordes' as suggested by Posener and earlier Gardiner.[230] Line 2, *ḥꜣw nbw*; on these, see most recently, Cl. Vandersleyen, *Les guerres d'Amosis*, 1971, pp. 139-174.

Line 3, *Nḫswt* is a fem. plural adjective, agreeing with *rswt*. The phrase *sk tpw ꜣbt ḫꜣkt-ỉb* lends itself to more than one rendering. That given above reflects the renderings of Posener and Blumenthal.[231] It is also possible to translate: 'who lops off heads, who brands disaffection', i.e. who brands as slaves, prisoners taken among crushed rebels. *Skỉ* is a 'forestry' term.[232] The epithet *wsḫ tꜣš* should not be confused with the common causative idiom *swsḫ tꜣšw*;[233] *pḏ-nmtt* is more familiar.[234]

In line 4, all previous translators have missed the *n* of the suffix *.sn* attached to *ḫꜣswt*, an *n* broken but clearly visible on Rowe's plate. Therefore, we have here[235] *ḫꜣswt.sn* followed by *ḫr(w) n šꜥt.f* (and NOT *sḫr. n šꜥt.f*). The Old Perfective ('Stative') *ḫrw* needs a masculine antecedent, and the *.sn* a plural one. This is provided by *snḏw* 'the fearful ones in their (foreign) countries, fallen to his slaughter/sword'. But then, a link is needed between *nb-ꜣt*, 'lord of striking-power' and *snḏw*, 'the fearful ones'. This may be readily furnished by restoring a lost *r* in the lacuna, directly below the largely-destroyed animal-head determinative of *ꜣt*; there is ample room for both signs. Hence, one reads *nb-ꜣt* [*r*] *snḏw m ḫꜣswt.sn*. As a result, *sbỉw* at the end of line 4 must go with *ꜣḳ(w)* (a possible Old Perfective/Stative) at the beginning of line 5.

In line 5 there is a horizontal break above the *b* of *bṯnw*, sufficient for an *.f* (with possible traces). Hence restore *sbỉw ꜣḳw n.f* and then *bṯnw.f n šꜥt ḥm.f*: 'rebels are perished because of him, and those who defy him are for H.M.'s slaughter/sword'. Rowe's adoption of Drioton's restoration of *sp*[*ḥ.n*]*.f ḫftyw.f* is followed by all subsequent commentators,[236] and is supported by the extant traces. The *wr* at the line-end appears to be an epithet of the king, not just 'chief' (as used of foreign princes) but 'great one *par excellence*', more usually with a complement ('great of . . . '). Posener[237] reads *wr-bnrỉt*, but this assumes a very irregular spelling of *bnrỉt*, and is therefore not accepted here.

In line 6, just a trace of *bnr* can be seen, followed by *bỉt*, regularly spelt but without determinative.[238] These phrases, *bnr-bỉt n šms sw, dd ṯꜣw-n-ꜥnḫ n dwꜣ sw*, are directly reminiscent of the 'loyalist' wisdom instructions, with their injunctions to honour the king as fount of rewards for the faithful, although these phrases are not actual citations from such works.[239] Near the line-end, the reading *ỉmyt.f* (replacing Rowe's *ꜥnḫt.f*) is owed to Clère.[240]

In line 8, *ỉnw* is an old word for messengers/emissaries, going back into the Old Kingdom,[241] as is also *ḥwwtyw* (similar meaning) used in parallel with *ỉnw*.[242] Hor thus gives a flavour of distinguished antiquity to his eulogy of the king.[243] *Imyt ỉrty.f(y)* has given rise to very divergent opinions. Drioton (in Rowe, p. 190) took it as 'what is in his eyes' = 'what he sees' = 'his domain'. Following an ingenious suggestion by Vercoutter, Blumenthal would render:[244] 'his expedition-leaders are in the *nbwt* (coastlands/isles) and deserts', understanding *ỉmyw-ỉrty* - an Old Kingdom title for ships' captains.[245] Unfortunately, this title (i) is only Old Kingdom, (ii) fits *nbwt* but not *ḫꜣswt* (deserts), and (iii) would require emendation of the *t* out of *ỉmyt*. Therefore it seems wiser to retain a fairly literal translation of the phrase: 'what is in his sight', i.e. what is within the king's purview, which includes all regions, whether maritime or inland.

Line 9, *n.f-ỉm(y)* is the possessive construction (Gardiner, §§ 113,3; 114,4) relating here to *šnnt ỉtn*. The phrases that follow are the most obscure in the entire text. *Inw* may be a Perfective Relative Form, rather than a noun or simple *sḏm.f, ỉrt* ('Eye') being the subject. Thus, *šnnt ỉtn* and *ỉnw* (for *ỉnt*?) *n.f Irt* would form a parallel pair of phrases. The three small circles after '*ỉm-m*' appear to be a plural determinative (as in *ḫprw*, just after), hence read *m ỉmyw.s*, 'from what is ('are') in her'. *Nbt ḫprw* may then be a sobriquet in parallel with *Irt*, 'Eye' and *m ḳmꜣ.s nb* in parallel with *m ỉmyw.s*. The resulting translation (given above) seems simpler and smoother than Blumenthal's; Drioton's is perhaps equally possible: 'one brings to him the Eye with what is in her, the Lady of beings with all that she has created'.

In line 10, *mrrw* and *dwꜣw* can be either Imperfective Passive Participles (Gardiner, § 358) or Imperfective Relative Forms (*ibid.*, § 387).[246] The lacuna after *Nbt-ḫnt* shows a horizontal sign and trace above a vertical trace of a sign; *nt* plus *ḳbḥ* would give *ḫnt ḳbḥw*, 'presiding over the Cataract', an appropriate title for Satis, cf. 'Satis, Lady of Elephantine' at the head of this stela.[247]

Lines 11f. introduce the author of the stela with numerous titles. Of these, *ỉmy-r sšw, ỉmy-r pr-ḳbḥw(y),* and (line 12) *ỉmy-r ʿb wḥmt šwt nšmwt* belong closely together. The second title most likely refers to the domain devoted to waterfowl (rather than a bathroom).[248] The third title is found with other stewards of the Middle Kingdom[249] and was studied by Loret.[250] On the significance of stewards in relation to these desert expeditions, see on WH 1 above, with note 11. The name Hor is a common Middle Kingdom one (*PN*, I, 245:18). Line 12, *ḏd* is either Perfective *sḏm.f* with suffix suppressed after a noun subject (Gardiner, §§ 450, 1; 486 middle) or possibly a Perfective Active Participle. *Wḏ* is certainly a participle, qualifying *nṯr pn* and epithets. As *kȝt* is feminine, the *ʿn sw* of line 13 (beginning) cannot well refer back to it (despite Rowe), but must surely be an interjected phrase in honour of the king;[251] he inspires affection even in this howling wilderness! Then, *dy* is a *y*-form of the Old Perfective (*dy* for *dỉw*) like those from other *3ae inf.* verbs cited by Gardiner, § 309. Here, *(r)dy m ḫt* seems almost synonymous with *rdỉ m ḥr* or *(rdỉ) r ḫt*. *Mrrt* is Imperfective Relative Form. Ta-Seti here (as in WH 4, etc.) appears clearly to refer to (Lower) Nubia, not the 1st Upper-Egyptian nome (Aswan), as a source of amethyst. Thus, the Iuntyu of Ta-Seti are 'natives of Nubia' (line 15), not people (*rmṯ*) of Upper Egypt, while Horus-gods belong to Nubia,[252] not to Aswan and Elephantine where Khnum is supreme. So, Horus of Ta-Seti is a Horus of Nubia, not Aswan, which is represented here by the goddess Satis, who was also (with Anukis) known in Nubia.

Line 14, *ỉn.k(wỉ)*, and Old Perfective ('Stative') in its residual active role in the 1st person of verbs of motion (Gardiner, § 312, 3). *Sḫnn.ỉ*, a geminating *sḏm.f*, is here a circumstantial tense ('when'). Hor here appears to boast of gathering or scooping up amethyst as one would shovel up grain at the mouth of a grain-bin at a granary; an appropriate metaphor, in view of his connection with the state granaries (*ỉmy-r šnwty*, line 11). *Itḥw* and *ȝtpw* are both Old Perfectives. *Sṯȝt* may signify a flat tray or pallet (here placed on sledges?) to take the lumps of amethyst; or perhaps better, wooden boxes or containers (i.e., crates) that could equally be dragged away on sledges. In favour of a flat object, cf. the single 'sheet' of copper beaten out to cover a door;[253] in favour of a container, cf. the old word for a transportable container.[254] Faulkner's translation 'rollers' would fit his cited context,[255] but not this stela. One could not load the amethyst straight onto rollers, but onto trays/containers on rollers.

In line 15, *bȝkt.f* could not be feminine if it qualified *Iwnty nb n Tȝ-Stỉ*, hence its interpretation as *bȝkty.fy*, 'who shall pay tax/render service', by Drioton, Säve-Söderbergh and Blumenthal,[256] to which they attach the phrase *bỉt.f wnn mn n ḏt*, taken to mean 'his people shall be, enduring forever'. However, as Posener has noted,[257] the *wnn mn(w) n ḏt* cannot be understood thus, in the light of its occurrence in WH 14:14. There, it can only refer to the gods and their decree, or to the king himself. Therefore, it could hardly be applied here to the Nubian workforce. Moreover, there is no further evidence for Drioton's translation of *bỉty* (written with bee-phonogram) as 'race, people'. Rather, *m bȝw nṯr pn* and *m mnḫw bỉty.f* are surely two parallel phrases both qualifying *ḥm ỉrr*, 'a servant who acts' and 'by the might of this god, and by the effectualness of his (L.-Eg.) king', keeping *bỉty* in its normal meaning. In this situation, *wnn mn(w) n ḏt* easily fits the king (*nṯr pn, bỉty*), and be so understood in WH 14:14 also. (Here, *wnn* has been regarded as a participle; it might just be a geminated Old Perfective.)

This still leaves the *bȝkt.f mỉ* (after *Iwnty nb n Tȝ-Stỉ*). The *bȝkt.f* could be *bȝk.t(w).f*: 'every Nubian native, he shall be worked' (as a serf),[258] 'like any servant who acts . . '. Or even more simply *bȝkt* can be treated as a feminine substantive, for taxes to be paid or wages to be drawn: '(As for) every Nubian, his taxes/wages will be like a(ny) servant who acts . . . '.

Overall, this stela is remarkable in several respects. It is of limestone, and so was imported specially into Wadi Hudi from either Thebes or (more likely?) the northern Residence. As the only formal, properly sculptured stela of the entire Wadi Hudi series, none even approach its quality. Its one serious omission is a year-date. One may ask whether it was perhaps brought on the first, official and inaugural expedition of the reign, or simply when a specially important official was sent to push the production. Hence its official nature.

The Hor of Wadi Hudi may well be the same high official of whom a group of four monuments survives from Abydos, probably constituting a cenotaph or chapel.[259] Especially on the stela Louvre C.2,[260] there recur several titles held by Hor at Wadi Hudi, e.g. 'Superintendent of Horn, Hoof, Feather and Scale', '(Chief) Steward', besides the commoner 'Seal-bearer of the King of Lower Egypt' and 'Sole Companion'. Louvre C.2 is explicitly dated to Year 9 of Sesostris I (equivalent to Year 29 of Amenemhat I), on the eve of Sesostris's sole reign. Given the high titles already borne by Hor in Year 9, it would be prudent not to date his Wadi Hudi expedition too much later in time, as there is no indication of the overall length of Hor's career. One might, therefore, incline to place this Wadi Hudi stela within about Years 10-25 of Sesostris I. So far, the earliest certain date of this reign at Wadi Hudi is Year 17 (WH 6), followed by Years 20 (WH 7, 8, 14A) and 22 (WH 9, 10, 11), etc. If that of Year 17 were indeed the first of the reign, and Hor's stela an 'inaugural' one, then WH 143 might indeed date to Year 17. Hor would have been the King's representative, over Hotepu and Resuwi of WH 6; against this, is only the negative fact that they do not mention their preseumed senior colleague. So the matter of date remains beyond final solution at present.

The long eulogy of 10 lines followed by 'facts' in 5 is a fore-runner of New Kingdom royal usage, as Posener has also noted.[261] Twofold character of the king (fierce; gracious) is found also in Sinuhe and royally inspired stelae, etc.

225. Cf. Blu, *Unt.*, p. 231, F.3.16, references.
226. A clear pun on the royal name Se-n-Wosret, 'Man of (the goddess) Wosret', as seen by Rowe (*ASAE* 39 (1939), p.190, n.2) and by Blumenthal (Blu, *Unt.*, p.229, F.3.11).
227. Parallels for *'rf Ḥ3w-nbw*, cf. Blu, *Unt.*, p.190, E.3.5.
228. Synonymous with *in pḥwy*, cf. A.M. Blackman, H.W. Fairman, *JEA* 30 (1944), p.16, § 34.
229. *BIFAO* 48 (1949), p.162, followed by Blu, *Unt.*, p. 189f., E.3.3.
230. Posener, *Littérature et Politique dans L'Egypte de la XIIe Dynastie*, Paris, 1956, p.133, and Gardiner, *Egyptian Grammar*, 1957, p.512: T.13.
231. Rowe, *ASAE* 39, p.190; Posener, *op.cit.*, p.133; Blu, *Unt.*, p. 229f., F.3.12.
232. Cf. 'to fell tress' (Admonitions, 4:14), cited by Faulkner, *Dict.*, p.251.
233. As is done by Blu, *Unt.*, p.187, E.2.11.
234. Cf. Blu, *Unt.*, p.215, F.2.2, plus Sinuhe B.56f. (*ibid.*, F.2.3).
235. Contrary to Blu, *Unt.*, pp.211, F.1.21, and 212, F.1.23.
236. E.g., Blu, *Unt.*, p.227, F.3.8, cf. her F.3.7.
237. *Loc.cit.* (n.231, above).
238. Cf. variants, *Wb.*, I, p. 441 end.
239. Cf. publications of G. Posener, *L'Enseignement loyaliste*, Geneva, 1976, and K.A. Kitchen, *Oriens Antiquus* 8 (1969), pp.189-208.
240. Cf. Posener, *Littérature et Politique . . .* , p.133, and n.4. For the whole passage in lines 6-7, cf. Blu, *Unt.*, pp.196-7, E.3.30, 34.
241. E.g. Pyramid Texts, § 1675; cf. *Wb.*, I, p.91:19.
242. Pyr. Texts, § 1675*c*; cf. *Wb.*, III, p.44:4, 5.
243. Cf. M. Vallogia, *Recherche sur les 'messagers' (wpwtyw) dans les sources égyptiens profanes*, Geneva, 1976, p.233.
244. Vercoutter, *BIFAO* 46 (1947), p.149, n.3; Blu, *Unt.*, p.199, E.4.2.
245. Cf. W. Helck, *Untersuchungen zur den Beamtentitlen des ägyptischen Alten Reiches*, Glückstadt, 1954, p.101.
246. Cf. Also Blu, *Unt.*, p.75, B.2.10.
247. For *ḳbḥw*, cf. *Wb.*, V, p. 29:5-6.
248. As noted by Rowe, *ASAE* 39, p.191 and n.2; cf. title *ỉmy-r ḳbḥw* of Henenu in the late Eleventh Dynasty, W.C. Hayes, *JEA* 35 (1949), p.47*c*, pl. IV.
249. Hayes, *loc.cit.*
250. *RT* 38 (1916), pp. 61-68.
251. Dependent pronoun with participle as an adjectival predicate, cf. Gardiner, §§ 44,3; 48,2; 137.
252. Cf. the later Horuses of Baki, Miam, Buhen and Meha, in the New Kingdom.
253. *Wb.*, IV, p.356:8.
254. *Ibid.*, p.354:7.
255. *Dict.*, p.235, third entry from bottom, using Glanville, *ZÄS* 68 (1932), p.11.
256. In *ASAE* 39 (1939), p.191, *Ägypten und Nubien*, Lund, 1941, p.71, and Blu, *Unt.*, p.430, note G.152a, respectively.
257. In *Littérature et Politique . . .* , 1956, p.133, n.7.
258. Cf. references given by Faulkner, *Dict.*, p.78, to 'working' horses and 'enslaving' people.
259. W.K. Simpson, *The Terrace of the Great God at Abydos*, Philadelphia, 1974, pp.19, 23:ANOC 29, 1-4, and pls. 43-45.
260. *Ibid.*, pl.44.
261. *Littérature et Politique . . .* , p.132f.

WH, No. 144. Rowe, II; Cairo Museum JdE. 71900; PM, 111.
Date: Sesostris I, Year 29 (*c.*1943 BC).
Bibliography: A. Rowe, *ASAE* 39 (1939), pp. 191-2, pl. 26a.
Description: Sandstone stela with man in kilt (facing right) framed with a horizontal line of text above him and three columns before him. Height 34 cm, width 23 cm. From Site B (Site 5).

Normalised Text:

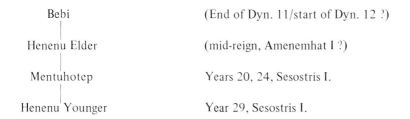

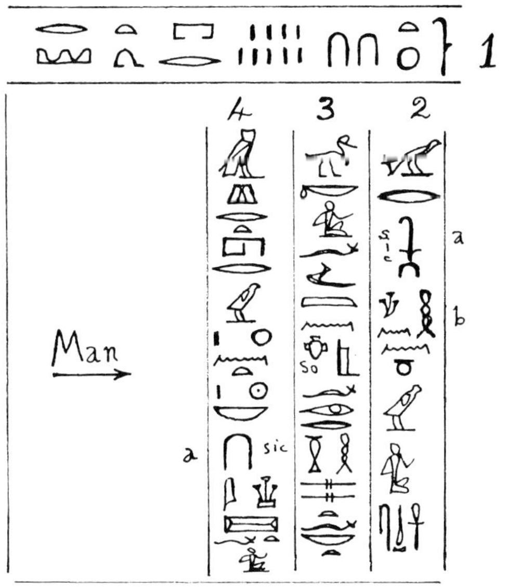

Textual Notes: 2a: reversed form. 2b: cursive *ḥn*-plant (cf. WH 145). 4a: a simple loop, standing for either *sḏ3wty* or *sš*, see Commentary.

Translation: (1) Year 29; going out into the desert. (2) Chief of the Southern Tens, Henenu, L.P.H. (3) His true and favourite servitor, who does all that he praises (4) in the course of every day, daily, the Seal-bearer?/Scribe?, Ha-ishtef.

Commentary: Attribution of 'Year 29' to Sesostris I is assured by the more explicit dating by the same Henenu son of Mentuhotep (cf. WH 145) of his stela at the diorite quarries in the western desert.[262] The actual originators of WH 144, 145, however, appear to have been Henenu's lieutenants, in this case Ha-ishtef. Henenu's title 'Chief of Southern Tens' is one also borne by the Mentuhotep son of Henenu and grandson of Bebi who led two expeditions to Wadi Hudi in Years 20 and 24 of Sesostris I (WH 14:6-8, 19). It is at least possible that our present Henenu was the son and successor-in-office of that Mentuhotep, and hence grandson of the earlier Henenu. The following succession would result:

Bebi	(End of Dyn. 11/start of Dyn. 12 ?)
Henenu Elder	(mid-reign, Amenemhat I ?)
Mentuhotep	Years 20, 24, Sesostris I.
Henenu Younger	Year 29, Sesostris I.

The reading of Ha-ishtef's own title remains uncertain. It could be a pure hieratic form for 'Scribe' (*sš*), cf. *HP*, I, No. 537. But none of the rest of the inscription is in hieratic, so Helck's suggestion[263] to read *sḏ3wty*, 'seal-bearer', may be the better one. Cf. the summary forms of this sign in earlier texts of this series, e.g. WH 4:3, 15.

The proper names in this inscription are all well-attested elsewhere: Mentuhotep, cf. *PN*, I, 154:21; Henenu, *ibid.*, 245:1; Ha-ishtef, *ibid.*, 231:25 and reference.

262. R. Engelbach, *ASAE* 33 (1933), p.71, § 5, pl. II:3; Rowe, *ASAE* 39 (1939), p. 193f., fig.9.
263. *OLZ* 50 (1955), col. 213.

WH, No. 145. Rowe, III; Cairo Museum JdE. 71899; PM, 112.
Date: Sesostris I, Year 29 (*c.* 1943 BC).
Bibliography: A. Rowe, *ASAE* 39 (1939), pp. 193-4, pl. 26b.
Description: Ovoid sandstone stela, with man facing right, framed within two lines above and two columns at right, similar to WH 144. Height 35.5 cm, width 24 cm. From Site B (Site 5).

Normalised Text:

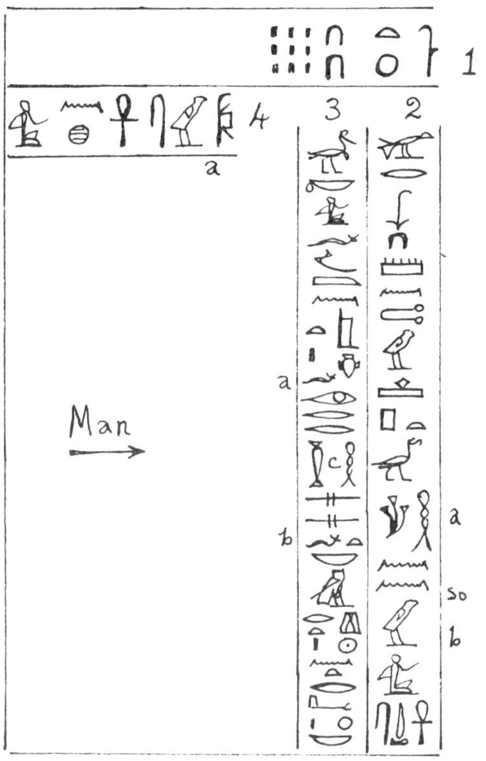

Textual Notes: 2a: cursive form of *ḥn*-plant, cf. WH 144. 2b: no *nw*-pot. 3a,b: hieratic *fs*. 3c: hieratic *ḥ* and *ḥs*. 4a: hieratic form of *šms*.

Translation: (1) Year 29: (2) Chief of Southern Tens, Mentuhotep's son Henenu, L.P.H. (3) His true and favourite servitor, who does all that he praises daily, in the course of every day, (4) the retainer Sankh.

Commentary: For attribution of the year-date to Sesostris I, and the expedition-leader Henenu, see above under WH 144. The name Sankh is a good Middle-Kingdom one, cf. *PN*, I, 300:22.

WH, No. 146. Present location unknown ('Document A').
Date: Sesostris I, Year 28 (*c.* 1944 BC).
Bibliography: None; hitherto unpublished.
Description: Rectangular quartzite stela, broken at top left corner. Eight horizontal lines of text within frame-lines, below a date-line; lightly and poorly engraved. This text is published from a photograph (cf. Plates) which I owe to the courtesy of Dr. Labib Habachi.

Normalised Text:

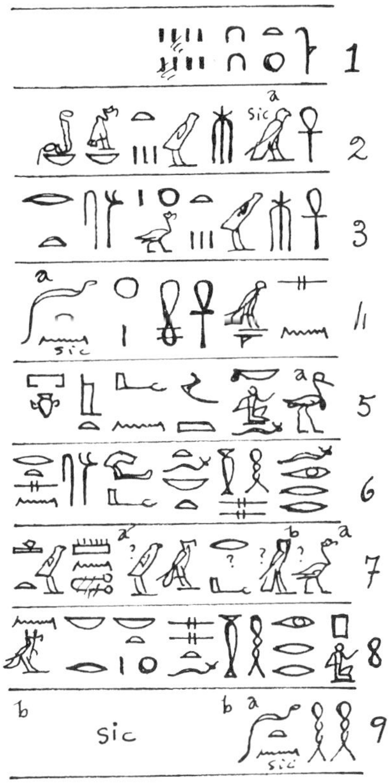

Textual Notes: 2a: emend to <*ꜥnḫ*>-*mswt*. 4a, 9a: *n* for *tꜣ*. 5a: hieratic form of *bꜣ*-bird. 7a-a: highly ambiguous forms here. 7b: hieratic *m* or *k* or *ỉb*? 9b-b: rest of line left blank.

Translation: Year 28: (2) (Long) live the Horus, '<Life>-of-Births', Two-Goddesses, (3) 'Life-of-Births', the Son of Re, Seso- (4) tris I, may he live like Re for ever.

(5) His true and favourite servitor, (6) who does all that he praises, (7/8/9) the Count Senwosret's son, the Caravan-leader Mentuhotep (*or*: the Count Senwosret. The servant, Neb-ꜥa's son, Mentuhotep), who does all that he praises daily, forever (9) and ever.

Commentary: Line 1, date damaged but certain. Lines 6-8 contain the crux of this badly written text, which turns on the bird-hieroglyphs of line 7. If here the first bird and the last one before Mentuhotep are both read as *sꜣ*, then we would have a normal threefold filiation: 'the Count Senwosret's son, X's son, Mentuhotep'. Against this solution stand two points, neither insoluble. First, one would not expect a repetition of the formula *ỉrr ḥsst.f nbt (rꜥ nb)*, it applying twice to one person, although this should not be impossible. Second, the middle name poses acute problems, especially the first sign. That sign is peculiarly difficult (see alternatives, Textual Notes above), while the sign following it could be *nb*, *r* or even *ꜥꜣ*. An *m* plus *r* and *ꜥ*, *ꜣ*, *w*, would yield *ỉmy-r ꜥꜣw*,'caravan-leader', as the title of Mentuhotep. For *ꜥꜣw* rather than just *ꜥw* (as often written), cf. *PN*, I, 58:22 in a name.

The best alternative to the foregoing is to read the first bird of line 7 as *bꜣ*, and the sign after it as a bad *k* (cf. line 5), giving *bꜣk* or *bꜣk*<*f*>. Then one might have the reading and filiation *Nb-ꜥꜣ sꜣ Mnṯw-ḥtp*. This solution would give us two individuals, Senwosret and Mentuhotep son of Neb-ꜥa, each having the *ỉrr ḥsst.f nbt* formula. Again, two main objections may be raised, neither decisive. First, the name *Nb-ꜥꜣ* cannot be readily paralled; *PN*, I,, 183:23 has only a *Nb-ꜥꜣw-wr* of New Kingdom date. Second, one would expect to find mentioned the filiation of the 'great man' (Count Senwosret) rather than of his servant; however, this usage does occur on WH 6 and probably 7. If the lesser man is the dedicator in each case, this is understandable, since he focusses on his own line, not another's.

WH, No. 147. Aswan Museum, storage court (no number); 'Document B'.
Date: Sesostris I, Year 28 (*c.*1944 BC).
Bibliography: None; hitherto unpublished.
Description: Pink granite stela engraved as a vertical rectangle (twelve horizontally-ruled lines of text), having a shallow rounded top, upon an irregularly-shaped block. Wadi Hudi provenance confirmed by the Aswan Museum curator (1975). Height 50 cm, max. width 37.5 cm, thickness 7 cm.

Normalised Text:

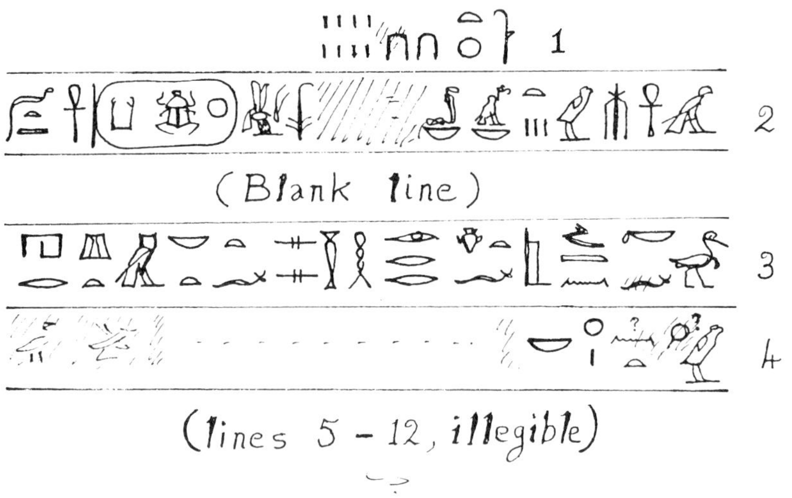

Translation: (1) Year 28: (2) Horus, 'Life-of-Births', Two-Goddesses, ['Life-of-Births'], King of Upper & Lower Egypt, Kheperkare, may he live forever.

(Blank spacer line.)

(3) His true and favourite servitor, who does all that he praises in the course of the day, daily, ... (*rest illegible*).

Commentary: Same date as WH 13, 146. The blank line puts a respectful space between the royal titulary and the text of the official concerned.

WH, No. 148. Dabod; Staatliche Museen zu Berlin, Aeg. Abteilung, Inv. 1203.
Date: Amenemhat II, no year-date. (*c.* 1929/1892 BC).
Bibliography: PM, VII, p. 5; Lepsius, *Denkmäler*, II, 123*b*; Lepsius, *Denkmäler, Text*, V, p. 8; *Aeg. Inschriften, Mus. Berlin*, I, 1913, p. 256.

Description: Rectangular sandstone stela, with one line and eleven columns of text, to be read in retrograde order, the last line ending with a space. Bottom ends of all other lines are lost; badly worn in middle. Photo, kind courtesy of Dr. Steffen Wenig, formerly Keeper, Berlin Museum.

Normalised Text:

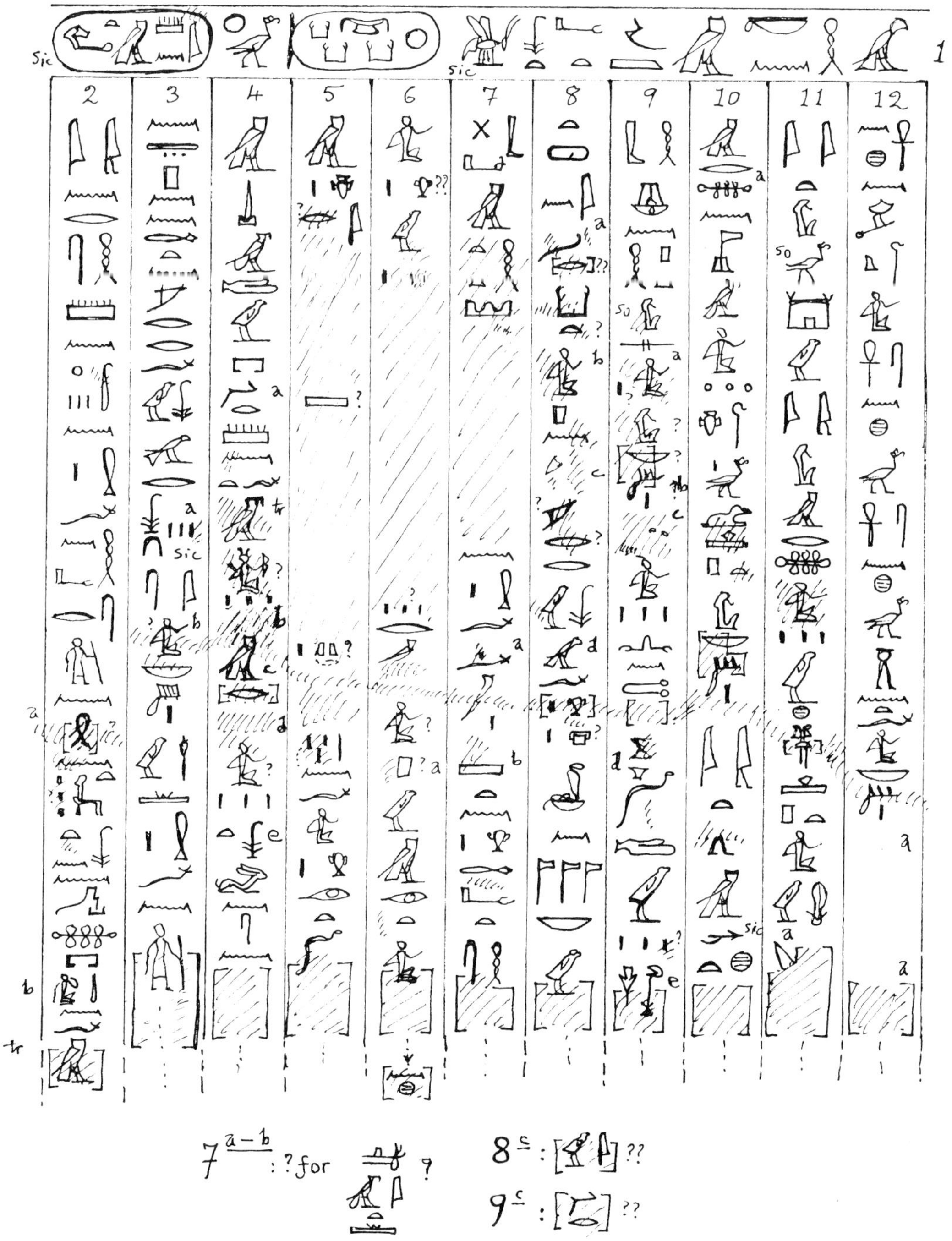

Textual Notes: 2a: one sign or group lost, probably *šn*. 2b: hieratic form, cf. *HP*, I, No. 35. 3a: three small, regular strokes are visible on the photo. 3b: space, context, and possible tiny traces require a seated-man determinative. 4a: traces and context suggest *ỉmy-r* written with tongue-sign, cf. hieratic forms (*HP*, I, No. 161), but lacking top left tick. 4b: one group illegible here. 4c-d: possibly *m*-bird over lost *r* plus another horizontal sign lost; *ỉmy-r sꜣw*? Cf. lines 10, 11. 4e: reed is clear on photo. 6a: either *p* or *ḥ*? 7a-b: interpretation of traces as *bỉꜣt* is very conjectural but just possible. 8a-b: also a conjectural reading. 8c: *ỉw* is conjectural, but possible? 8d: falcon, to be read *nb*? 8e: again, conjectural restoration [*ḥr*]*-sꜣ*. 9a-b: a probable reading of the traces, better than Leps., *Denk, Text, skr*. . . 9c: a compact horizontal group lost here; [*ỉmy-r*] *mšʿ* (?) is a guess on context and spacing. 9d: status of these traces is uncertain; not for *mḏw* ? 9e: right-hand sign like *ḥꜣ* '1000', left-hand one, obscure. 10a: best reading is *sꜣ* as in line 11 and perhaps line 4; not *gs*. 11a: perhaps a reversed *mr*; dubious sign. 12a-a: this space was left blank, signifying the end of the text, and so proving that its columns must be read from left to right, i.e. retrograde. The list of expeditionaries in lines 9-12 is also what one tends to find near the end of a text of this kind, not at its commencement.

Translation: (1) Horus, 'Truly acclaimed', King of Upper & Lower Egypt, Nubkaure, Son of Re, Amenemhat II.

(2) I came for amethyst, on behalf of His Majesty, together with a dignitary of the King's entourage, (he) belonging to the Palace, who had been spoken to (?)/instructed (?) concerning [. . . this expedition? . . . , one placed at the head?] (3) of this land, because so greatly, did he (= the King) love him:- the Chief of Southern Tens, Is(i), possessing veneration.

His Majesty made command for [? this] dignitary [. . . at a session, etc.? . . .] (4) in the audience-hall. The general of troops [and?] the commander of [contingents?] of the South, (when) they were [. . . . .] (5) in heart. As for (??) [. . . . .], [the one instru] cted (?) making se[arch?? . . . . .], (6) (one) [. .] ing (?) [. . . . .] he/it was a [. . . . .] from my doing (?) . . [. . . . .] (7) [ope] ned as/in a mine [. . . . . .]; His Majesty [? praised] this wonder (?), because of the amount ('greatness') of the ame[thyst? . . . . brought from Nu-] (8) -bia by this Superintendent of Works(?). His lord loved him next to the Lady of all the gods [. . . .] . [? List of the expedition?]:

[. . . . .]; (9) the Lector-priest of Ptah, Se, possessing veneration; the [gener] al (?) Nentji; . . . [. . . .] . (10) The Commander of contingents of stonemasons, Heqaib's son Sobkhotep, possessing veneration.

Coming after (i.e., accompanying) [them were: . . . . . . the *x*, Si-Wadj-] (11) -yt's son, Shesmu-iyi; the Commander of contingents, Ukh-hotep; the sandalmaker, Mer(?) - [. . . . .]; (and) (12) the member of the Ruler's crew, Sankh's son Sankh's son Intef, possessing veneration.

Commentary: This monument is the only one of our series dated to Amenemhat II's reign. As in the case of the Khor Dehmit stela (see WH 149 below), its discovery well away from Wadi Hudi itself, though mentioning amethyst, presents three possibilities. First, that this stela was originally set up at Wadi Hudi but has been removed subsequently over to Dabod, where Lepsius found it. Second that this stela was originally set up in the vicinity of Dabod by an ancient expedition that reached the Nile here from Wadi Hudi, before returning downriver. Third, that this stela commemorates an expedition to some amethyst mining location other than Wadi Hudi. While amethyst was also worked in the western desert some 40 miles (64 km) north of Abu Simbel,[264] this is so far away from Dabod (90 miles/145 km or more) that the Berlin stela is unlikely to commemorate an expedition conducted to this distant source. Therefore, either the first or second solutions would fit, hardly the third. In which case, this document fits into the annals of amethyst-mining at Wadi Hudi, and hence belongs within the scope of this work. The same considerations apply equally to the stela from Khor Dehmit (WH 149 below), found only a few miles upstream from Dabod.

In line 2, rather unusually, the originator of the inscription launches into sustained 1st-person narrative, without first naming himself.[265] Because of the break at the end of line 2, it is not clear whether the Chief of Southern Tens, Isi (line 3) is the court dignitary mentioned in line 2, or whether the text here shifts from 1st to 3rd person (via honorific epithets) so as actually to name Isi as author of this inscription. The restoration of *šnwt* would fit the context and also some tiny traces just visible; *n* of *n stp-s3* appears to relate back to *sr*. In the present context, *mdw m* must bear a positive connotation, and so not be the idiom 'speak against'. Rather, here, it will be to 'speak concerning'.[266] Here *mdw* may be a passive participle, *lit.* 'one spoken to him about . . . ', hence, 'one who had been instructed/spoken to, concerning' (the expedition, or the like).

In line 3, *mrr.f* will be geminating *sdm.f*, circumstantial after the preposition *n-ʿ3t-n* (cf. also Gardiner, § 181). On role of Isi, cf. above. This name, cf. *PN*, I, 45:26-27, and 46:1-7. For *wḏ n* of benefit, cf. Faulkner, *Dict.*, p. 73 end. At line-end, perhaps restore *sr* [*pn*].

In line 4, title *ỉmy-r mnf3t*, cf. above WH 6:6. After this title, one may restore [*ḫnʿ*], but there is no sufficient trace to justify this or any other suggestion. *Wn.sn* could be an adverbial clause of time (cf. Gardiner, § 454, 1). In line 5, the group . . *n.f*, seated-man, before *ḥr ỉrt* is damaged and obscure; no obvious term for a person ends in *-nf*. The vertical stroke and traces above *nf* could conceivably stand for the baton and seated-figure of *mdw* (cf. line 2). Then we would have (as in line 2) the phrase *mdw n.f*, 'the one instructed', but used as a compound noun, and so marked by the final seated-man determinative; cf. Gardiner, § 194 for other such compounds. At the end of the line, the tentative translation already given above presupposes the word *ḏ*[*ʿr*], 'to investigate/search out'.

In line 6, little is legible or therefore, intelligible. Near the end, . . *ḫw m ỉrt* is rather meaningless, but . . . *pw m ỉrt* is a feasible construction. The following seated-figure looks like *.ỉ*, but traces or scratches (?) could imply *mšꜥ*.

Line 7 begins part-way through a verb ending in *b* connected with mines or quarries (here, *ḥtt*). The obvious restoration is *nḫb*, 'to open' fresh mines/quarries,[267] which implies the former presence of *nḫ* at the lost end of line 6. This verb takes a direct object, not usually *m* as here. Therefore, it is preferable to understand [*nḫ*] *b(w)* here as either an Old Perfective ('Stative') or a passive participle, 'opened', plus *m* either preposition or of equivalence. After [*verb*]*.n ḥm.f*, tantalising traces might just possibly stand for *bỉꜣt*, 'wonder/ marvel' (it has to be a feminine noun because it is qualified by *tn*). The sentence structure is clear – 'H.M. [something] ed this [marvel?], because of the greatness (of) the *ḥs*[. .]'. The verb might easily be one 'to praise' or similar, and at the end it seems most fitting to restore *ḥs*[*mn pn* . .] as done in the translation given. Alternatively, one might restore something like *ḥs*[*t* . . .], 'because of the greatness of the fav[our granted by Hathor . .], or the like. But this seems less likely. At the end of the line, running into line 8, one must certainly restore *Stỉ* or *Tꜣ-Stỉ*, Nubia.

Line 8 is very difficult to restore to sense after *ỉn*. *Imy-r* (plus or minus *r*) rather than *.f* or a bird is just possible as in line 4 and conceivably in line 9 (*q.v.*). *Kꜣt* is very uncertain, but *pn* seems clear. *Imy-r kꜣt* may relate to the court official who accompanied the author of the stela. Thereafter, *ỉw* is tentative but *mrr sw* fits well; then *nb.f*? Vulture-on-basket is also used for a divine 'Lady' in WH 20:3 above.

Line 9, beginning with *ḥb* of *ẖry-ḥbt* assumes a lost *ẖr*-group at end of line 8. For the name Se, cf. *PN*, I, 278:21, and in compounds, 278-9 *passim*. The restoration of [*ỉmy-r*], and spelt as in line 4, is hypothetical; but the space admits of little more and it would agree well with the next sign (logogram for *mšꜥ* or *mnfꜣt*). The possible name *Nn-ṯ/Nn-ỉw* is not found in *PN*, but is of good Middle-Kingdom stamp (cf. *PN*, I, 204:17 - 205:12), while *PN*, I, 205:7, 11/12, may be variant spellings of either form possible here. After signs that are mainly unintelligible, the lost end of this line may have contained the heading *rḫt mšꜥ pn*, 'List of this expedition', and the start of the list, judging from the names that then follow.

Line 10, perhaps Heqaib's son Sobkhotep was the last of the senior personnel, as the next phrase (*ỉỉt m-ḫt* . . .) appears to set him apart from the names that follow. The title *ỉmy-r sꜣ n ẖrtyw-nṯr* recurs at Sinai.[268] Compare also *ỉmy-r sꜣ n ỉkyw* at Hammamat.[269] For the names Heqaib and Sobkhotep, cf. *PN*, I, 256:3 and 305:6. *Iỉt* is an infinitive serving as heading to what follows; perhaps restore *m-ḫt*[*.sn*], 'accompanying them'. Otherwise, perhaps 'Coming of the *ỉmy-ḫt* . . . (follower)'.[270]

Line 11, restoration of the first male name (. . . *yt*) is not certain, but probably a *Sꜣ-Wꜣḏyt. Sꜣ-ỉtyt*, or the like (cf. *PN*, I, 281:8,12). Ranke's citation of *Šsmw-ỉỉ* comes from this stela (*PN*, I, 329:24); for *Wḫ-ḥtp*, he cites others also (*PN*, I, 84:9).

Line 12, the title *ꜥnḫ-n-ẖnyt* appears to be formed on the same model as the common *ꜥnḫ-n-nỉwt*, 'citizen', and *ꜥnḫ-n-mšꜥ*, 'soldiers', besides *ꜥnh-n-ṯt-ḥḳꜣ*, 'dependent of the Ruler's table';[271] hence the rendering given. The names *Sꜥnḫ, In-ỉt.f*, cf. *PN*, I, 300:22, 34:5.

As set out above this text appears to show the following sequence. After the titles of the king, the expedition leader states his aim to fetch amethyst for the king and mentions a member of the court accompanying him. A royal command is given in the audience-hall, a 'general' and chief of southern contingents are involved. Then, a mine was (freshly?) opened, and possibly a surprisingly large quantity of amethyst obtained. Perhaps a message was immediately sent to the king, who then sent his congratulations at the 'marvel', a favour from the goddess (Hathor?). This climax to the expedition is followed by a list of leading personnel in two sections. Seen thus, the stela's text makes a co-ordinated whole.

264. Lucas, ed. Harris, *Ancient Egyptian Materials & Industries*, 1962, p.389.
265. In the translation, phrases within square brackets in the lost line endings are simply conjectural insertions, to give continuity of sense.
266. Faulkner, *Dict.*, p.122.
267. *Wb.*, II, p.307:9; Faulkner, *Dict.*, p.138.
268. Text 83, Year 2 of Amenemhat III; Gardiner, Peet, Černý, *Inscriptions of Sinai*, II, p.91.
269. Goyon, *NIH*, p.91, No. 70.
270. Cf. Hammamat examples, Couyat & Montet, I, p. 132 references.
271. All these, refs., Faulkner, *Dict.*, p.44.

WH, No. 149. Khor Dehmit, Lower Nubia; present location unknown.

Date: Amenemhat III, Year 11 (*c.* 1832 BC).

Bibliography: PM, VII, p. 39; A.E.P. Weigall, *A Report on the Antiquities of Lower Nubia,* 1907, p. 60, pl. 21:1; Weigall, *ASAE* 9 (1908), p. 109, fig. 4; cf. J.R. Harris, *Lexicographical Studies in Ancient Egyptian Minerals,* Berlin, 1961, p. 122, n.5.

Description: Small sandstone stela, date in lunette, 13 lines of text.

Normalised Text:

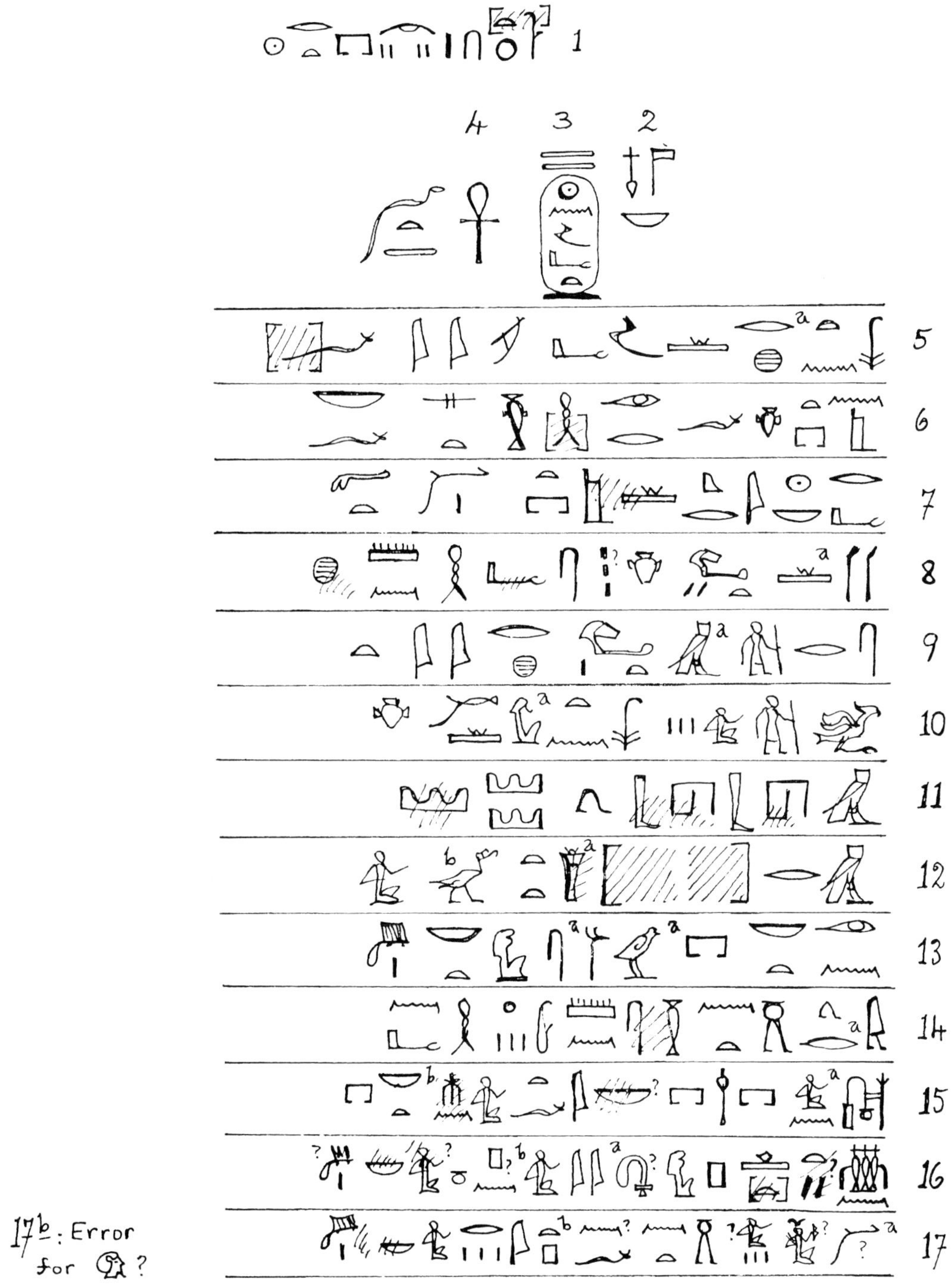

Textual Notes: NB: The readings adopted here result from close scrutiny of the *Report* photo under magnification along with the *ASAE* figure.

5a: here and almost throughout, *r* is engraved as a thick, elliptical line, not (as normally) as a 'hollow' outline. 8a: hieratic form, cf. *HP*, I, No. 538. 9a: here and in following lines, *m* is in hieratic form. 10a: hieratic form, cf. *HP*, I, No. 45. 12a: hieratic, cf. *HP*, I, No. 493. 12b: ditto, cf. *HP*, I, No. 216. 3a-a: hieratic forms. 14a: By its form (cf. 5a above), *r* not *n* - contrast *n* of *ỉnt*. 15a: hieratic group of seated-man over *n*, cf. *HP*, I, p. 74, No. LVII (Sinuhe example). 15b: hieratic form for *ms*; cf. *HP*, I, No. 408. 16a: form similar to that in Goyon, *NIH*, No. 64 (=Couyat & Montet, No. 123), horizontal line 3 middle, for which Goyon, p. 182, offers the reading, *sḏ3wty*, used here; the normal hieratic forms (*HP*, I, No. 423) are not so close. 16b-b: these readings are possible but tentative. 17a: except for *ỉnt . . f*, nearly all readings in this line remain tentative.

Translation: (1) Year 11, 4th Month of Peret, Day <1?>, (of): (2) the good god, Lord of (3) the Two Lands, Nema-'etre, (4) may he live forever.

(5) Real acquaintance of the King, whom he loves, (6) his favourite, who does what his lord praises, (7) daily, excellent in speech, reliable in (8) thoughts, an effective noble, (9) an official in front of the (10) people, confidant of the King (11) in traversing the deserts;
(12) Superintendent of [. . . . .] Si-Bastet, (13) born of the lady of the house, Woser, possessing veneration.
(14) (I/who) came to obtain amethyst, together with (15) the Treasury-scribe Neb-iotef, born of the lady of the house, (16) Khenti-hotep, (and with) the Treasurer (?) Pennu (?), possessing veneration (?), (and) (17) the general Intu-nef-tep-iru (?), possessing veneration (?).

Commentary: As in the case of WH 148, it is the mention of amethyst (line 14) that may link it with Wadi Hudi, either removed from there (cf. Harris, in Bibliography, above), or possibly set up by the Nile on the expedition's return from the desert.

Line 1, the date given would be late June in *c.* 1832 BC, a hot season for working in the desert; but cf. Sinai, No. 90, the famous text of Harwerre of this same reign, dispatched in summer heat to Sinai.[272] Lines 5-7, the sequence of epithets, *rḫ-nsw m3ʿ mry.f* and variants is well-known in the Middle Kingdom.[273] For *ỉrr ḥst nb.f rʿ nb*, cf. above on WH 9. In lines 7-8, the pair *ỉḳr st-ns* and *mty* (<*mtr*) *ḥ3t/ỉb* has parallels.[274] Closely comparable is the Eighteenth-Dynasty example (Sethe, *Urkunden IV*, 993:7) *ʿḳ3 st-ns, mty ḥ3tyw* with the plural form *ḥ3tyw* which is probably to be understood here in WH 149. *Sʿḥ mnḫ* is not unknown, either.[275]

Lines 9-11, also attested are *sr m-ḥ3t rḫyt* and *hbhb ḫ3swt*,[276] including in conjunction with *mḫ-ỉb nsw.*[277] Line 12, the entity of which Si-Bastet is superintendent is completely destroyed on the stone. He may have been an *ỉmy-r sḏ3yt*, 'Chief Treasurer'. If so, it is conceivable that he was the Si-Bastet who visited Wadi Hudi in Year 20 of Amenemhat III a mere nine years after this stela (cf. WH 19, above). Line 13, for Woser as a feminine name in the Middle Kingdom, cf. *PN*, I, 85:6.

Line 14, the initial *ỉỉ* may be either a Perfective *sḏm.f*, *ỉỉ.ỉ*, 'I came', or else a Perf. Active Participle *ỉỉ*, 'who came', qualifying Si-Bastet. The former would be a less usual variant for *ỉỉ .n(.ỉ)*, cf. WH 148:2, above, also followed by *r ỉnt ḥsmn*. Line 15, the title *sš n pr ḥḏ* recurs at Sinai.[278] The name *Nb-ỉt.f*, cf. *PN*, I, 183:19-20.

Line 16, for names *Ḫnty-ḥtpw* and *Pn(n)w*, 'mouse', cf. *PN*, I, 272:14, and 133:6. Line 17, initial title is probably *ỉmy-r mšʿ*, less general than commander of the expedition's labour-force. A name *In.tw n.f tp-ỉrw* is not otherwise known, but is comparable with similar long Middle Kingdom names, e.g. compounds of *In-ỉt.f* (*PN*, I, 34:2-4. 9, 11-14), and *Inḥr-n-Ptḥ-ʿnḫ* (*PN*, I, 35:15).

272. Gardiner, Peet, Cerny, *Inscriptions of Sinai*, I (2nd ed.), pls. 25a, 26; and II, pp.97ff.
273. Cf. Janssen, *TEA*, I, p.63, Aw:17, 18; Goyon, *NIH*, p. 91, No.70:2; Couyat & Montet, Nos. 43:2, 47:13-14, 108:4.
274. Cf. *TEA*, I, p.5, G: 44-48 (esp. 44-46) and p.23, Ac:13-14, 18-19.
275. *TEA*, I, p.21f., Aa:22, 25, 35.
276. For which cf. *TEA*, I, p.147f., Ax:1-3, 5, and p.85, Bp:1,3.
277. *Ibid.*, p.67f., Ax:14ff., esp. 32, 33.
278. Cf. Gardiner, Peet, Černý, *Inscriptions of Sinai*, II, pp. 18/19; p. 93, No.85:N.1; p.169, No.105:N.4.

G. Undated Inscriptions, II: Nos. 150-152.

WH, No. 150. Present location unknown.
Bibliography: Fakhry, pl. XXIIIB (not in text).
Description: Four signs scribbled on a rock-edge.

Normalised Text:

Translation: Iamu (?).

Commentary: For similar names, cf. *PN*, I, 6:18, 25, and 25:14.

WH, No. 151. Present location unknown.
Bibliography: Fakhry, pl. XXVB (not in text).
Description: One line of hieroglyphs on an isolated rock.

Normalised Text:

Translation: Harhotep('s son?) Pepi.

Textual Note: 1a: Reading of bird very doubtful.

Commentary: These names, cf. *PN*, I, 250:7 and 131:12. The juxtaposition of the two names in sequence may imply an unstated filiation.

WH, No. 152. Present location unknown.
Bibliography: Fakhry, pl. XXIVB (not in text).
Description: Across face of a boulder, line of signs across human figures.

Normalised Text:

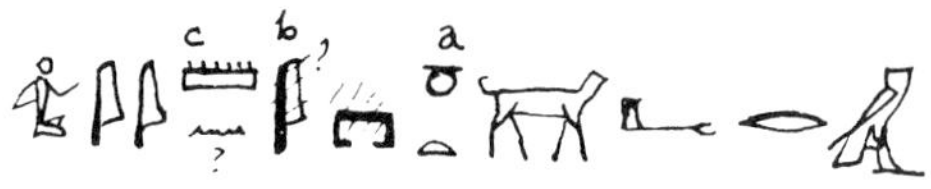

Textual Notes: 1a: inverted *t*. 1b: *ỉ* damaged badly. 1c: inverted *t* for *n*.

Translation: The chamberlain, Ameny.

Commentary: This name, *PN*, I, 31:13.

III: AMETHYST MINING EXPEDITIONS OF THE MIDDLE KINGDOM IN THE LIGHT OF THE INSCRIPTIONS.

Introduction.

The mining of amethyst during the Middle Kingdom at Wadi el-Hudi is on a par with the extraction of turquoise in Sinai, the quarrying of choice stone in Wadi Hammamat, and similar enterprises elsewhere. Such expeditions came at intervals by royal command, the gems secured going to the king (in practice to the royal and state treasury). In this part will be briefly reviewed the contribution of the Wadi Hudi texts and site to our knowledge of Egyptian gemstone mining activity.[279]

The Eleventh Dynasty.

The texts and workings at Wadi Hudi attest a sudden and considerable burst of mining and quarrying that took place in the first two years of Mentuhotep IV Nebtawyre, at the very end of the Eleventh Dynasty.

In that king's Year 1 we have three, perhaps four inscriptions (WH 1-3, perhaps 26) all engraved on the authority of the caravan-leader Intef, having as associates Khuyu (WH 3, property-administrator) and perhaps a director of works Didiu (WH 26) to handle the practical details. The scale, season and duration of this expedition are not given.

However, the results were sufficiently encouraging for Intef to be sent out with a large expedition in Year 2, ranked clearly as both Steward (his father's rank?) and chief caravan-leader. Our authority here is the long and difficult text WH 4. Referring back to Year 1, its first line confirms WH 3 in stating that amethyst then, as throughout these texts, was the objective of the expedition. Geographically, mining amethyst at Wadi Hudi was work done in Nubia (WH 4:4), a fact also stated in later texts in the series (e.g., WH 14:8-9). For that work, Intef gathered local Nubians from Wawat (south and north districts?), seemingly in considerable numbers (4:11, 'thousand after thousand', rank upon rank).

This claim (even if rhetorical to a degree) sheds a valuable sidelight on the power of the late Eleventh Dynasty and its officials in Lower Nubia. From the Abisko graffito,[280] it is known that Nubian warriors were recruited by the redoubtable Mentuhotep II Neb-hepet-re, but for service elsewhere, e.g. against Asiatics.[281] However, it appears that the Mentuhotep kings did not occupy Nubia forcibly by means of permanent fortress-garrisons as the Twelfth Dynasty was later to do,[282] but may have been content with a general 'protectorate' over the area (accepted by local chiefs?). Supposed evidence on graffiti for an Eleventh Dynasty occupation of Nubia in depth may in fact relate to the earlier part of the Twelfth Dynasty.[283] Thus, WH 4 does add significantly to the modest evidence of the Abisko graffito on the power of Eleventh Dynasty kings to levy manpower (voluntarily?) from Lower Nubia for their mining projects and wars.

The flurry of activity at Wadi Hudi under Mentuhotep IV coincides with similar endeavours in Wadi Hammamat, begun only in Year 2 of the reign.[284] However, unlike the Hudi expeditions run by 'middle rank' officials

(Intef, Khuyu, Didiu), the Hammamat enterprise was led by the vizier himself, that Amenemhat who may have founded the next dynasty.

The Twelfth Dynasty.

The reign of the founder, Amenemhat I, left no known mark at Wadi Hudi (enough amethyst being gained under his predecessor?), and very little of such works elsewhere. We have one stela each at the quarries of Hammamat (Couyat & Montet, No. 199) and for diorite north-west of Abu Simbel, the latter dating to the coregency with Sesostris I.[285] At the end of his reign, Amenemhat I sent a punitive expedition into Nubia (Year 29).[286]

With the accession to sole power of Sesostris I there came a crescendo of gemstone mining not equalled or surpassed until the time of Amenemhat III nearly 150 years later, nor again until the New Kingdom epoch. In his early years, Hammamat was quarried,[287] and at an unspecified date his agents re-opened the long neglected turquoise mines of Sinai (texts Nos. 64, 70 there). But the main focus of activity was in the south during Year 17 to 30; a campaign into Nubia in Year 18 (Buhen stela), followed by an expedition to the diorite quarries in Year 20 (two stelae).[288] Two years later still, in Year 22, a further expedition passed through the Eastern desert to the Red Sea en route for Punt, responsible to the vizier Intefoqer himself.[289]

But inscriptionally, at least, all these activities pale in comparison with the intensive efforts expended in mining amethyst at Wadi Hudi in Years 17 to 29, with expeditions at frequent intervals (4, 3, 2, even 1 year(s) apart), witnessed by fourteen or more inscriptions. Each expedition usually left two or three stelae each time. Only in Year 17 have we just WH 6 as sole witness, although a very important one (see below); unless WH 143 also belongs here. For Years 20, 22, 28, we have three stelae each (WH 7, 8, 14A; 9, 10, 11; 13, 146, 147), and in Years 24 and 29 two documents each (WH 12, 14B; 144, 145). Never again was Wadi Hudi so intensively worked by the Middle Kingdom pharaohs.

The leadership of these expeditions varied, but always fell to representatives of the king and his administration, especially the treasury. In Year 17, the Steward Hotepu was leader, and then (or later) the Steward and Granary-chief Hor, both administrators of royal property. Hotepu had an army commander to help run his 1500-strong expedition, and some troops for its security. In Years 20, 24 and 29, the leader in each case was from one class of court official, a Chief of Southern Tens. Interestingly enough, in Years 20/24, it was the same man Mentuhotep son of Henenu the Elder who had also worked the diorite/carnelian quarries; while in Year 29, this same man's son (and successor?) Henenu the Younger continued the work at Wadi Hudi. Leadership by a Chief of Southern Tens persisted later, down to Amenemhat II's time (WH 148). In each case the Chief had various aides. In Year 20 of Sesostris I, it was Weni, an assistant treasurer and emissary of the vizier Intefoqer, besides the 'practical men', the Intefs as chief and director of works. In Year 24, it was the courtier, 'Chief of Secrets', Hetepheru. In Year 29 we have record of only two lesser aides to Henenu, a scribe/sealbearer (?) Ha-ishtef and retainer Sankh. In the intervening Years 22 and 28, others directed the work. In Year 28, it clearly devolved upon the caravan-leader Mentuhotep (WH 146), accompanied by gemstone specialists (WH 13) and others (WH 147, details lost). But the expedition of Year 22 is (so far) attested only from the three stelae of quite subordinate officials, a retainer (WH 9), a servitor (WH 10) and one untitled (WH 11). Clearly, we either lack entirely a record of the leadership for this expedition (lost, destroyed?), or else it has gone unrecognised. Could it actually be the Steward Hor of the undated and splendid stela WH 143? This would still be a feasible date for him.

Besides the Wadi Hudi stela already referred to (WH 148, undated), other monuments show modest activity by Amenemhat II's agents in Sinai in Years 11 (?) and 24 (Nos. 71, 72; 47, 48), in Year 28 to the Red Sea,[290] and to the diorite and carnelian workings (date unknown).[291]

In the reign of Sesostris II, the evidence suggests even less activity. From Wadi Hudi, there is only the very doubtful witness of WH 15; Sinai was visited (Nos. 79, 80). In Year 1, a further expedition went to the Red Sea,[292] and in Year 8 (?) one to the diorite quarries, led by a Chamberlain (*ỉmy-r ʿ-ẖnwty*).[293]

In turn, the energetic Sesostris III is more famed for his military campaigns (four in Nubia, in Years 8, 10, 16, 19) than for mining. But fresh work was undertaken at Wadi Hudi in Year 13 (WH 16, 17, perhaps 18), besides quarrying in Hammamat in Year 14 (*NIH*, Nos. 68, 69). This time, like the diorite-expedition in the previous reign, the visitations to Wadi Hudi were led by a chamberlain, with whom went a seal-bearer.

The long reign of Amenemhat III saw further changes in both emphasis and leadership. First, the focus of interest (mineralogically) shifted northwards. In Years 4 and 6 (and one unknown), two or more expeditions went for carnelian and diorite.[294] To Hammamat there went two 'twin' series of expeditions, in Years 2, 3 (Montet, 43; Goyon, 7) and Years 19, 20 (Montet, 17, 19, 48; 42). Wadi Hudi ranks with these, with expeditions sent thither at roughly decade intervals, in Years 11, 20 and 28 (WH 149, 19, 20). Two of these expeditions in Years 11 (probably) and 28 were led by Si-Bastet, a Shipmaster;[295] who led the intervening one in Year 20 remains uncertain. In striking contrast to all these relatively modest and limited undertakings is the frenzy of almost non-stop mining for turquoise in Sinai. The intensity of effort here can be seen forcefully from a simple listing of regnal years and texts: Years 2 (Nos. 23-25), 4 (85), 5 (86, 87, 112, 113), 6 (88-90, 406), 8 (91), 13 (92), 15 (93-99), 18 (115), 20 (25, W. Nasb), 23 (102, 131), 25 (103), 27 (104), 27/29? (50), 30 (26, 105). Then, after an eight-year interval, Years 38 (51, 52, 409), 40 (106). 41 (27), 42 (28, 29; 142?), 43 (30), 44 (53, 107), and 45 (54, 108-110?).[296]

On a much smaller scale, the same pattern appears in the brief reign of Amenemhat IV; one solitary text of Year 2 at Wadi Hudi (WH 21), of an assistant treasurer and probably a shipmaster (as in the previous reign). But in Sinai, again, a series of expeditions in close succession - Years 4 (118), 6 (33-35, 59; 119, 120?), 8 (121) and 9 (122, 123).[297] Of Queen Sobknofru, we have no expeditionary records at all.

The Thirteenth Dynasty.

The nature and content of the Thirteenth Dynasty records from Wadi Hudi faithfully reflects the profile of fluctuating royal power then. Significantly, there is no surviving record at any period save one - that of the powerful 'inner dynasty' of Neferhotep I and his brother and successor Sobkhotep 'IV' (Khaneferre). Of this latter king, we have a single, compact group of four stelae, two certainly and one most probably dated to his Year 6 (WH 22, 24, 25); and there is no reason to date WH 23 any differently from these. This group, therefore, would appear to be the record of just one major expedition under this king, in stark contrast to the repeated quests for amethyst in the Twelfth Dynasty. Significant also is the interesting fact that, on this occasion, amethyst was not the sole objective; on the evidence of WH 23, garnet, green felspar, black and white quartz, and other prized stones were sought along with amethyst. This general foraging expedition for 'anything and everything' is a far cry from the specialised ventures to Hudi, Sinai and the Western Desert respectively for precisely amethyst, turquoise, carnelian, according to location.[298] The leadership came from court circles, Iunefer, Deputy to an unnamed High Steward, with a Retainer of the Judgement Hall as principal lieutenant. They were assisted by a posse of middle rank officials, by a chief of recruits, and the usual specialists (prospectors, stonemasons, etc.). The vizier and the court were also specifically represented by the Chief Scribe of the Vizier and a Seal-bearer of the King (WH 25), and a chamberlain and a courtier (WH 24).

Composition and Scope of the Expeditions.

Alongside the changing classes of leader on the various expeditions from reign to reign, the texts from Wadi Hudi give a broad picture of the other personnel present on these enterprises.[299] For general quarrying and mining of rock, there were contingents (*sꜣ*) of stonemasons (*ẖrtyw-nṯr*), and for general labouring work, clearing away of waste, transport of the amethyst and so on, large forces of 'recruits' (*ḏꜣmw*), 'braves' (*ꜥḥꜣwtyw*), labourers (*ḥsbw*), and others. Specialists included the *ḥr-ḥrww*, 'supreme artisans', and *msw-ꜥꜣt*, 'prospectors' (and their chiefs), men who could recognise, expertly extract and work the actual lumps of semi-precious stone, readying it for transport to the Nile valley and down to the Residence and its treasuries. Various titles were borne by the men controlling the gangs; chiefs of contingents (*ỉmy-r sꜣ*), commanders of forces (*ỉmy-r mšꜥ*), not needfully military. But some soldiery was present under commanders; *pḏt*, 'troops', led by 'generals' (*ỉmy-r mnfꜣt*). Less obvious is the role of lector-priests on more than one occasion. Interesting is the presence of shipmasters in the later Twelfth Dynasty, presumably a reflexion of their importance in shipping the spoils of mining back down the Nile. Some classes of people, chief hunters and dog handlers, occur only in independent graffiti, not in the formal dated texts. It may be that they travelled this way out on game hunting expeditions, unless in fact they went with the expeditions and kept their leaders in fresh meat from desert game.

Very few of these texts give any conspectus of the personnel involved (e.g., WH 6, 23, 148), and fewer still any statistics. Thus, WH 4 speaks of 'rank upon rank' (lit. 'thousand after thousand'), while the figures, if any, in WH 23: 6 are now totally lost. Only WH 6 gives a straight set of numbers of people, and so is of unique value. But none of the texts ever attempts to give any idea of precisely what weight or quantity of amethyst, or any other gemstone, was secured on any particular expedition.

The inscription WH 6 is perhaps the most informative of all the Wadi Hudi texts, itemising the make-up of an expedition. It is for Wadi Hudi what the Montet texts Nos. 87, 192, and Goyon No. 61 are for Wadi Hammamat at this period, but more modestly.

The relative proportions and size of this expedition deserve note:

The responsible official, the Steward Hotepu	1
The general, Resuwi	1
The strong men from all Thebes	1000
The 'braves' from Elephantine	200
The 'braves' from Ombi (Kom Ombo)	100
The Residence: chief prospectors	41
: officers of the Steward Hotepu	56 (?)
Caravan-leaders (?)	50
Archers, from Department of the 'Head of the South'	61
Total:	1510 men.

(This figure assumes that Neni and Neferhor depicted below the main text are included somewhere in the list of people given).

It is also worth noting the geographical composition of the force. The leader Hotepu was certainly a royal administrator (on 'steward', cf. above, comments to WH 1, with n.11), and almost certainly came from the Residence, i.e. the administrative capital of Egypt, Ithet-tawy just south of Memphis. With him came 56 officers (*ḫrpw*) and 41 chief prospectors. So some 92 of the leading personnel and specialists came upstream from the north to direct the expedition.

By contrast, the large numbers of 'lower ranks' were all local, belonging to the Thebaid and southernmost Upper Egypt proper. Here belong the 1,000 strong recruits from 'all (of) the Southern City' (Thebes; with possibly its nome?), obviously the principal 'brawn' for all the heavy work, carrying supplies out and minerals back, digging and clearing rock, etc. To them, one adds the 300 local militia from the south and north centres of the Elephantine nome, stiffened and protected by the 61 troops (or, archers) from the southland. To these 1,361 men one most probably should add the 56 caravan-leaders, especially if they were in fact Egyptianised and 'naturalised' Nubians as Bell has suggested. This would give a total of 1,417 southerners under the command of 92 northerners. Alone, the general Resuwi cannot be definitely assigned to either origin, and guesswork is pointless. The odd units in the totals of 41 chief prospectors and 61 archers call for remark. They may well indicate groups of 40 and 60 men, respectively each under its own leader, in turn subject to the steward and general.

The nature, numbers and proportions of personnel in WH 6 will bear comparison with what is to be found in other records of Middle Kingdom desert expeditions, especially to Wadi Hammamat and Sinai. Detailed comparisons of titles and office bearers is impracticable here, as the terminology in Sinai, Hammamat and Wadi Hudi differs considerably; others may find a fruitful field for study here. Naturally the skills for extracting large blocks of stone, whole, for buildings and statuary will have differed somewhat from the abilities required to locate and ferret out deposits of gemstones. Therefore, some differences in workforces are to be expected as between Hammamat on the one hand and Sinai and Wadi Hudi on the other. But differences also exist between these latter two for several reasons. For example, as Sinai was so much nearer the capital than was Hudi, the Sinai expeditions included more officials from the central treasury in their ranks.[300]

In terms of size, again, much larger numbers of men were deployed at Hammamat to move large blocks of stone, than for extracting the smaller volume of gemstones and waste at Wadi Hudi or in Sinai. Neither of the latter can compare with the imposing Hammamat musters, 3,000 men in Year 8 of Mentuhotep III Sankhkare (CMH, No. 114:12), 10,000 and 3,000 sailors in Year 2 of Mentuhotep IV (CMH, No. 192:12, 20), 5,000 men in Year 16 of Sesostris I (CMH, No. 123/*NIH*, No. 64), the almost 19,000 men (i.e., 17,000 plus 2,000 'other ranks') in Year 38 of Sesostris I (*NIH*, No. 61; cf. CMH, No. 87 - part of same text?), and the 2,080 men in Year 19 of Amenemhat III (CMH, No. 19).

But in Sinai we find at the most 734 men in Year 2 of Amenemhat III (Sinai, No. 23), then 262 men in his Year 4 (No. 85), 361+*x* men in Year 40 (No. 106), 209 men with 284 donkeys (No. 114) and 205+*x* men (No. 117) in undated contexts of this king. Then, 285 men in Year 6 of Amenemhat IV (No. 120); and in two undated Middle Kingdom texts, 470 men tabulated plus 67+*x* men and 500 donkeys in one case (No. 137), and 170 men with 50 donkeys in the other (No. 412). Here, the numbers, varying from over 700 men down to 200 men or less, are much more modest, and all of them far less than the 1510 men of the Wadi Hudi amethyst expedition commemorated on WH 6 which, by this scale, reflects an unusually large undertaking. More closely comparable than most of the Sinai visits is the stela of the herald Horemsaf from Year 4 of Amenemhat II at Toshkeh, commemorating his expedition to obtain carnelian (*mḥnmt*) with 1,006 men, 250 specialists and 1,000 donkeys;[301] this total of 1,256 men is quite close in scale to the 1,510 men of the WH 6 text.[302]

Religious Aspects.

By far the most popular deity to whom dedications appear in the Wadi Hudi texts is 'Hathor, Lady of Amethyst'.[303] She was patron of the local desert product here, as of turquoise in Sinai and carnelian in the Nubian desert (N.W. of Abu Simbel). Her nearest rival (and well behind her) was Satis, 'Lady of Elephantine', a patron goddess of the nearest inhabited centre and starting point of the expeditions - a goddess, too, recognised in Nubia to which in some measure Wadi Hudi was geographically reckoned.[304] The great Theban gods Amun and Montu make an isolated appearance in WH 14 as patrons of the king, likewise Horus of Nubia (precursor of the New Kingdom Horus gods of Nubian localities) in WH 143 of the same reign (Sesostris I). The role of other deities is negligible, Osiris twice under Amenemhat III in *ḥtp-dỉ-nsw* formulae, Ptah in a title, and Re solely in royal clichés.

No clear evidence of the practice of the worship of the gods has so far been isolated at Wadi Hudi. Fakhry spoke[305] of the illicit removal of 'two small obelisks and an offering table', whether funerary, or for the cult of a deity. These have never reappeared since their removal. Perhaps some day they will, together with other relics of Wadi Hudi for some future publication. It is possible that, unlike Sinai and Hammamat, the lengths of stay in Wadi Hudi by visiting expeditions were simply too brief to justify any permanent provision for religious activity.

Physical Conditions.

In such a barren place, all food, and probably some water, had to be brought from the Nile valley by the expeditionaries themselves. Abundant broken pottery attests this fact. From the remains seen, it is clear that the workmen had to sleep in roughly made huts of dry stone walling. These were of various types; completely freestanding, three walls with cliff-face as fourth, or a cave in the rock-face with a simple front wall and doorway, or one room outside and one under the overhanging rock. If Fakhry was right in dating a fort (Site 9) to the Twelfth Dynasty, then the leaders at least had more spacious quarters, but hardly less spartan except for any comforts brought with them. With hot days and cold nights, the expeditions doubtless sought to complete their work in the minimum span of time to obtain a sufficient and worthwhile quantity of amethyst. The actual mines were long excavations in the ground, hacked out of the rock, and two or three metres or more deep, with heaps of waste thrown out. Occasionally, the inscriptions give glimpses of the opening of fresh mines (**WH** 143, 148), and indicate the mode of removal of the lumps of amethyst on sledges, loaded with pallets or boxes (?) of the mineral. The well and waste at Site 8 may illustrate the preliminary sorting, cleaning and dressing of the mineral lumps for ultimate transport back to the Nile. At any time, these expeditions must have been serious and quite difficult undertakings; they bear witness to the vigour, drive and exploratory sense of the Egyptians of the Middle Kingdom.

279. The outline synthesis given here has been deliberately restricted to essentials, partly because the main task of this work is to present reliably the WH texts themselves, and partly because other works of synthesis on Egyptian mining and quarrying at all periods are in the course of preparation. For such, this book should serve as a source.
280. For which see G. Posener, *Archiv Orientální* 20 (1952), pp.163ff.
281. Cf. H.S. Smith, *The Fortress of Buhen, II: The Inscriptions*, London, 1976, p.61.
282. On the Twelfth Dynasty founding of (e.g.) Buhen, cf. Smith, *op. cit.*, pp.61ff., esp. p.63.
283. See Smith, *JEA* 58 (1972), pp.51-55, esp. 55.
284. His texts of Year 2 are: CMH, Nos. 110, 113, 191, 192, and implicitly No. 205; Goyon, *NIH*, Nos. 53, 54, 57. Without year-date are: CMH, Nos. 1, 40, 55, 105, 112, 241; Goyon, Nos. 52, 55, 56, 58, 59, 60.
285. For the latter, see Engelbach, *ASAE* 33 (1933), p.70, No.3 (Cairo, JdE. 59505), cartouches only.
286. PM, VII, p.84, references.
287. In Years 2 (*NIH*, No.67), 11 (CMH, No. 104), 14 (CMH, No.47) and 16 (CMH, No.123/*NIH*, No.64).
288. The Year 20 stela, Engelbach, *ASAE* 33 (1933), p.70, No.4 (Cairo, JdE. 59504); undated stela of Chief of Southern Tens, Henenu, *ibid.*, p.71, No.5 (Cairo, JdE. 59483), pl.II:3.
289. See latterly, A.M.A.H. Sayed, *RdE* 29 (1977), pp.150-173, especially pp.159ff. and 169ff.
290. Stela of Khenty-khety-wer, reproduced after Birch by A.M.A.H. Sayed, *op. cit.*, pl.8*b*.
291. Engelbach, *ASAE* 33 (1933), p.71, No.6, fig.2 (Cairo, JdE. 59480).
292. Stela of the Chamberlain Khnumhotep, cf. Sayed, *op. cit.*, pl.8*a*, after Birch.
293. *ASAE* 33 (1933), pp.71-72, No.7 (Cairo, JdE.59485), pl. II:4.
294. *Ibid.*, pp.72-74, Nos.9-12, etc.
295. Entirely distinct from the Si-Bastet, a treasurer, who went to the diorite quarries.
296. To which add: Year 20+*x* (Nos.31, 32); Year *x*+17 (143), and several undated (Nos. 56, 100, 101, 111, 114A, 116+164, 117, 132, 405).
297. Plus the undated texts, Nos.124-130.
298. The only other known Thirteenth Dynasty ventures of this kind were to Hammamat in Year 7 of Sobkemsaf I (Lepsius, *Denkmäler*, II, 151k; plus undated graffito, CMH, No.111; both, W. Helck, *Historisch-Biographische Texte der 2. Zwischenzeit* . . . . ,Wiesbaden, 1975, p.61, No.89A/B), and one under Sobkhotep IV (unpublished, cf. Drioton, *CdE* 25 (1950), p.239). For date of Sobkemsaf I, cf. Kitchen, *Orientalia NS* 36 (1967), p.45f., n.5; on numbering of the Sobkhoteps, cf. *ibid.*, p.46, n.2.
299. The best conspectus of the detailed range of titles and functions of members of Wadi Hudi expeditions can be gained by consulting Index 5, Titles, below.
300. On Sinai personnel, cf. W.J. Murnane, *Göttinger Miszellen* 15 (1975), pp.22-33.
301. Published in W.K. Simpson, *Heka-nefer*, New Haven/Philadelphia, 1963, p.52 with figure. The Red Sea/Punt expedition of Sesostris I under the responsibility of the vizier Intefoqer totalled 3,756 men; cf. figures from stela, A.M.A.H. Sayed, *RdE* 29 (1977), p.170 and pl.16.
302. Against Goedicke's ingenious suggestion to understand all these figures (especially at Hammamat) as simply man/work units (as in Papyrus Reisner I-III), in *American Journal of Archeology* 68 (1964), pp.403-4, see the remarks by D. Müller, *Orientalia NS* 36 (1967), pp.359ff.
303. See below, Index 1, for the relative occurrences of deities.
304. Her influence in the northern half of Lower Nubia is still seen centuries later in (e.g.) her presence in the Ramesside temples of Gerf Hussein and Wadi es-Sebua; studied by Mr. A. Et-Tambouli, in a paper (unpublished) which he very kindly gave me to consult in 1976.
305. His p.2, § 3.

IV: INDEXES

The following abbreviations are used here: asst. = assistant; -b. = -bearer; cf. = compare; ch. = chief; dept. = department; f. = feminine; fa. = father (of), gfa. = grandfather (of), gs. = grandson (of), L. Eg. – Lower Egypt, mo. – mother (of); -n. = -name; rdg. = reading (in a text); s. = son (of); S. = Southern; supr. = supreme; Supt. = Superintendent; trans. = transitive (verb); treas. = treasury-/treasurer.

1. Deities.

Imn, Amun, *nb nswt tꜣwy*, Lord of the Thrones of the Two Lands, 14:14.
Wsỉr, Osiris, *nb Ḏdw*, Lord of Busiris, 19:2; 20:4.
Psḏt, Ennead, in title, 14:18-19.
Ptḥ, Ptah, in title, 148:9.
Mꜣꜥt, Maet/Truth, in title, 14:7, 18.
Mnṯw, Montu, *ḥry-ỉb Iwny*, residing in Armant, 14:13-14.
Rꜥ, Re, in tag *mỉ Rꜥ ḏt*, like Re forever, 3:1; 7:3; 11:2; 13:5; 15:2; 143:10; 146:4; in title *sꜣ Rꜥ*, see Vocabulary.
Ḥr, Horus, of *Stỉ*, Nubia, 143:10; as title, see Vocabulary.
Ḥwtḥr, Hathor, *nbt ḥsmn*, Lady of Amethyst, 16:3; 17:3; 20:3; 22:4, 5; 24:4; 25:3; *ḫntt ꜣbw*, chief of Elephantine, 20:3; broken context, 15:4; 28:1 (?); hypothetical reading, 4:4.
Ḫnmw, Khnum, *nb ḳbḥw*, Lord of the Cataract, 20:3.
Stt, Satis, *nbt ꜣbw*, Lady of Elephantine, 22:4; [25:4]; 143:A.4; *nbt ỉnt*, Lady of the Wadi, 2:6.
Gb, Geb, 143:7.

2. Royal Names.

Imnmḥꜣt, nomen, Amenemhat II, 148:1.
ꜥnḫ-ỉb-tꜣwy, Horus-name, Sobkhotep IV, 22:2.
ꜥnḫ-mswt, Horus-n., Sesostris I, 7:1-2; 9:2; 10:4; 13:2; 14:2, 15; 143:A.1, B.1; 146:2; 147:2.
ꜥnḫ-mswt, Nebty-n., Sesostris I, 13:3; 14:2, 15; 143:B.1; 146:2-3; [147:2].
ꜥnḫ-mswt, Golden Horus-n., Ses. I, 14:2.
Mꜣꜥtḫrwrꜥ, prenomen, Amenemhat IV, 21:2.
Mnṯwḥtp, nomen, Mentuhotep IV, 5:3.
Nỉ-mꜣꜥtrꜥ, prenomen, Amenemhat III, 19:2; 20:2; 149:3.
Nbwkꜣwrꜥ, prenomen, Amenemhat II, 148:1.
Nb-tꜣwyrꜥ, prenomen, Mentuhotep IV, 1:2; 2:1; 3:1; 4:2; 5:1.
Ḥkn-m-mꜣꜥt, Horus-n., Amenemhat II, 148:1.
Ḫꜥ-nfr-rꜥ, prenomen, Sobkhotep IV, 22:3; 23:A.1; 24:2; 25:1.
Ḫꜥ-ḫpr-rꜥ, prenomen, Sesostris II, 15:2?
Ḫꜥkꜣwrꜥ, prenomen, Sesostris III, 15:2?; 16:2; 17:2; 18:1.
Ḫpr-kꜣrꜥ, prenomen, Sesostris I, 6:2; 7:3; 10:5; 11:2; 13:4; 14:3,16; 15:2?; 143:B.1,10; 147:2.
Sbk-ḥtp, nomen, Sobkhotep IV, 22:3; 24:2 25:2.
Snwsrt, nomen, Sesostris I, 9:3, 10:6; 11:2; 12:2; 14:4,16; 143:A.2,B.1; 146:3-4.
Snwsrt, nomen, Sesostris I?, II?, or III?, 15:2; 95:1.
. . . . . *rꜥ*, prenomen, (Mentuhotep IV?), 26:1.
. . . . . . ,nomen, unknown king, 28:3.

3. Datelines.

Mentuhotep IV, Year 1, 1:1; 2:1; 3:1; 4:1; 26:1?
------, Year 2, 4:2.
------, no year, 5:1-3.
Sesostris I, Year 17, 6:1; (15:1?);
------, Year 20, 7:1; 8:1; 14:1.
------, Year 22, 9:1; 10:1; 11:1.
------, Year 24, 12:1; 14:15.
------, Year 28, 13:1; 146:1; 147:1.
------, Year 29, 144:1; 145:1.
------, no year, 95?; 143.
Amenemhat II, no year, 148:1.
Sesostris II, Year [1]6/[1]7; 15:1?
Sesostris III, Year 11+*x*, 18:1.
------, Year 13, 16:1; 17:1.
------, Year [1]6/[1]7, 15:1?
Amenemhat III, Year 11, 149:1.
------, Year 20, 19:1.
------, Year 28, 20:1.
Amenemhat IV, Year 2, 21:1.
Sobkhotep IV, Year 6, 22:1; 24:1; 25:[1?]
------, no year, 23.

4. Place Names.

ꜣbw, Elephantine, 200 warriors, 6:10; title of Satis, *nbt ꜣbw* 22:4; 25:4; 143:A.5; title of Hathor, *ḫntt ꜣbw*, 20:3.
Iwny, Armant, title of Montu, *ḥry-ỉb Iwny*, 14:14.
wꜣwꜣt, Wawat, Lower Nubia, Nubians and regions of, 4:4-5; cf. *(Tꜣ)-Stỉ*.
mḥ, north (region), of Wawat, 4:5.
nỉwt rst, Southern City (Thebes), 6:9.
Nbwyt, Ombi (Kom Ombo), 100 warriors, 6:11.
Nḥs(w), Nubian(s), of Wawat, 4:4; producing amethyst?, 4:14; rebel hordes, 143:B.3.
rs, south, 148:4; hypothetical reading, 6:6; cf. *tp-rst*, *šmꜥw*.
Ḥꜣw-nbw, remote northerners, 14:12; 143:B.2.
Stỉ, Nubia, 4:4; (S.& N.), 4:5; of Horus, 143:10; 148:8; cf. *Wꜣwꜣt*, *Tꜣ-Stỉ*.
Sṯt, Asia, 143:B.2.
Šꜣw, Shau, Wadi Hudi?, 21:9-10.
Šmꜥw, Southland, 4:5,10; cf. *rs*.
Kꜣs, Kush, 8:6.
Tꜣ-Stỉ, Nubia, amethyst-source, 14:7; 143:13; natives of, 143:14; cf. 4:4; 148:8; cf. *Wꜣwꜣt*, *Stỉ*.
Tp-rst, 'Head of the South', admin. region; troops of, 6:14.
Gbtyw, Koptos, in title, 23:6.
Ḏdw, Busiris, title of Osiris, *nb Ḏdw*, 19:2; 20:4.

5. Titles of Personnel.

ỉmy-r[. . .], Supt. of [. . .], Si-Bastet, 149:12 (cf. 20:5?).
ỉmy-r ꜥ(ꜣ)w, caravan-leader, Intef (s. of Ptahshedwy), 1:3; 3:4; 4:17; 26:4(?); 37:1; -- *n nb.f*, of his lord, idem., 2:4; *n ỉmyw-rꜥw*, - - of caravan-leaders, idem, 4:7; Iku, 31:3; Iyemhotep, 88; Ka, 97:1; Mentuhotep, 146:7; Montemhat, 66:1; Senwosret-iaꜥu, 20:8; 50 unnamed, 6:13; *ḥsbw*, of workforce, Nebnufer, 53:4.

ỉmy-r ꜥb wḥm, šwt, nšmt, Supt. of horn, hoof, feather and scale, Hor, 143:12.
ỉmy-r ꜥḥꜥw, shipmaster, Si-Bastet, 20:5 (cf. 149:12?); Mentjebu, 21:10 (?); Reswi, 93:7.
ỉmy-r ꜥḫnwty, chamberlain, Ameny, 152; Intefoqer (s. of Senankh), 16:8-9; Henui, 51:3; Heqaib, 97:2; Tjeb-uy, 92; - - *n kꜣp,* of the palace, Senbeb, 24:6.
ỉmy-r wꜥrt n Gbtyw, District Supt. of Koptos, Bebiy, 23:B.6.
ỉmy-r pr, steward, Ptahshedwy & s. Intef, 1:5; 2:2; 3:2; Intef, 4:3,9; Intef (s. of Senwosret), 66:3-4; ꜥAwenti, 53:3; Hor, 143:12; Hotepu, 6:4, 12.
ỉmy-r pr wr, high steward, see *ỉdnw.*
ỉmy-r pr-ḳbḥwy, Supt. of waterfowl dept., Hor, 143:11.
ỉmy-r mnỉw ṯsmw, Supt. of dog-handlers, Nakht, 65:1.
ỉmy-r mnfꜣt, general of troops, Resuwy, 6:6; name lost, 148:4.
ỉmy-r ms-ꜥꜣt, chief prospector, 41 unnamed, 6:12.
ỉmy-r mšꜥ, commander of a force, Intefoqer (vizier), 8:3; Intunef-tepiru, 149:17; Nentji, 148:9.
ỉmy-r mḏḥ, chief carpenter, Renefankh-senut, 20:12.
ỉmy-r nỉwt, city governor, Intefoqer, (vizier), 8:4.
ỉmy-r nww, chief hunter, Kamose, 32:1.
ỉmy-r ḥwwt 6 wrt, Supt. of the Six Great Mansions, Intefoqer (vizier), 8:4.
ỉmy-r ḥmw-nṯr, Overseer of Prophets, Nakht-ankh, 29.
ỉmy-r ḫnrt ꜥḥ, Supt. of council-chamber (?) of palace, Hepu, 51:2.
ỉmy-r sꜣw, chief of contingents, Intef, 49:2; Ukh-hotep, 148:11; unnamed, 148:4; – *n ḥrtyw-nṯr,* of stonemasons, Sobkhotep (s. of Heqaib), 148:10.
ỉmy-r sšw, Supt. of wildfowl pools, Hor, 143:11.
ỉmy-r sḏꜣyt, Supt. of Treasury/Seal, Iku, 61:4; Si- . . , 19:4 (?); cf. *ḥry-ꜥ.*
ỉmy-r šnwty, Supt. of Double Granary, Hor, 143:11.
ỉmy-r kꜣt, chief of works, Intef, 7:4; unnamed, 148:8.
ỉmy-ḫt, follower, Dwa/Sba, 74.
ỉry-ꜥt n pr-ḥḏ, petty official of the treasury, Ankhu, 46:1.
ỉry-pꜥt, see *r-pꜥt.*
ỉdnw n ỉmy-r pr wr, Iunefer, 23:A.3, B.1.
ꜥꜣw, ꜥw, caravaneer, P . . tiu, 60:1.
ꜥfty, brewer, Nuby, 93:8.
ꜥnḫ-n-nỉwt, citizen, Waꜥti . ., 23:B.2.
ꜥnḫ-n-ḫn n ḥḳꜣ, crewman of the Ruler, Intef, 148:12.
ꜥnḫ n tt ḥḳꜣ, dependent of the Ruler's table, Hor, 63:1.
ꜥḥꜣ(wty), brave, warrior, Mimi, 84:1; 200 Elephantine, 100 Ombi, 6:10-11.
wꜥrtw, district officer, Ameny, 94:1; Didiu?, 23:A.5 (?); Sobekre, 23:A.3; cf. *ỉmy-r wꜥrtw n Gbtyw.*
wpwty, messenger, Kamose, 32:3.
wr n ḏꜣmw, chief of recruits, unnamed, 23:B.4.
wr šmꜥ mḏwt, chief of Southern Tens, Mentuhotep, 14:6, 19; Henenu, 144:2; 145:2; Isi, 148:3; Sobekre, 28:4.
wdpw, butler, Senbebu, 17:11; Sobkhotep, Kemaꜥni, 20:7.
mnỉw-ṯsmw, dog-handler, Nakht, 93:1; Nebꜥan, 93:2; Kai, 93:3; Didiu, 94:3; cf. *ỉmy-r mnỉw-ṯsmw.*
ms-ꜥꜣt, prospector, Ipi, 57:3; Kheperkare, 20:11; Si-Hathor, 13:10; 30 unnamed, 20:14; unnamed, 23:B.5; cf. *ỉmy-r ms-ꜥꜣt.*
nbt-pr, lady of the house, Benrit, 23:B.1; Sit-Sobk, Senbeb, 23:B.6; Didit-Anuqet, Senebtisi, 24:7, 8; Woser, 149:13; Khentihotep, 149:15.
r-pꜥt, hereditary prince, Hotep, 18:5.
rḫ-nsw, King's acquaintance, Senbebu-ankh, 23:B.5; Rehu-ankh, 24:5, 7.
rḫ-nsw mꜣꜥ, real King's acquaintance, Hetepheru, 12:3; plus *mry.f n st-ỉb.f,* beloved and favourite, Intefoqer, 16:4; Senbebu, 17:4; Hotep, 18:2; Si-Hathor, 21:3; Si-Bastet, 149:5.
ḥꜣty-ꜥ, count, Hotep, 18:5; Nakht-ankh, 29; Senwosret, 146:6; in plural, 60:1.
ḥr-ḥrww, supreme artisan, Woser, 13:7-8; Senwosret, 36.
ḥry-sštꜣ, chief of secrets, (vizier) Intefoqer, 8:4; Hetepheru, both, 12:3, 4; Thutwedjaꜥef, 59.
ḥry n tm, chief of the *tm,* Bebi, 23:B.2.
ḥḳꜣ ḥwt, ruler of a domain, Ameny, 94:1; Intef, 53:2; 54:1.
ḫrp(w), director/officer, Intef, 4:16; 56 (of Steward), 6:12-13.
ḫrp ḫt(?) nsw, director of royal property(?), Ankhu, 46:1.
ḫrp (n) kꜣt, director of works, 4:11; Didiu, 7:7 (?); 26:5 (?).
ḫtmw, seal-bearer, see *sḏwty.*
ḫry-ꜥ, assistant (to chief treasurer), Weni, 8:2; Si-Hathor, 21:6.
ḫry-ḥbt, lector, Intef, 48:1; 53:2; 54:1.
ḫry-ḥbt n Ptḥ, lector of Ptah, Se, 148:9.
ḫrty-nṯr, stonemason, Intef (?), 43/44; group of, 23:b.5; cf. *ỉmy-r sꜣw n . . .*
sꜣ-nsw, king's son, Sobkhotep, 23:A.2.
sꜣw, guardian, Heribsen, 58:4; Intef, 90A:1.
smr wꜥty, sole companion, Hor, 143:11.
sḥḏ-šmsw, inspector of retainers, Rehu-iry, 23:B.2.
sš, scribe, Intefꜥo, 38; Didi-Montu, 55; Meni, 56A.
sš or *sḏꜣwty?*, scribe/seal-bearer? (reading uncertain), Nakht, 65:1; Khentikhety, 75; Ha-ishtef, 144:4; (of *Mꜣꜥt*) Mentuhotep, 14:7; 14:18-19 (& of Ennead).
sš wr, chief scribe, Irynebef (?), 20:9; – of vizier, Bebi, 25:6.
sš n pr-ḥḏ, scribe of the treasury, Nebiot, 149:15.
sš n ḫnrt, scribe of harim/prison, Si-Sobk, 23:B.3.
sḏꜣwty, seal-bearer/treasurer, Intef, 4:3; Men-tjebu, 21:10; Pennu (?), 149:16(?); plus *kfꜣ-ỉb,* trusty, Senbebu, 17:5.
sḏꜣwty/sš, seal-bearer/scribe?, see above under *sš/sḏꜣwty.*
sḏꜣwty bỉty, Seal-bearer of King L. Eg., Irenre, 25:4; Ka, 97:1; Hor, 143:11.
sḏꜣwty n pr-ḥḏ, seal-bearer of treasury, Ankhu (?), 20:8.
sḏꜣwty-nṯr, seal-bearer of the god, Intef, 4:15.
sḏꜣwty ḫr-ꜥ (n) ỉmy-r sḏꜣyt, see above under *ḫry-ꜥ.*
šmsw, retainer, Resuwy, 6:6; Nesu-Montu, 9:9; 85; name lost, 26:3?; Nemti, 53:4; Inpu, 59; Iqeri, 62:1; Henui, 91:4; Ameny, 94:1; Sankh, 145:4.
šmsw n ꜥrryt (wr. *ꜥrdyt*), retainer of the judgement hall, Didiu-tjeni, 23:B.2.
ṯꜣw ꜥ-n-sš, obscure, plus 'holding the seal of Head-of-the-South', Sobkhotep, 23:B.3.
ṯꜣty, vizier, Intefoqer, 8:4; unnamed, ch. scribe of, 25:6.
ṯbw, sandalmaker, Hesi, 45; Mer . . . , 148:11.
ṯsw, commander, Senwosret, 30:1.
. . . *w,* ?, Mentu-woser, 90B:1.

6. Personal Names.

Iꜣmw, Iamu, 150:1.
Iỉ-m-ḥtp, Iyemhotep, caravan-leader, 88.
Iy (f.), Ay, 12:3.
Iꜥy, Iaꜥy, 34.
Iw-nfr, Iunefer, deputy of high steward, 23:A.3, B.1.
Ibỉ, Ibi, 48.
Ipỉ, Ipi, prospector, 57:3.
Imny, Ameny, fa. of Neni, 6:15; no title, 81:2; ruler of domain, etc., s. of Mentuhotep, 94:1; chamberlain, 152.
Imn-nḫt, Amennakht, s. of Mentuhotep & Sobkhotep, 96:1.
In-ỉt.f, Intef, s. of Ptahshedwy, caravan leader and steward, 1:3,4; 2:3; 3:3,4; 4:3 (seal-b.), 7, 9, 15 (god's seal-b.), 16 (*ḫrpw*), 17; 26:4; 37:1 (steward); Intef s. of Senwosret, steward, 66:4; fa. of Resuwy, s. of Rensi, 6:7; director of works, 7:4,8 (s. of Didiu); chief of S. tens, s. of Sobekre, 28:5; no title, 40:2; 71; stonemason, 43/44; lector, 48; plus etc., 53:2; 54:1; chief of contingents, 49:2; guardian, 90A; crewman of Ruler, s. & gs. of Sankh, 148:12.
In-ỉt.f-ỉḳr, Intefoqer, vizier, 8:5; chamberlain etc., 16:9; warrior (*In-ỉḳr*), 52:2; no title (*In-ỉḳr*) 57:1.
In-it.f-ꜥꜣ, Intefꜥo, scribe, 38.
In.ỉḳr, see *In-ỉt.f-ỉḳr,* end.
Inpw, Inpu, retainer, 59.
In.tw-n.f-tp.ỉrw, Intunef-tepiru, 'general', 149:17.
Ir (?)*-n-rꜥ,* Irenre (?) [OR: *Nb-n-rꜥ*?], seal-b.

of king of L. Eg., 25:5.
Iry-nb.f (?), Irynebef (?) [OR: *Sꜣw-nb.f*?], chamberlain & ch. scribe, 20:9.
Irr, Irer, 76.
Isỉ, Isi, no title, 20:6; chief of S. tens, 148:3.
Iḳw, Iqu, 52:3.
Iḳr, Iqer, 31:2.
Iḳrỉ, Iqeri, 62:1.
Iḳrw, Iqeru, s. Mentuhotep & Sobkemsaes, 99.
Ikw, Iku, caravan-leader & Supt. of seal, 61:4.
It, Ita, fa. of lector Intef, 53:2; 54:1.
Idỉ, Idi, fa. of Hetepi, gfa. of Nesu-Montu, 9:9; (f.), 47.
ʿwntỉ, ʿAwenti, steward, 53:3.
ʿnḫw, ʿAnkhu, seal-b. of treasury, 20:8; title illegible, 20:10; no title, s. of Hetepi (f.), 40:1; director of royal property & treasury official, s. of Hepy (f.), 46:2-3.
Wʿtỉ. . . , Waʿti. . ., 23:A.5, B.2.
Wn(ỉ), Weni, assistant treasurer, 8:2.
Wnn, Wenen, supr. artisan, s. of Senwosret, 10:7; 36.
Wḫ-ḥtp, Ukh-hotep, chief of contingents, 148:11.
Wsr, Woser, supr. artisan, 13:8; (f.), mo. of Si-Bastet, 149:13.
Bbỉ, Bebi, fa. of Henenu, gfa. of Mentuhotep, 14:7, 19; chief of *tm*, 23:B.2; ch. scribe of vizier, 25:6; no title, 56B; s. of Henenu, 63:3.
Bbỉy, Bebiy, Supt., District of Koptos, 23:B.6.
Bnrỉt, (f.), Benrit, mo. of Deputy Iunefer, 23:B.1.
Brt. . , Beret. . , 78:2.
Bšt, Beshet, Ombite, 93:5.
Ppỉ, Pepi, s. of Harhotep, 151.
Pnnw (?), Pennu (?), treasurer(?), 149:16.
P. . *tỉw*, Pe . . tiu, caravaneer, 60:2.
Ptḥ-šdwy, Ptah-shedwy (or, Shedwy-Ptah), fa. of Intef, 1:5; 2:2-3; 3:2.
Mỉmỉ, Mimi, warrior (of Thebes?), 84:1; no title, 64:1.
Mn, Meni, scribe, 56A.
Mnf (?), Menef (?), 77.
Mnṯw-wsr, Mentu-woser, s. of Iaʿy, 34; no title, 89; 90A:2; broken title, 90B.2.
Mnṯw-m-ḥꜣt, Montemhat, caravan-leader, s. of Mentuhotep, 66:1-2; no title, 79:1-2 (fa. of Kanefer?).
Mnṯw-ḥtp, Mentuhotep, s. of Henenu, gs. of Bebi, ch. of S. tens, etc., 14:7-8, 19; fa. of ch. S. tens Henenu, 145:2; fa. of prospector Kheperkare, 20:11; fa. of caravan-leader, Montemhat, 66:1; fa. of domain ruler, etc., Ameny, 94:1; fa. of Amennakht, 96:1; no title, 61:2; 81:1; 91:2; fa. of Iqeru, s. Keri, 99:1; caravan-leader, s. of count Senwosret, 146:7.
Mn-ṯbt (?), Men-tjebet (?), seal-b., ship (master?), 21:10.
Mr-ʿnḫ, Merankh, 94:2.
Mr(y)-Ḫnty, Merykhenty, 69.
Mrryt (f.), Mereryt, mo. of Si-Hathor, 21:7.
Mḥ-ỉb-Ḥr, Meh-ib-Hor, 83.
Nb-ỉt(.f), Nebiot(ef), treas.-scribe, s. of Khentihotep (f.), 149:15.
Nb-ʿ, Nebʿa, hypothetical rdg., 146:7.
Nb-ʿn, Nebʿan, a dog-handler, 93:2.
Nb-nfr, Nebnufer, caravan-leader of work-force, 53:4.
Nb-n-nỉwt, Nebenniut, 70.
Nb-n-rʿ, hypothetical rdg., see *Ir-n-rʿ* above (25:5).
Nb-n-. . , Neben . . , 78:1.
Nbwy, Nuby, brewer, 93:9.
Nfr-ḥr, Neferhor, 6:16.
Nmtỉ, Nemti, retainer, 53:4.
Nnỉ, Neni s. of Ameny, 6:15
Nnṯỉ, Nentji, 'general', 148:9.
Nḫt, Nakht, no title, 39; 67; 68; dog-handler, 93:1; ch. dog-handler, 65:1-2.
Nḫt-ʿnḫ, Nakht-ankh, Count, ch. of prophets, etc., 29.
Nsỉ-sw, Nesisu, s. of Idi (f.), 47.
Ns-sw-Mnṯw, Nesu-Montu, retainer, s. Hetepi, gs. Idi, 9:10; 85.
Rn.ỉ-ʿnḫ, Reni-ankh, fa. of Renef-ankh-senut, 20:12.
Rn-ỉḳr, Renoqer, 93:6.
Rn.f-ʿnḫ-snwt, Renef-ankh-senut, chief carpenter, 20:12.
Rnsỉ, Rensi, fa, Intef, gfa. Resuwy, 6:6.
Rḥw-ỉrỉ, Rehu-iry, retainer, 23:B.2.
Rḥw-ʿnḫ, Rehu-ankh, king's acquaintance, 24:5, 7.
Rsw, Resu, shipmaster, 93:7.
Rsw-wỉ, Resuwy, general, s. Intef, gs. Rensi, 6:7.
Hnwỉ, Henui, Supt. of audience-hall, 51:3.
Hr-ỉb.sn, Heribsen, guardian, 58:4-5.
Ḥꜣ-ỉšt.f, Ha-ishtef, scribe/seal-b., 144:4.
Ḥpy (f.), Hepy, mo. of treas. Ankhu, 46:3.
Ḥpw, Hepu, Supt. of palace council-chamber 51:2.
Ḥnnw, Henenu, s. of Bebi, fa. of Mentuhotep (ch. S. tens), 14:7, 19; ch. S. tens, 144:2; 145:2 (s. of Mentuhotep); retainer, 91:1, 3, 4; gfa. Senwosret, fa. Hetepi, 30:1; fa. of Bebi, 63:2; no title, 57:2; 82:1; 86; 87.
Ḥr, Hor, steward, etc., 143:12; dependent, ruler's table, 63:2.
Ḥr-ḥtp, Harhotep, fa. Pepi, 151.
Ḥsỉ, Hesi, sandalmaker, 45.
Ḥḳꜣ-ỉb, Heqaib, warrior, 52:2; chamberlain, 97:2; ch. of contingents of stonemasons, 148:10.
Ḥtp, Hotep, prince and count, 18:4.5; retainer, 49:1.
Ḥtpỉ, Hetepi, fa. Nesu-Montu, s. of Idi, 9:9; (f.) mo. of Ankhu, 40:1.
Ḥtpy, Hetepy, s. of Henenu, fa. of Senwosret, 30:2.
Ḥtpw, Hotepu, steward, 6:4, 13.
Ḥtp-nbw, Hotepnebu, 98.
Ḥtp-ḥrw, Hetepheru, ch. of secrets, fa. & s., 12:3, 4.
Ḫwyw, Khuyu, house-supt., 3:6.
Ḫpr-kꜣ-rʿ, Kheperkare, prospector, 20:11.
Ḫnty, Khenty, 72; 73.
Ḫntỉ-ḥtp, (f.), Khentihotep, mo. of treasurer Nebiot (ef), 149:16.
Ḫnty-ḫty, Khentikhety, scribe/seal-b., 75.
S, Se, lector of Ptah, 148:9.
Sꜣ-ỉpw, Sa-ipu, 35.
Sꜣ-Bꜣstt, Si-Bastet, shipmaster, 20:5; 149:12.
Sꜣ-Mwt, Simut, 64:2.
Sꜣ-Ḥwtḥr, Si-Hathor, prospector, 13:10; asst. treasurer, 21:7.
Sꜣ-Sbk, Si-Sobk, prison scribe, 23:B.3.
Sꜣ-. . . ,Si- . . . , Supt., 19:4.
Sꜣt-Rʿ, (f.), Sitre, mo. of Iqeri, 62:2.
Sꜣt-Sbk (f.), Sit-Sobk, 23:B.6.
Sꜣw-nb.f (?), Sau-nebef (?) [OR: Iry-nebef?] see *Irỉ-nb.f* above.
Sʿnḫ, Sankh, retainer, 145:4; fa. & gfa. Intef, ruler's crewman, 148:12.
Sbꜣ, Sba, [OR: *Dwꜣ*], follower, 74.
Sbk, Sobek, s. of Keti, 11:3.
Sbk-m-sꜣ.s, (f.), Sobk-em-saes, mo. of Iqeru, 99:2.
Sbk-rʿ, Sobekre, fa. Senbebu & Senwosret, 17:5, 10; fa. of Deputy Iunefer, 23:A.3; fa. ch. S. tens, Intef, 28:4.
Sbk-ḥtp, Sobkhotep, King's Son, 23:A.2; butler, 20:7; *ṯꜣw-ʿ-n-sš*, etc., 23:B.3; commander, contingents of stonemasons, 148:10; (f.), mo. of Amennakht, 96:1.
Sn-ʿnḫ, Senankh, 16:9.
S-n-wsrt, Senwosret, commander, 30:3; supr. artisan, 36; fa. steward Intef, 66:3; count, 146:6; no title, son of Wenen, 10:7; s. of Sobekre, 17:10.
Snwsrt-ỉʿw, Senwosret-ia'u, caravan-leader, 20:8-9.
Snb (f.), Sonb, Lady of House, 23:B.6.
Snbb, Senbeb, palace-chamberlain, 24:6.
Snbbw, Senbebu, treasurer, 17:5, 7, 9; butler, 17:11.
Snbbw-ʿnḫ, Senbebuankh, King's acquaintance, 23:B.6.
Snbtỉsỉ, (f.), Senebtisi, lady of house, 24:8.
Snt (f.), Senet, mo. of Hetepheru, 12:4.
Ššmw-ỉỉ, Shesmu-iy, 148:11.
Šd-ỉt.f-ʿnḫ, Shediotefankh, 27:3.
Šd.wy-ʿnḫ, Shedwy-ankh, 80.
Kꜣ, Ka, seal-b., King L. Eg., etc., 97:1.
Kꜣỉ, Kai, dog-handler, 93:4.
Kꜣpw, Kapu, 20:11.
Kꜣ-ms, Kamose, ch. hunter, messenger, 32:1-3.
Kꜣ-nfr, Kanefer, 79:2.
Kꜣ-hr(yt), Kaherit, 33.
Kmʿ, (f.), Kama, mo. of count Nakht-ankh, 29.
Kmʿ.n.ỉ, Kema'ni, butler, 20:7.
Krỉ, Keri, fa. Mentuhotep, gfa. of Iqeri, 99.
Ktỉ, Keti, fa. of Sobek, 11:3.
Twtw, Tutu, 82:2.
Ṯbwy (?), Tjebuy (?), chamberlain, 92.
Dwꜣ (?), Dwa (?) [OR: *Sbꜣ*], 74.
Ddw, Didiu, fa. Intef, 7:8; director of works, 26:5; dog-handler, 94:4.
Dd(w)-Mn(ṯ)w, Didi-Montu, scribe, 55.
Ddw-ṯnỉ, Didiu-tjeni, retainer of judgement hall, etc., 23:A.5, B.2.
Ddt-ʿnḳt, (f.), Didit-Anuquet, lady of house,

24:7.
Ḏḥwty-wḏꜥ.f, Thut-wedja'ef, ch. of secrets, 59.
. . . . *yt*, . . . yt, fa. of Shesmy-iy, 148:11.

7. General Vocabulary.

ꜣt, striking-power, 143:4.
ꜣw-ꜥ, gifts, 51:1.
ꜣbỉ, to brand, 143:3?
ꜣbd, month, (4th Akhet) 20:1; (4th Peret) 149:1.
ꜣpdw, fowl, 17:8; 19:3; 20:5; 27:3.
ꜣḫt, Akhet, 'Season of Inundation', 20:1.
ꜣḳ, to perish, 143:5.
ꜣṯp, to load, 143:14.

.ỉ, my, 14:8 (wr. as stroke).
ỉꜣš, to summon/summons, 16:6.
ỉꜣt, official post, 18:4.
ỉỉ, to come, for amethyst, 3:3; 46:1; 61:4; 148:2; 149:14; (general) 4:5 (?); 14:11 (?); to return home, 148:10.
ỉw, to be, as auxiliary, 14:8; 148:8 (?).
ỉw, to come, 4:11; 8:2 (?); 21:3 (?) - or *šms*?; for amethyst, 58:1; to return, 4:1, 13.
ỉwn, character, 14:18 (twice?).
Iwntyw, (Nubian) tribesfolk, 143:1; 143:15 (singular).
ỉwty, be without, 4:6.
ỉb, heart, mind, 3:6; 148:5; *wꜣḥ-ỉb*, patient, 17:4; *mḥ-ỉb*, confidant, 4:10; 149:10; *kfꜣ-ỉb*, trusty/discreet, 17:5; for *n st-ỉb.f*, favourite, see under *st-ỉb*.
ỉm, therefrom, 8:7; 14:9; 143:14; whereon, 19:3-4.
ỉmꜣ, to show favour, 143:7.
ỉmꜣḫ, veneration, reverence, in epithet *nb-ỉmꜣḫ*, possessing veneration, 2:6 (?); 16:9; 17:5, 7, 9, 10; 20:6, 9; 23:B.3; 25:5; 148:3,10,12; 149:16,17; *nbt-ỉmꜣḫ*, 149:13.
ỉmꜣḫy, revered one, 2:6?; 17:8; 19:4 (?); 28:4; 40:1,2; 48:1; 61:1,3; 99.
ỉmy(w), whatis/are in . . , 143:9; f. *ỉmyt*, 14:13; 143:6, 8; *ỉmyw-Sṯt*, Asiatic people, 143:B.2.
ỉmy-r. . , see Index 5, Titles.
ỉmnt, hidden products, 143:5.
ỉn, of agent, 'it is . . . who', 3:2; 14:11.
ỉn, by, 14:17; 58:1; 148:8.
ỉnỉ, obtain/fetch/bring (amethyst), 3:3; 4:14; 6:5; 7:[5]; 8:6; 14:8; 46:2; 66:2; 149:14; in quantity, 8:7; 14:10; 143:14; desired, 37; (general) 143:9; *ỉnỉ ḏrw*, make an end of (foes), 143:B.2.
ỉnw, emissaries, 143:8.
ỉnt, wadi, title of goddess (*nbt-ỉnt*), 2:6; 4:9? (if not *nbt n smt*).
ỉnr, lump, block, (of amethyst), 14:10.
ỉnk, I, 84:2 (unusual spelling).
ỉr, as for . . , 11:3; 148:5.
ỉrỉ, to do/make/perform, in *ỉrr ḥsst nbt*, etc., see under *ḥsỉ*; do, 2:5 (king's command); 4:6, 8 (wrong); 22:5 (right); 4:7 (jobs); 14:10, 17 (achieve); 143:8, 13 (wishes); make, 4:17 (text); 11:3 (stela); 17:6 (character); 148:5 (search?); act, 143:15; 148:6; become (?), 2:6 (?).
ỉrỉ, to beget, in *ỉr.n*, begotten by, 16:9; 17:5, 10; 20:6, 9, 11 (*ỉr* omitted), 12; 21:7; 23:A.3, 5, B.2, 3.
ỉrỉ, to bear, in *ỉr.n* born of (a woman), 23:B.1; 149:13.
ỉrt, eye, 143:9; in dual, 143:8.
ỉry-ꜥt, petty official, 46:1; Index 5.
ỉry-ṯsmw, see *mnỉw-ṯsmw*, Index 5.
ỉsft, wrong, falsehood, in *šw m* (*ỉrt*) *ỉsft*, 2:5; 4:6, 8.
ỉḳr, excellent (of speech, *st-ns*), 149:7.
ỉty, Sovereign, 143:B.2.
ỉtn, sun's disc, 143:9.
ỉṯḥ, to drag, 143:14.
ỉdnw, deputy, see Index 5.

ꜥ, document?, in obscure title, *ṯꜣw ꜥ-n-sš*, 23:B.3.
ꜥ, in *wḥm-ꜥ*, again, 4:3; 14:17.
ꜥ, obscure, 23:B.5.
ꜥt, department, in *ỉry-ꜥt*, 46:1.
ꜥꜣmw, Asiatic, 31:1, 3; 17:11 (butler).
ꜥꜣt, precious stone, 23:B.5; in titles, *ms-ꜥꜣt*, see Index 5.
ꜥꜣt, greatly in phrase *r-ꜥꜣt-wrt*, very greatly, 8:7; 14:10; 143:14; amount (of amethyst), 148:7; in phrase *n-ꜥꜣt-n*, so greatly, 148:3.
ꜥ(ꜣ)w, caravaneer, see Index 5.
ꜥb, horn, in title *ỉmy-r ꜥb* etc., see Index 5.
ꜥn, beautiful, 143:13.
ꜥnḫ, life, 143:6 (breath of life); to live, 19:3 (of gods); 143:B.1; 146:2 (of king); *ꜥnḫ-mswt* (Sobk-hotep IV), 22:5; in oath, 28:3 –, in royal cliches, *ꜥnḫ ḏt*, may he live forever, 4:2; 9:3; 12:2; 14:4, 16; 18:1; 19:2; 147:2; 149:4; in *ꜥnḫ ḏt r nḥḥ*, 6:3; 10:6; 16:2; 17:2; 20:2; 21:2; 22:3; 23:A.1; 24:3; 25:2; 95:1-2; in *ꜥnḫ mỉ Rꜥ ḏt*, 7:3; 11:2; 13:5; 146:4; in *dỉ ꜥnḫ mỉ Rꜥḏt*, 143:A.3; in *dỉ ꜥnḫ ḏd wꜣs*, 22:4; in *dỉ ꜥnḫ ḏd wꜣs mỉ Rꜥ ḏt*, 15:2; 143:10; in tag *ꜥnḫ, wḏꜣ, snb*, Life, Prosperity, Health (L.P.H.), of king, 6:4, 5; 14:8; 23:B.1; of prince, 23:A.2; of commoners, 8:5; 30:3; 63:2; 94:1; 96:2; 144:2; 145:2; in *wḥm-ꜥnḫ*, see under *wḥm*.
ꜥrf, to hem in, 143:B.2.
ꜥrryt, judgement-hall, in title, 23.B.2.
ꜥrdyt, error for *ꜥrryt*, see above.
ꜥḥ, palace, in title, 51:2.
ꜥḥꜣ(wty), brave, warrior, 6:10, 11; 52:2 (twice).
ꜥḥꜥw, ships, see *ỉmy-r* . . , Index 5.
ꜥẖnwty, palace-chambers, see *ỉmy-r*. . . , Index 5.
ꜥšꜣ, to abound, 143:7.
ꜥḳw, provisions, 27:1.
wꜣt, way, road, 4:12 (?); in *mḏd wꜣt nt smnḫ sw*, 9:7; 18:3; 21:5.
wꜣḥ-ỉb, patient, 16:5.
wꜣs, dominion, in cliches, 15:2; 22:4; 143:10.
wỉ, me, 8:5, 8; 14:8; 143:12.
wꜥ, unique one, 14:18.
wꜥb, pure, fingers, 17:11; offerings, 19:3.
wꜥrt, district/department, Head of South, 6:14; 23:B.3; – of Koptos, 23:B.6.
wꜥty, see Index 5 (*smr wꜥty*).
wbꜣ, to open, 3:5 (of hearts).
wpwt, (official) mission, 3:4.
wpwty, messenger, 32:3; hypothetical readings, 2:4; 4:16.
wnn, to be, 4:10; 148:4; enduring, 14:14; 143:15.
wnt, fault, 4:6.
wnf, be elated, 4:12.
wnš, sledge, 143:14.
wr, great, 4:6; 22:5; 143:B.5; in titles, see Index 5 (*wr n ḏꜣmw, wr šmꜥ mḏwt, sš wr, ỉmy-r ḥwwt 6 wrt, ỉdnw ỉmy-r pr wr*).
wrt, greatly, see above, under *ꜥꜣt*.
wḥꜣ; to hew out (lumps of stone), 14:10.
wḥm(t), hoof, in title *ỉmy-r ꜥb, wḥm*, etc., see Index 5.
wḥm-ꜥ, again, 4:3; 14:7.
wḥm-ꜥnḫ, repeating life, epithet, 23:A.3 (twice), 5, B.1, B.2 (twice), B.3 (twice); 24:5, 6; 46:3; 81:2.
wsrt, throat, 143:2.
wsḫ, broad, of bounds, 143:3.
wḏ, to command, by king, 2:5; 23:B.1; 143:12; 148:3; by gods, 143:6.
wḏ, a command, of king, 21:9; of gods, 14:13; a stela, 11:3.
wḏꜣ, prosperity, see under *ꜥnḫ* . . .

bꜣw, power, might, 14:11; 143:15.
bꜣḥ: *m-bꜣḥ*, before, 28:3.
bꜣk, servitor, in phrase, *bꜣk.f mꜣꜥ n st-ỉb.f*, 1:4; 6:4; 7:6; 9:4; 13:9; 14:5; 26:3; 66:3-4; 143:11; 144:3; 145:3; 146:5; 147:3; in *bꜣk mry nb.f*, 14:17; in *bꜣk mḏd wꜣt nt smnḫ sw*, 18:3; **bꜣk**, 8:8; 10:7.
bꜣk, to work (for), 14:13.
bꜣkt, impost/wages?, 143:15.
bỉꜣt, wonder/marvel, 148:7 (?).
bỉty, King (of Lower Egypt), 143:15; in title *sḏꜣwty-bỉty*, Index 5.
bnrt, sweetness, 143:6 (*wr-bnrỉt*).
bṯn, to defy, 143:5.

pw, is, 27:1; 148:6.
pn, this, 3:4; 4:1, 10; 11:3; 27:1; 61:4; 143:12, 13, 15; 148:3, 8.
pr, house(hold), 3:5; 4:7; in titles, *ỉmy-r pr, nbt-pr*, cf. Index 5.
pr-ḥḏ, treasury, in titles, 20:8; 46:1; 149:15.
pr-ḳbḥwy, dept. of waterfowl, in title, 143:11.
prỉ, to go out, (for amethyst, etc.), 4:1, 3; 6:5; 7:4; 10:2; 27:2; to desert, 21:9; 23:B.4; 144:1; to survey it, 21:8.
prt, Peret, 'Winter Season', 149:1.
prt-ḫrw, invocation-offerings, 19:3; 20:4.

psḏt, Ennead, 14:18-19.
pḏ, wide, 143:B.3.
pḏt, troops, archers, 6:13.

.f, he, his, him, passim.

m, of equivalence, 4:11, 14 (?); 148:7.
m, by, 14:13.
m, in, 4:6; 11:3; 14:12, 18; 143:8, 13; 148:4. 5.
m, during/throughout (*m ẖrt-hrw*), 8:4; 9:6; 14:6; 21:4; 58:3; 144:4; 145:3; 147:3;
m, with/on, 4:1 (?); on, 3:4; 4:12.
m, from, 143:9 (twice); 14:12; (*šw m*, free from), 2:5; 4:6, 8.
m with Infinitive, 10:10; 4:13; etc., 148:2 end. See also *bꜣḥ, ḥꜣt, ḫt*.
mꜣꜣ , look, see, 14:17.
mꜣt, new/fresh, 14:9.
mꜣʿ, to proceed, 23:B.3; to send, 143:12; to produce, 143:6.
mꜣʿ, true, in phrase *bꜣk.f mꜣʿ n st-ỉb.f*, see *bꜣk*; in epithet *rḫ-nsw mꜣʿ*, see Index 5.
mꜣʿ(w), truly, in *mry nb.f mꜣʿ(w)*, 4:10; 58:2.
mꜣʿt, truth/right/Maet, 14:7, 18 (in title); 22:5 (*ỉrw-mꜣʿt*); 28:4 (in truth); 4:6 (hypothetical reading).
mꜣʿ-ḫrw, justified, epithet, 3:6; 7:9; 9:10; 23:B.1, 2, 6; 28:5; 40:2; 43/44; 47; 48; 61:2 (?); 82:2; 93:5 (?).
mỉ, like, 4:12; 143:14, 15; in cliché, like Re, 3:1; see under *ʿnḫ*; *mỉ-ḳd*, entirely, 4:13?
mỉtw(w), equal(s), 28:2.
mn, to abide, endure, 14:14; 143:15; *mn-ṯbt*, firm of tread, 16:4; 21:5.
mnỉw, keeper, see Index 5.
mnw, quartz, 23:B.4; *ḥḏ, km*, white, 23:B.4.
mnfꜣt, troops, see Index 5 (*ỉmy-r* . .).
mnf(ꜣ)t(y), warrior, 4:10.
mnḫ, effective, 14:18; 16:5; 149:8.
mnḫw, effectiveness, 14:11; 143:15.
mnḫt, linen, 17:8.
mrỉ: *mry*, beloved, of gods, 2:6; 16:3; 17:3; 20:3; 22:4, 5 (?); 143:A.4; of King (in title), 12:3; 16:4; 17:4; 18:2; 21:3; 149:5; cf. 148:3; *mry nb.f*, 4:9; 14:17; 37; 49:2; 58:2; 148:8; of city, 84:3; *mrrw*, 143:10; *mrỉ*, desire, 143:8, 13.
mrwt: *n-mrwt*, for sake of, 4:5; so that, 8:6, 7.
mḥ-ỉb, confidant, 4:10; 17:6; 149:10.
msỉ, to bear; *ms*, born (of), 12:3, 4; 62:2; 96:1; *ms.n*, ditto, 8:9; 24:8; 29; 40:1; 46:1; 47; 48; 99:2; 149:15; see Index 5 (*ms-ʿꜣt*).
mswt, birth, in *ʿnḫ-mswt*, 22:5, and Index 2.
mšʿ, expedition, 4:10, 13; 6:4; 20:6; 23:B.5; army in *ỉmy-r mšʿ*, 8:3.
mty, reliable, *mty-ḥꜣt*, 149:7-8.
mdw, to speak, 4:8; 148:2,5 (?).
mḏwt, tens, Index 5 (*wr šmʿ mḏwt*).
mḏd, to stick (to), in *mḏd wꜣt nt smnḫ sw*, 9:7; 18:3; 21:5.

n, of, passim; *nt*, ditto, passim; *nw*, plural, of, 6:5; 14:10.
n, for, 10:3; 27:3; 28:3 (in oath); 60:1; 61:1. 3; 143:6, 7, 9; of time, 14:14; to, 3:6; 143:B.4, 5, 6. (twice).
n, because (of), 4:8; 6:5; 61:4; 143:B.5; on behalf of, 148:2.
n-mrwt, see *mrwt*.
n-ḥr, before, 4:7.
n . . . -ỉm, to . . belongs, 143:9.
n, not, 14:9.
nỉwt, city, 84:1; in titles, 8:4; 23:B.2; *nỉwt rst*, Thebes, 6:9.
nww, hunters, in title, 32:2.
nb, possessor, 16:6; *nb-ỉmꜣḫ*, see *ỉmꜣḫ*; *nb-tꜣwy*, 7:2, 14:16; 149:3; *nb-nswt-tꜣwy* (Amun), 14:14; *nb-ḳbḥw* (Khnum), 20:3; *nb-Ḏdw* (Osiris), 19:2; 20:4;
nb, lord/master, 2:4; 3:5; 4:6; 7:9; 8:8; 9:7; 14:17; 17:6; 18:3, 4; 37; 49:1, 2; 51:2; 58:2; 60:2; 148:8; 149:6; lord, L.P.H. (king), 6:5 (twice); 14:8; cf. 46:2 (falcon); 143:4, 12.
nbt, possessor (f.), lady; *nbt-pr*, see Index 5; *nbt-ỉmꜣḫ*, see *ỉmꜣḫ*; *nbt n smt* (?), 4:9; other *nbt*-titles, goddesses, see Index 1; *nbt n nṯrw nbw*, 148:8; *Nbt*, Lady, 143:10; – of Forms, 143:9.
Nbty, (patron of) Two Goddesses, royal title, 13:3; 14:2, 15; 22:2; 143:B.1; 146:2; 147:2.
nbw, coastlands, 143:8.
nb, every, 4:4, 10; 19:3; 143:9, 15; *nbt*, every, 143:7; see also under *ḥsỉ*; *nb*, all, plural, 6:5; 14:12; 143:8; 148:8; *nbt*, all, 6:9; 18:3 (?); cf. *ḥsỉ*.
nbw, gold, 16:7.
nbwy, Ombite, 93:5.
nfr, good, 19:3; well, 4:13 (?); cf. *nṯr nfr*.
nfrw, beauty, 143:B.4.
nfrw, recruits, 6:8.
nmtwt, goings, in *šms nb.f r nmtwt.f*, 9:6-7; 18:3 (?); in *hr-nmtwt*, 16:5; 21:5; in *pḏ-nmtt*, 143:B.3.
nḥḥ, forever, *r-nḥḥ ḏt*, 146:8-9; in *ʿnḫ ḏt r nḥḥ*, etc., see *ʿnḫ*.
nḥsy(w), Nubian(s), see Index 4.
nḫb, to open (mines), 148:[6]-7.
nḫt, strong, 6:8.
ns, tongue, in *st-ns*, speech, 149:7.
nst, throne, in *nb-nswt-tꜣwy*, 14:14.
nsw, king, 22:5; 148:2; 149:10; 17:6; in formula *ḥtp-dỉ-nsw*, 19:2; 20:4; 24:3; 25:3; 48; 61:1, 3; in titles, see Index 5 (*rḫ-nsw, sꜣ-nsw, ḫrp-ḥt-nsw*).
nsw-bỉt, King of Upper & Lower Egypt, 1:1; 3:1; 4:2; 5:1; 7:1; 10:5; 11:2; 12:2; 13:4; 14:3, 16; 15:2; 16:2; 17:2; 18:1; 19:1; 20:2; 21:2; 24:1; 26:1; 143:B.1, 10; 147:2; 148:1; inside cartouche, 6:2.
nšmt, fish-scale(s), in title, 143:12.
nšmt, green felspar, 23:B.4.
nty, who, which, 11:3; 20:6.
nṯr, god, 19:3; (plural), 148:8; (the king), 143:12, 15; *nṯr nfr*, the good god (king), 7:2; 9:3; 10:4; 14:16; 143:B.1; 149:2. See Index 5 (*ḫrtyw-nṯr; sḏꜣwty-nṯr*).
nḏ, to protect, 22:5.

r, to (of place, after *prỉ*), 21:9; 23:B.3 (1st); 144:1; on (road), 4:11; at (time, occasion), *r-nmtwt.f*, 9:7; 18:3 (?); *ḏt r nḥḥ*, see under *ʿnḫ*.
r, for (amethyst, after *prỉ*), 4:3; 10:2; 27:2; after *ỉw*, 58:1; after *ỉỉ*, 148:2; *šms r*, seek for amethyst, 12:1; 14:17; etc., 16:8.
r, in order to (fetch . .),6:5; 8:5; 14:8; 23:B.3 (2nd); 46:2; 149:14; to survey, 21:8
r, adverbial uses, *r ʿꜣt wrt*, see *ʿꜣt*, *r-ḫrw*, freely (of speech), 4:8; *r-ḏr*., entire(ly), 4:13(?); 84:2.
r-šꜣʿ-r, as far as, 4:4.
r-20, 1/20th (part), 27:1.
r, door (of granary), 143:14.
rỉt, obscure (architectural term?), 41.
rʿ, day, in *rʿ nb*, daily, 4:10; 18:3 (?); see under *ḥsỉ* ; for Re, see Index 1.
rmṯ, men, 4:12.
rnpt, year, 4:13? (hypothetical reading).
rḫ, to know; knowledgeable man, 4:7; for *rḫ-nsw*, see Index 5.
rḫt, list, of expeditionaries, 6:4; 20:6; 23:B.4.
rḫyt, the people, 149:9-10.
rst, southern, of city, Thebes, 6:9.
rswt, rebel hordes, 143:B.2.
rdỉ, to give, yield, 14:13; 19:3; 20:4; 143:6, 7.
- - -, to place, set, 14:18; in *dy m ḫt*, put in someone's charge, 143:13; in *ḥtp dỉ nsw*, see *nsw; dỉ ʿnḫ*, see *ʿnḫ*.

hꜣỉ, to return, 11:3; *hꜣỉ ḥr*, to fall behind (others' production), 14:9-10.
hꜣb, to send, 8:5; 14:8.
hbhb, to traverse, explore, 17:6; 66:2; 149:11.
hr, easy (of gait, *nmtwt*), 16:5; 21:5.
hrw, day, 16:6; *hrw, ẖrt-hrw*, see also under *ḥsỉ*.

ḥꜣt(w), chief(s), 18:4 (?).
ḥꜣt(y), heart/thoughts, 4:12; 149:8.
ḥꜣt: *m-ḥꜣt*, before, 149:9.
ḥꜣt-sp, regnal year; for occurences, see Index 3, with years of kings.
Ḥꜣw-nbw, distant northerners, 14:12; 143:B.2.
ḥwt, mansion, domain, see Index 5 (*ỉmy-r ḥwwt 6 wrt; ḥḳꜣ ḥwt*).
ḥwt(wt), mine(s), 14:9.
ḥwtyw, messengers, 143:8.
ḥm, servant, 143:15; cf. Index 5 (*ỉmy-r ḥmw-nṯr*).
ḥm, majesty (of), 9:2; 12:2; 14:1, 15; 16:1; 17:1; 19:1; 20:2; 21:1; 24:1; 143:12; *ḥm.f*, His Majesty, 2:5; 8:8; 21:9; 21:9; 23:B.1; 27:2; 143:B.5; 148:2, 3, 7.
ḥmꜣgt, garnet, 23:B.4.
ḥmwt, green stone, 23:B.4.
ḥmwt: *st-ḥmwt*, workshop, 16:8.

ḥmt, wife, 8:9; 24:7.
ḥn, to charge (with a task), 8:8.
ḥnt, business, 4:13.
ḥnꜥ, (together) with, 4:5; 20:6; 148:2; 149:14; and, 16:7.
ḥnḳt, beer, 17:8; 19:3; 20:5; 27:3.
ḥnk, to make offering, 143:7.
Ḥr, the Horus, royal title, 7:1; 9:2; 10:4; 13:2; 14:1, 15; 22:2; 143:A.1, B.1; 146:2; 14/:2; 148:1.
Ḥr-nbw, the Golden Horus (ditto), 14:2.
ḥr, face, 4:12 (nḏm/ỉmȝ ḥr).
ḥr, on, 143:14; at, 4:8; because of, 148:7; holding, 23:B.3; behind (in ḥȝỉ ḥr), 14: 9-10; with Infinitive, 4:10; 14:11; 143: 7, 8; 148:5.
ḥr-sȝ, next to, 148:8.
n-ḥr, before, 4:7.
ḥry-ỉb, residing in, 14:13.
ḥry n tm, title, 23:B.2.
ḥry-tp, chief (over household), 3:5.
ḥry-tp-tȝwy, ruling the Two Lands (of king), 143:12.
ḥsỉ, to praise/favour, 2:4; ḥsy, favourite, 3: 6; 11:3; ḥsw, protégé, 8:2; one praised, 84:2. Idiom, who does what his lord praises (OR: what is praised), during every day: variants are:
(1) ỉr ḥsst, who does what is praised, 2: 5.
(2) ỉr(r) ḥsst.f nbt, 1:5; 7:7; 13:7; 146:6;
(3) ỉr ḥs.f n rꜥ nb, 4:10;
(4) ỉr(r) ḥsst.f nbt rꜥ nb, 18:2; 146:8-9 (adding r-nḥḥ);
(5) ỉr(r) ḥst nb.f rꜥnb, 149:6;
(6) ỉrr ḥst nbt m hrt-hrw, rꜥ nb, 58:2;
(7) ỉr(r) ḥsst.f nbt ḫrt-hrw nt rꜥ nb, 8:3-4; 9:5-6; 14:5-6; 21:4; 144:3; 145:3; 147:3.
ḥsbw, workforce, in title, 53:4.
ḥsmn, amethyst, 50; lumps, 14:10-11; desert of, 21:8; amount, 148:7; bring (ỉnỉ), 66:2-3; ỉỉ r ỉnt, coming to obtain, 3:3; 6:5; 8:6; 14:9; 23:B.3; 46: 2; 149:14; prỉ r, go for, 4:4; 10:2; 27: 2; ỉỉ r, come for, 148:2; ỉỉ n, 61:4; ỉw r, 58:1; šms r, seek for, 12:1; 14: 17; return, etc. m ḥsmn, 4:1, 14; 143: 13; Hathor, lady of ḥsmn, 16:3; 17:3; 20:3; 22:4, 5; 24:4; 25:3.
ḥḳȝ, ruler, in titles, 63:1; 148:12.
ḥtp, offering (table), 42;`100; m ḥtp, in peace/safely, 11:3; ḥtp dỉ nsw, see under nsw,
ḥtt, mine, 148:7.
ḥḏ, white, quartz, 23:B.4; silver, 16:7 (cf. pr-ḥḏ).
ḥḏt, white crown, 22:6.

ḫt, thing(s), 4:7; ḫt nbt, all things (offerings), 19:3; ḫt-nsw?, royal property?, 46:1.
ḫȝ, thousand, 6:9; 17:8; 20:4; ranks, 4: 11 (twice); obscure, 148:9?
ḫȝỉ, to survey, 21:8.
ḫȝst, desert, 23:B.4; 143:13; 144:1; of amethyst, 21:8; 23:B.3; of Shau, 21:9; (plural), 14:13; 17:6; 66:2; 143:B.4, 7; 149:1.
ḫȝstyw, foreigners, 14:12.
ḫprw, forms, 143:9.
ḫpsw, able-bodied men, 6:9.
ḫft, (royal) presence, 14:18;
ḫft, according to, 21:9.
ḫftyw, foes, 143:B.4.
ḫnrt, harim/prison, in titles, 23:B.3; 51:2.
ḫnt, before, 18:4.
ḫnt(w), forward (adverb), 14:17.
ḫnt(y)t, presiding, 20:3; 143:10.
ḫr, for/by, 51:1; under (king), 7:1; 9:2; 14:1, 15; 16:1; 17:1; 19:1; 20:1; 21: 1; 24:1; 26:1.
ḫr(t), necessities, 4:5.
ḫr, to fall, 14:12; 143:B.4.
ḫrw, voice, in r-ḫrw, freely (of speech), 4:8; see also prt-ḫrw, mȝ-ḫrw.
ḫrp, see Index 5.
ḫt: m-ḫt, after, 148:10; (m)-ḫt, 4:11.
ḫt: rdỉ m ḫt, put in charge of, 143:13.
ḫtm, to seal, 16:7; seal, 23:B.3.

ẖȝkt-ỉb, disaffection, 143:B.3.
ẖn(yt), crew, in title, 148:12.
ẖnw, Residence, 4:12; 6:12.
ẖry-ꜥ, assistant, 8:2; 21:6.
ẖry-ḥbt, see Index 5.
ẖrt(-hrw), during (day), see ḥsỉ.
ẖrtyw-nṯr, stonemasons, 23:B.5; 148:10 (in title).

.s, she, her, 143:A.5.
.sn, they,their, 148:4; written as .s(n)?, 4:6.
s, man, member, 3:5; 200, 100, 61 men, 6:10, 11, 14.
st, place: st-nbt, everywhere, 143:7; st-ḥmwt, workshop, 16:8.
st, state: st-ns, speech, 149:7; st-ỉb, favourite, see bȝk.
sȝ, son, 1:6; 3:2; 6:7 (twice), 15; 7:8; 9: 9; 10:7; 11:3; 12:4; 14:7 (twice), 19 (twice); 28:5; 30:1, 2; 34; 36; 53:2; 59; 63:3; 66:1, 3; 72; 94:1; 96:1; 99: 1 (twice); 145:2; 146:7; 148:10, 11, 12 (twice).
sȝ-nsw, king's son, 23:A.2.
sȝ Rꜥ, Son of Re, king's title, 5:2; 10:4, 5-6; 11:2; 12:2; 14:3, 14; 15:2; 22: 3; 24:2; 28:3; 143:A.2, B.1; 146:3; 148:1.
sȝ(w), contingent(s), in titles, 49:2; 148: 4, 10, 11.
sȝ: m-sȝ, following, 4:13; ḥr-sȝ, next to, 148:8.
sȝw, guardian, 16:7.
sȝw ṯsmw, see mnỉw-ṯsmw, Index 5.
sꜥḥ, noble, 149:8.
sꜥḳ, to present, 8:8.
sw, he, him, himself, it, 4:8; 9:8; 11:3; 18:3; 21:6; 143:6 (twice), 13; 148:3, 8.
sw, day (in dates), 20:1 (Day 24).
sbỉ, to send, 23:B.1.
sbỉw, rebels, 143:B.4.
sp, occasion, 14:18; sp 4, 4 times, 23:A.4.
spḥ, to lasso, 143:B.5.
smt, desert, 4:9 (?); pl., 143:8.
smȝ, to unite, join, 4:8; 143:B.4.
smnḫ, to advance (trans.), 9:8; 18:3.
smr (wꜥty), companion, 143:11.
sn, brother, 17:10.
sn, to slit (throats), 143:B.2.
snb, health, in ꜥnḫ-wḏȝ-snb, see ꜥnḫ.
snḫt, make strong, 14:11 (hypothetical reading).
snḏw, fearful, 143:B.4.
sr, dignatary, official, 148:2, 3; 149:9.
srs, to keep vigilant, 14:11.
sḥ, council, 4:8.
sḥtp, to please, 8:8 (hypothetical reading).
sḫnn, to collect, 143:14.
sḫnt, to promote, 18:4.
sḫr, plan, 4:9.
sḫr, to overthrow, 31:1.
sš, scribe, see Index 5; writing(s) in obscure title, 23:B.3.
sšw, wildfowl pools, in title, 143:11.
skỉ, to lop (heads), 143:B.3.
stp-sȝ, palace, 148:2.
sṯȝt, pallet, 143:14.
sḏḫ, to conceal, 143:7.
sḏȝyt, seal/treasury, see Index 5 (ỉmy-r. .).
sḏȝwty (bỉty), treasurer/seal-bearer, etc., see Index 5.

šȝ, to order, 14:9.
šȝ ꜥ, in r-šȝꜥ-r, as far as, 4:4.
šꜥt, onset, 14:12; 143:B.4, 5.
šw (m), free (from), 2:5; 4:6, 8.
šwt, feather, in title, 143:12.
špsỉ, noble, 8:9.
šft, renown, 14:11.
šfyt, respect, 16:6.
šmꜥ, see Index 5 (wr šmꜥ mḏwt).
šms, follower, 4:11, 14 (?).
šms, to follow, 9:6-7; 18:3; to seek (amethyst), 12:1; 14:17.
šmsw, retainer, see Index 5.
šnỉ, to encircle, 143:9.
šn(y)t, entourage, 148:2.
šnwt, granary, in title, 143:11; in simile, 143:14.
šs, alabaster, 17:8.
ššȝ, skilled, 2:4.
šd, to read out, 11:3.

ḳỉ, character, 17:7.
ḳbḥw, (1st) Cataract, 20:3; 143:10.
ḳbḥwy, waterfowl, in title, 143:11.
ḳmȝ, to fashion, 16:8; creation, 143:9.
ḳnbt, magistrates' assembly, 3:5.
ḳd, see mỉ-ḳd.

kȝ, ka in n-kȝ-n, 25:4, 5; 17:8; 20:5; 24:4.
kȝ will, wishes, of king, 6:5; 143:13.
kȝ, ox(en), 17:8; 19:3; 20:5; 27:3.
kȝt, work(s), 4:1; 143:12; 148:8; in titles, Index 5 (ỉmy-r. . , ḫrp).
kȝp, palace, in title, 24:6.
kyw, others, 14:10.

8. Select General Index.

9. Concordance of Text-Numbers & Designations.

PM, VII, 319f.	Fakhry/Sadek
1	15?
26	1?
29	53?
38	54?
39	46
42	2?
49	3?
72	4?
110	143
111	144
112	145
113	6
114	7
115	8
116	9
117	11
118	14
119	10
120	13
121	15?
122	16
123	17
124	19
126	25
127	22
128	23
129	12
130	28
132	31
135	29
Others	not identifiable.

– – – – – – – – – – – –

Cairo, JdE	Rowe	Sadek
71899	III	145
71900	II	144
71901	I	143

– – – – – – – – – – – – – – – –

Other Sources	Sadek
Berlin, Inv. 1203 (Dabod)	148
Document A (AIS)	146
Document B (AIS) (Aswan, no No.)	147
Khor Dehmit	149
Wadi Hudi, unedited	150-2

———

Aswan Museum, acc. no.	Excav. nos.	F/Sadek.
1471	1	6
1472	2	7
1473	3	8
1474	4	9
1475	5	11
1476	6	12
1477	7	13
1478	8	14
1479	9	16
1480	10	17
1481	11	18
1482	12	20
1483	13	21
1484	14	22
1485	15	23
1486	16	24
1487	17	25
1488	18	27
1489	19	28
1490	20	29
1491	21	30
1492	22	31
1493	23	32
1494	24	33
1495	25	34
1496	26	35
1497	27	36
1498	28	37
1499	29	38
1500	30	39
1501	38 (sic)	100
1502	32	103
1504	34 (so)	112
1505	33 (so)	109
1507	37	10
1508	38 (sic)	19
(no No.)	35 (so)	140
(no No.?)		114
(no No.)		145

– – – – – – – – – – – – – –

Schenkel, *MHT* nos.	F/Sadek nos.
435	1
436	2
437	3
438	4, A.
439	4, B.
440	4, C.

– – – – – – – – – – – – – –

Fakhry/Sadek – All Sources

See headings to texts in Part II.

V: MAPS

Map 1 (from the Archaeological Survey of Nubia 1908)

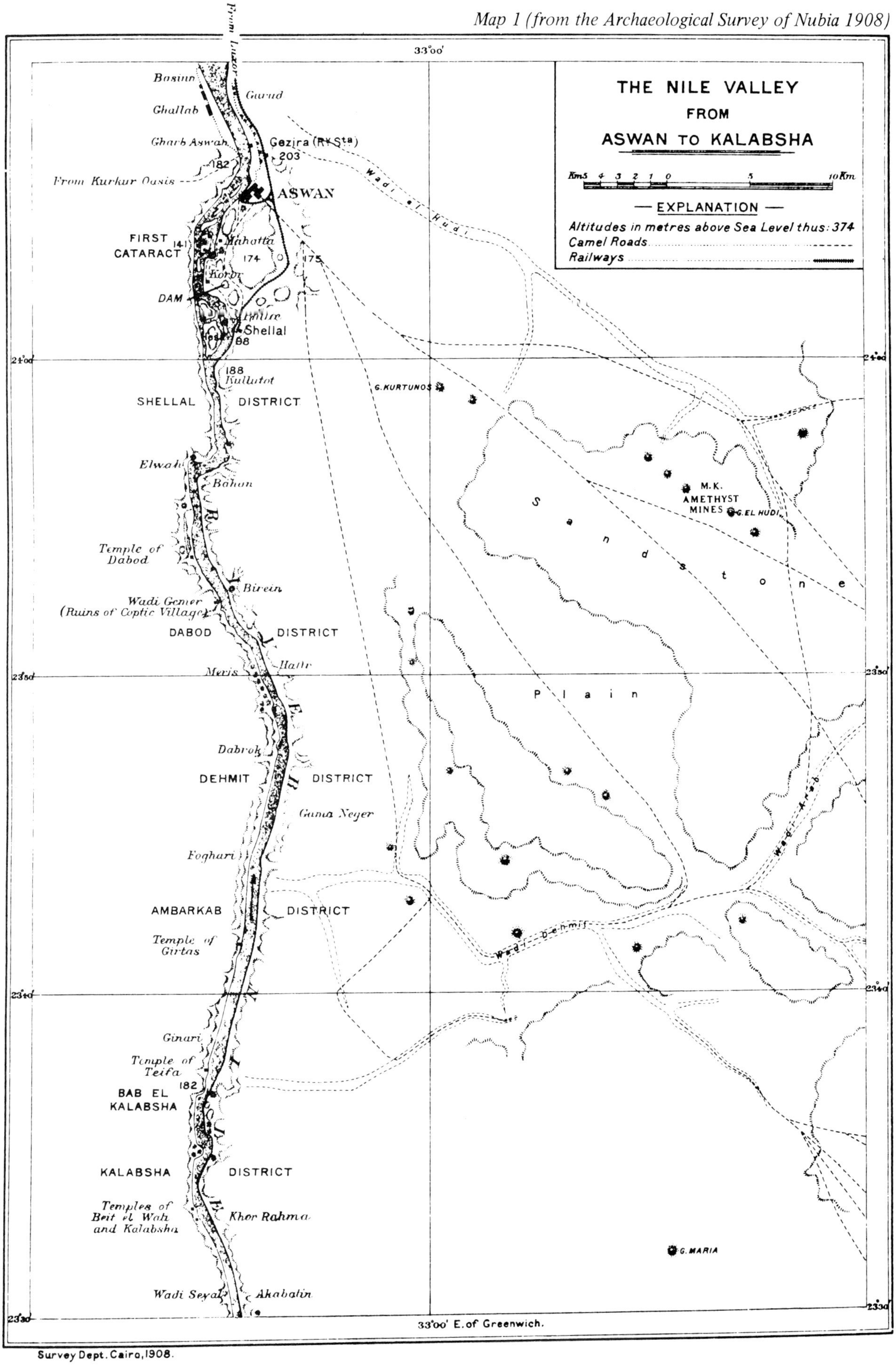

Map 2 (adapted from Fakhry)

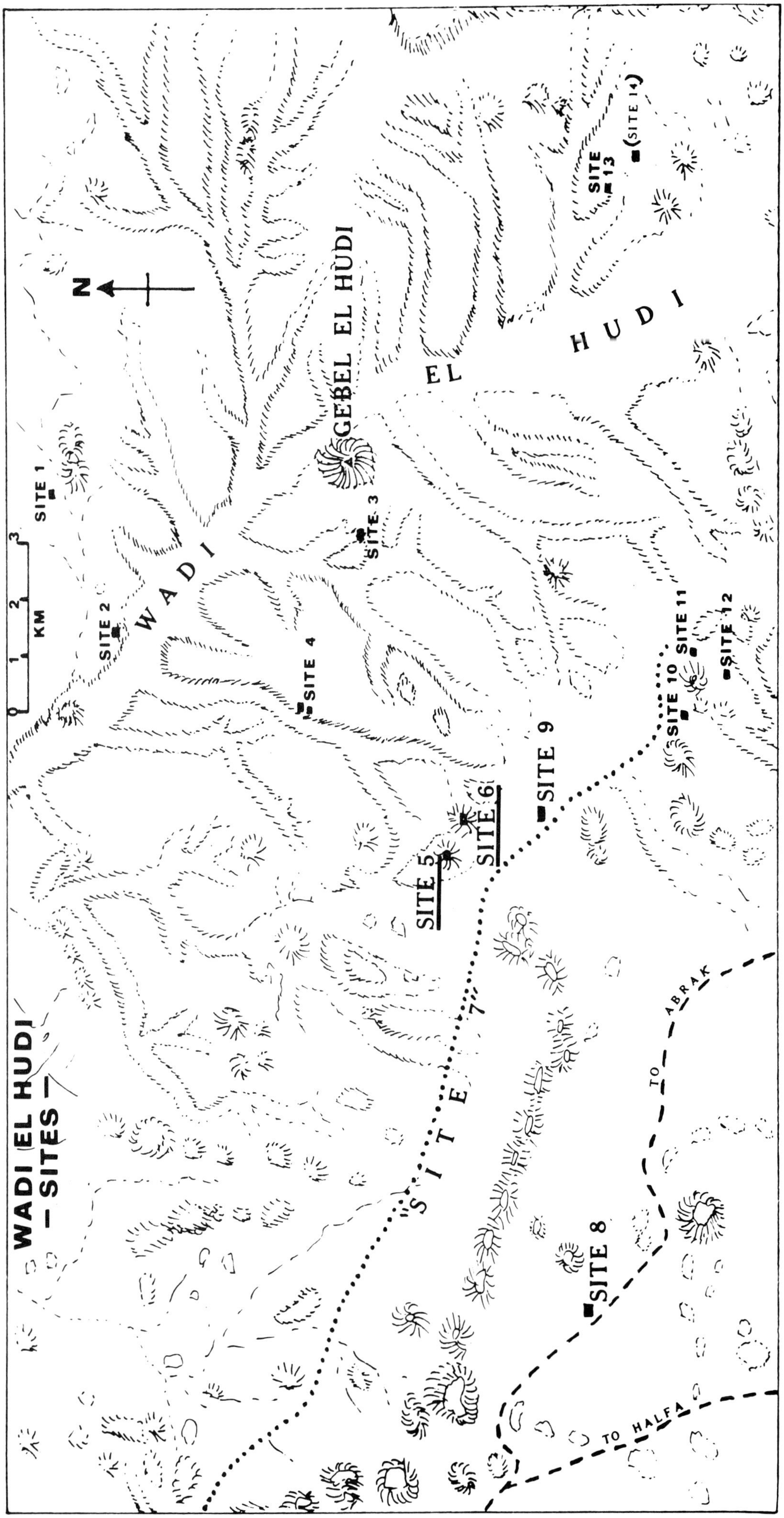

ARIS & PHILLIPS LTD : EGYPTOLOGY SERIES